THE WAR
IN SOUTH AFRICA

ITS CAUSES AND EFFECTS

WITH AN ESSAY FROM
The War in South Africa
BY A. CONAN DOYLE

By

J. A. HOBSON

First published in 1900

This edition published by Read Books Ltd.
Copyright © 2019 Read Books Ltd.
This book is copyright and may not be
reproduced or copied in any way without
the express permission of the publisher in writing

British Library Cataloguing-in-Publication Data
A catalogue record for this book is available
from the British Library

"We must see the first images which the external world casts upon the dark mirror of his mind; or must hear the first words which awaken the sleeping powers of thought, and standby his earliest efforts, if we would understand the prejudices, the habits, and the passions that will rule his life. The entire man is, so to speak, to be found in the cradle of the child."

— Alexis de Tocqueville.

THE OTHER SIDE OF THE QUESTION

AN EXCERPT FROM
The War In South Africa
BY A. CONAN DOYLE

Writing in November 1900, after hearing an expression of opinion from many officers from various parts of the seat of war, I stated in 'The Great Boer War': 'The Boers have been the victims of a great deal of cheap slander in the press. The men who have seen most of the Boers in the field are the most generous in estimating their character. That the white flag was hoisted by the Boers as a cold-blooded device for luring our men into the open, is an absolute calumny. To discredit their valour is to discredit our victory.' My own opinion would have been worthless, but this was, as I say, the result of considerable inquiry. General Porter said: 'On a few occasions the white flag was abused, but in what large community would you not find a few miscreants?' General Lyttelton said: 'The Boers are brave men, and I do not think that the atrocities which have been reported are the acts of the regular Dutch burghers, but of the riff-raff who get into all armies.'

It is a painful fact, but the words could not possibly be written to-day. Had the war only ended when it should have ended, the combatants might have separated each with a chivalrous feeling of respect for a knightly antagonist. But the Boers having appealed to the God of battles and heard the judgment, appealed once more against it. Hence came the long, bitter, and fruitless struggle which has cost so many lives, so much suffering, and a lowering of the whole character of the war.

It is true that during the first year there were many things to exasperate the troops. The Boers were a nation of hunters and they used many a ruse which seemed to the straightforward soldier to be cowardly and unfair. Individuals undoubtedly played the white-flag trick, and individuals were guilty of holding up their hands in order to lure the soldiers from their cover. There are many instances of this—indeed, in one case Lord Roberts was himself a witness of it. Appended is his official protest:

'Another instance having occurred of a gross abuse of the white flag and of the signal of holding up the hands in token of surrender, it is my duty to inform your Honour that if such abuse occurs again I shall most reluctantly be compelled to order my troops to disregard the white flag entirely.

'The instance occurred on the kopje east of Driefontein Farm yesterday evening, and was witnessed by several of my own staff officers, as well as by myself, and resulted in the wounding of several of my officers and men.

'A large quantity of explosive bullets of three different kinds was found in Cronje's laager, and after every engagement with your Honour's troops.

'Such breaches of the recognised usages of war and of the Geneva Convention are a disgrace to any civilised power.'

But British officers were not unreasonable. They understood that they were fighting against a force in which the individual was a law unto himself. It was not fair to impute to deliberate treachery upon the part of the leaders every slim trick of an unscrupulous burgher. Again, it was understood that a coward may hoist an unauthorised white flag and his braver companions may refuse to recognise it, as our own people might on more than one occasion have done with advantage. For these reasons there was very little bitterness against the enemy, and most officers would, I believe, have subscribed the opinion which I have expressed.

From the first the position of the Boers was entirely irregular as regards the recognised rules of warfare. The first article of the Conventions of The Hague insists that an army in order to claim belligerent rights must first wear some emblem which is visible at a distance. It is true that the second article is to the effect that a population which has no time to organise themselves and who are defending themselves may be excused from this rule; but the Boers were the invaders at the outset of the war, and in view of their long and elaborate preparations it is absurd to say that they could not have furnished burghers on commando with some distinctive badge. When they made a change it was for the worse, for they finally dressed themselves in the khaki uniforms of our own soldiers, and by this means effected several surprises. It is typical of the good humour of the British that very many of these khaki-clad burghers have passed through our hands, and[135] that no penalty has ever been inflicted upon them for their dangerous breach of the rules of war. In this, as in the case of the train hostages, we have gone too far in the direction of clemency. Had the first six khaki-clad burghers been shot, the lives of many of our soldiers would have been saved.

The question of uniform was condoned, however, just as the white-flag incidents were condoned. We made allowance for the peculiarities of the warfare, and for the difficulties of our enemies. We tried to think that they were playing the game as fairly as they could. Already their methods were certainly rough

PREFACE

DURING the summer and autumn of 1899 I spent several months in South Africa examining the political situation in the Transvaal and Cape Colony. I was at Pretoria during the most critical period of the negotiations, at Bloemfontein when the Raad of the Free State decided to stand by the Transvaal, and at Cape Town when the war began, and I had the opportunity of personal intercourse with many men of political prominence in the Republics and the Colony. The earlier chapters of this book are chiefly revised and amplified impressions of what I saw and heard, and include detailed studies of "Outlander grievances" and of the feelings of Dutch and British Afrikanders upon the eve of the present conflict. Several of the chief issues I have detached for separate treatment, fortifying personal experience and intercourse by documentary evidence, some of which has not been before published in this country.

The latter part of the volume is chiefly devoted to an economic and political analysis of those factors in the situation which throw light upon the possibilities of a stable settlement upon the termination of the war, and of a peaceful and prosperous future for South Africa.

PREFACE

There is no attempt to work out the details of a scheme of settlement, but merely to point out some of the essential facts and forces which demand most careful consideration.

A considerable part of the earlier chapters appeared in the form of letters to the *Manchester Guardian*, and some of the substance of the later chapters was published in the *Speaker*. I am indebted to the proprietors of these papers for their kind permission to reprint these passages.

J. A. H.

PART I

THE BOER REPUBLICS IN 1899

CHAP.		PAGE
I.	POLITICAL POSITION IN CAPE COLONY	3
II.	JOHANNESBURG IN THE SUMMER OF 1899	10
III.	PERSONAGES AND PARTIES IN THE TRANSVAAL	15
IV.	THE PERSONALITY OF PRESIDENT KRUGER	22
V.	OTHER FORCES IN TRANSVAAL POLITICS	32
VI.	THE WAR SPIRIT IN PRETORIA	40
VII.	THE RACE CONFLICT IN SOUTH AFRICA	46
VIII.	THE HELOTS IN JOHANNESBURG	52
IX.	THE DEMAND FOR THE FRANCHISE	63
X.	OFFICIAL CORRUPTION AND INCOMPETENCY	73
XI.	THE NEED OF FINANCIAL REFORM	84
XII.	THE DYNAMITE MONOPOLY	88
XIII.	A GENERAL ESTIMATE OF GRIEVANCES	96
XIV.	THE ALLEGED DUTCH CONSPIRACY	99
XV.	THE DUTCH FEELING IN THE COLONY: AN INTERVIEW WITH OLIVE SCHREINER	119
XVI.	TRANSVAAL ARMAMENTS	126
XVII.	THE CASE OF THE FREE STATE	136
XVIII.	THE SUZERAINTY ISSUE	146
XIX.	WHY DID THE BOERS ISSUE THE ULTIMATUM?	155
XX.	DIPLOMACY LEADING UP TO WAR	161

PART II

THE POLICY OF RAND CAPITALISTS

CHAP.	PAGE
I. FOR WHOM ARE WE FIGHTING?	189
II. THE POLITICAL METHODS OF THE OUTLANDERS	198
III. A CHARTERED PRESS	206
IV. FOR WHAT ARE WE FIGHTING?	229

PART III

TOWARDS A SETTLEMENT

I. DUTCH AND BRITISH IN SOUTH AFRICA	243
II. THE AGRICULTURAL OUTLOOK	250
III. THE PROBABLE INDUSTRIAL FUTURE OF SOUTH AFRICA	257
IV. THE NATIVES IN SOUTH AFRICA	279
V. FEDERATION OF STATES	296
VI. THE TRUE LINE OF BRITISH POLICY	306
INDEX	317

PART I
THE BOER REPUBLICS IN 1899

CHAPTER I

POLITICAL POSITION IN CAPE COLONY

SOUTH AFRICA is proverbially a land of surprises, and for a sojourner to express any confident judgment upon the delicate relations between the Colonial Government and the Imperial policy during the recent crisis of public affairs would be the pinnacle of folly. But having occupied myself at Cape Town chiefly in canvassing opinion on this matter, and having got, in conversation with different members of the Ministry and other political leaders, clear and outspoken judgments, I venture to present a fairly representative summary of a situation which is not unlikely to mark the beginning of a serious constitutional struggle. Whether the Colonial Secretary and the High Commissioner were justified or not in their espousal of the cause of the Outlander, and in the use of him to urge upon the Transvaal a sort of suzerainty neither set forth nor, in my judgment, implied in the Conventions, is not a point to be argued here. But it is of urgent importance that Englishmen should understand how sternly and strongly the policy of Downing Street was resented by the elective Assembly of what has hitherto been held to be, and distinctly holds itself to be by right, a substantially self-governing colony. The Home Government and the High Commissioner are felt to have ignored and overridden the judgment of a strong Ministry, representing a people whose commercial and political interests and experience entitle them to paramount consideration in the settlement of this Transvaal issue. The press and the voice of a British minority must not be allowed to conceal the essential facts of the situation. Here is a very strong Colonial Government, commanding a majority of twelve in an Assembly of ninety-five (thus corresponding to a majority of over eighty in the English House of Commons), and likely to be returned with fresh reinforcements if, as is rashly suggested in some quarters, the Governor dissolves the Assembly and appeals to the country. Nor is this likely to be a merely transient condition of affairs. A clear race cleavage, such as the present Imperial policy promotes, is likely to mean a permanent majority of Dutch Afrikanders in the Assembly, for it is unlikely that any new scheme of redistribution can be adopted enabling the British Afrikanders to triumph over the higher natural increase of the Dutch population and the greater influence which their broader dispersion rightly gives them in the country.

At the head of this majority, with seven exceptions entirely Dutch, sits a Ministry of experienced politicians (chiefly British and with but two Dutch Afrikanders), under a Premier (Mr. Schreiner) whose ability and force of character are admitted even by his adversaries. Men like Mr. Merriman, Mr. Sauer, and Mr. Solomon are no raw carpetbaggers hoisted into power by some sudden swell in the stream of party politics; they are men thoroughly conversant with the life and needs of the people and trained in the arts of administration. Such men feel that they know a hundred times more about the really salient points of the situation—the character of the Boer, the possible union of South African States, the native question—than the Colonial Office and a brand-new High Commissioner from Egypt. Their general diagnosis of the Transvaal situation and its bearing on the larger questions of South African politics has been firm and consistent. They have been freely accused by the Jingo press of inciting the Transvaal Government to an obstinate refusal of British claims. So far is this from being true, that, when history comes to displace journalistic fabrication, it will be known that friendly representations from Cape Colony have been far more effectual to wring concessions and reforms from Mr. Kruger than the threats of the British Government. Mr. Schreiner and his Ministers were absolutely united in recognising the reality of grievances and the necessity of reforms along the lines proposed, but they regarded the grievances as gravely exaggerated and the forceful methods of reform adopted as foolish, unjust, and fraught with dangerous reactions on the peace and progress of South Africa. The concluding words of General Butler's speech at Grahamstown a year ago, generally held to have occasioned his recall, concisely express their judgment: "What South Africa needs is rest, and not a surgical operation." Holding that the Outlanders were not seriously threatened in life, liberty, or property, they deprecated alike the violence and the precipitancy of the present policy. Though progress in reform was slower than they would desire, there had been progress. The economic and other influences of the Rand had already acted as solvents of the old Boer conservatism. A few more years and the death of Mr.

Kruger would, they argued, in all probability, work a fairly rapid and peaceful transformation in the politics of the Transvaal. One and all held that in the more distant future England would and must, in the natural course of events, control the Transvaal politically as well as economically, and that to force the pace by abrupt and artificial interference was injurious. Mr. Schreiner, Mr. Merriman, and their colleagues, were as firmly convinced as the most pronounced Jingo that England must in effect control the destinies of the whole of South Africa, but they deprecated the doctrine of force as the midwife of progress, seeing—what the Imperial Government fails to see—the moral and political reactions of menace and war upon the race questions which underlie the political future of the country.

Upon the immediate policy of the Transvaal I found no absolute agreement. Several of the leading politicians were convinced that the proposal of a joint inquiry was deliberately conceived in order to force on Mr. Kruger an admission of the suzerainty he has always denied. The Premier thought otherwise, holding that no such implication was involved, even if it were intended. His view was that Mr. Kruger might accept the inquiry as a step in the friendly intercourse entered upon at Bloemfontein, and that, as a first result of the report of such inquiry, the conference might be resumed between Sir A. Milner and the President with a view to final settlement.

It was impossible to go far in such a political inquiry as that which I undertook without perceiving that the most serious obstacle to an amicable settlement was the profound distrust of one another's motives entertained by the negotiating parties. Sir A. Milner did not hesitate to pronounce duplicity to be the distinctive trait of the Boer Government. When I reached Pretoria, I found that the same word contained the essence of Boer criticism upon British diplomacy. How could a real and lasting understanding be reached between such controversialists? The Cape Ministers, divided in their estimate of Mr. Kruger's policy, were united in denouncing the tactlessness of the Chamberlain-Milner method. Sir A. Milner, they held, utterly failed to understand the Boer character, and could not get at any point into sympathetic touch with it. This was made manifest by the proceedings at Bloemfontein. "How differently," one of them put it to me, "would Rhodes have handled the business in the days before the Raid had made him an impossible negotiator! Instead of bombarding the old man with a display of officialism, and seeking to wrest from him admissions by dint of academic argument, Rhodes would have said to his attachés, 'Now all you fellows, clear out,' and then he would have sat down by the fire, lighting cigarettes, while the old man smoked his long pipe; and they would have talked over things for a couple of days, so as to get to really understand one another before entering on any formal attempt at settlement." Sir A. Milner's method was to treat Kruger as a nineteenth-century up-to-date European diplomatist, instead of a slow-thinking, suspicious, seventeenth-century Puritan farmer, and a conference upon these lines was foredoomed to failure. The Dutch Afrikanders were, indeed, convinced that a peaceful conference was not intended to succeed; that Mr. Rhodes had got a clear understanding with Mr. Chamberlain after the Raid, whereby the latter undertook to direct the next attack upon the independence of the Republic; and that in Sir A. Milner there had been found an apt and sympathetic agent of this plan of campaign.

Although Cape Ministers did not in so many words commit themselves to this interpretation, it indubitably expressed their underlying conviction. The real aim, as they saw it, was not redress of grievances on the Rand, but the application of the new Imperialism to the affairs of South Africa. The optimist notion that a few months must see a final settlement; that, by the display or the actual use of arms, we should drive the Boers to a recognition of our power, and that after this moral or physical drubbing they would at once get to "know their place," was rejected by them as utterly fantastic. The dogs of war, once let loose, could not be so easily leashed again; force applied as a remedy to the stubborn Boers could not be soon replaced by sympathetic and enlightened democratic institutions; annexation would be inevitable, and could only be sustained by permanent militarism and the autocracy which pertains to it. What Cape Ministers first and chiefly dreaded was the effect of this upon the general governmental policy of South Africa. Government from Downing Street has ever been the bane of colonial statesmen of every party. Intensely loyal to the British flag, they constantly chafe against the bit of the Colonial Office when employed to drive them along roads which they know far better than Imperial Ministers can know them. The real unity of South Africa—a mere sounding phrase in the mouths of party politicians in England—is brought home to them by concrete facts, and gives them a clear right to exercise a prevailing voice in affairs which so vitally affect their interests. The Transvaal is a plain case in point. The Imperial Government, in the early stages of the controversy, treated the issue as if it only affected Outlanders. But the Jameson Raid, and the policy which was its sequel, had already exercised most disastrous influences upon colonial trade. The proposals of taxation, which were hotly dividing parties in Cape Colony last summer, were directly due to the necessities arising from damage to commercial confidence and that diversion of railway traffic from the Cape Colony lines which has been a chief object of Transvaal endeavour during recent years. The colony suffered more than it was possible to compute from this policy of menace, and a catastrophic solution of the problem, attended by a *régime* of militarism and a close Imperial control over matters of vital domestic import, was dreaded by all who understood what it signified in the development of colonial life and institutions.

CHAPTER II

JOHANNESBURG IN THE SUMMER OF 1899

AFTER one has travelled for a thousand miles through a bare and desolate country, in which no single human settlement, with the solitary exception of Bloemfontein, the Free State capital, can even pretend to be a town, Johannesburg, the golden city of Africa, with its eighty miles of streets and its hundred thousand inhabitants, makes a powerful impression. It offers a weird mixture of civilisation and savagedom. Laid out in leisurely fashion, with broad and ample streets, where a handsome stone building breaks occasionally the meagre and ugly effect of hastily improvised shop fronts and boarding-houses, it has the potentiality of a splendid modern city of the Paris or Vienna order. There is plenty of room in Africa, and no inducement to overcrowding. In fact, Johannesburg covers an immense area, reaching out its tentacles on every side, and wearing the large gold reef, the Witwatersrand, with its mining villages, as a sort of long double flapping tail. The entire city is the product of thirteen years' growth, and the amount of energy put into this little stretch of forty miles of gold reef has been prodigious. Even during the period of slackness and depression last summer, when gloom and terror were hanging over the place, when all business was suspended, and the gaiety and social licence of the town were suffering a total eclipse, the outward signs of multifarious enterprise could not fail to strike a stranger. Here, seven thousand miles from

England, in the heart of a Republic of rude farmers of Dutch descent, has grown up in a single decade a great city, which, so far as the language and habits of the white population is concerned, is almost absolutely English. In Johannesburg the Boer population is a mere handful of officials and their families, some five thousand of the population; the rest is about evenly divided between white settlers, mostly English-speaking, and the Kaffirs, who are everywhere in White Man's Africa the hewers of wood and drawers of water. The town is in some respects dominantly, and even aggressively, British, but British with a difference which it takes some little time to understand. That difference is mostly due to the Jewish factor. If one takes the recent figures of the census, there appears to be less than seven thousand Jews in Johannesburg, but the experience of the streets rapidly exposes this fallacy of figures. The shop fronts and business houses, the market-place, the saloons, the "stoeps" of the smart suburban houses, are sufficient to convince one of the large presence of the chosen people. If any doubt remains, a walk outside the Exchange, where, in the street "between the chains," the financial side of the gold business is transacted, will dispel it. So far as wealth and power, and even numbers are concerned, Johannesburg is essentially a Jewish town. Most of these Jews figure as British subjects, though many are, in fact, German and Russian Jews who have come to Africa after a brief sojourn in England. The rich, vigorous, and energetic financial and commercial families are chiefly German Jews. I lay stress upon this fact because, while every one knows the Jews are strong, their real strength here is much under-estimated. Though figures are so misleading, it is worth while to mention that the directory of Johannesburg shows sixty-eight Cohens against twenty-four Joneses and fifty-three Browns. The Jews mostly took little active part in the Outlander agitation; they let others do that sort of work. But since half of the land and nine-tenths of the wealth of the Transvaal claimed for the Outlander are chiefly theirs, they will be chief gainers by any settlement advantageous to the Outlander.

In ordinary times Johannesburg is a strong type of modern cosmopolitan civilisation, with some of its good and all its bad features. Of its extraordinary wealth and reckless luxury signs exist everywhere. Saloons, gambling hells, and other dens of vice abound, while only two years ago the prize-ring of Johannesburg was the most famous in the world and had a virtual monopoly of the best talent. That the best society is very mixed it is needless to add when one remembers that a very few years has drawn from all quarters of the globe adventurous men and women in search of gold. That there are many sound and solid business men with their families, especially among the engineering and professional classes, men of grit and force of character as well as of business capacity, may well be admitted. But the strange taint of gold lust—*auri sacra fames*—everywhere pervades the atmosphere and dominates the life even of the shopkeeping and professional classes. Gambling in mining shares is well-nigh universal. I was assured that half the Cornish miners were always dabbling in them, seeking to make their thrift as profitable as they could by watching the market. Lotteries, horse-racing, and gambling of every sort are prevalent and absorbing pastimes. These, of course, are statements applicable to many places; but there can be no manner of doubt that the conditions under which this golden city has arisen have made it one of the most terrible haunts of greed, gambling, and every form of depravity which the world has ever seen. There are, of course, qualities which balance, screen, and in some eyes perhaps redeem the character of such a place. Never have I been so struck with the intellect and the audacious enterprise and foresight of great business men as here. Nor are these qualities confined to the Beits and Barnatos and other great capitalists; the town bristles and throbs with industrial and commercial energy; the bracing physical atmosphere (Johannesburg stands 6000 feet above the sea) has marvellous tonic influences to evoke and stimulate mental energy. Every one seems alert and tense, eager to grasp the skirts of some happy chance and raise himself, as he has seen some scores of others no better than himself raised, to sudden affluence. The utter dependence upon financial "booms" and "slumps," conjoined with the strain and kaleidoscopic changes of the political situation, has bred by selection and by education a type of man and of society which is as different from that of Manchester as the latter is from the life of Hankow or Buenos Ayres.

All this stands on an external basis of picturesque barbarism. The essentially serf civilisation of South Africa is represented by the prevalence of Kaffir servants; all the hard manual labour is done by them, and strange flashes of savagedom gave piquancy to the street life; as, for instance, the sight of Kaffirs, grotesquely painted and decorated, dashing through the streets harnessed to light rickshaws, carrying daintily-dressed English ladies to evening parties. Ordinary street life is indeed a babel of races and tongues; not only the European languages, but the voices of Hindoos, Chinamen, Malays, chime in with the various Kaffir dialects. The Boer, who is supposed in some obscure way to be the proprietor of this country, makes very little show. He is officially represented by the policeman or *Zarp* (a word-composition of the initial letters of the Dutch words for "South African Republic Police"), an innocent lump of stolidity, who stands at the street corner. If you want to see the real Boer, you have to get up early and visit the market. There you find him *in propria persona*, often with his family, and always with his waggon and team of oxen, with which he has brought his farm produce to market; often travelling a hundred miles, and taking several days and nights on his patient journey, sleeping by night in a sort of upper loft of his waggon; by day tramping along with his team, or smoking on the waggon-seat, while his Kaffir boy leads the oxen. Many scores of these Boers you can see any morning as the auctioneer is wheeled round the market, and stops before each waggon to sell the produce. There is no mistake about the physical prowess of these men; almost to a man they are tall, powerful-limbed, and vigorous, with strong, calm, enduring faces—men difficult to dislodge from any position they have taken in bargain or in battle. These are the sons of the country; their fathers conquered and brought the land under rude cultivation and control; yet almost their only real connection with this treasure-centre of their country is these brief early morning visits to the market, where they sell their farm-produce to the horde of foreigners who are living in luxury upon the natural wealth they extract (through Kaffir labour) from the strip of land on which they settle. They take no part whatever either as capitalists, miners, professional men, or shopkeepers in this curious scramble, but only pay these early morning calls with their oxen and drive back again.

CHAPTER III

PERSONAGES AND PARTIES IN THE TRANSVAAL

THE common English notion that the Boers are a single, solid, and compact body of obstinate and reactionary farmers, dominated by the personality of one strong and cunning man, who is incapable of education and spontaneous progress, is largely a mischievous perversion of history and of present conditions. It is put forward to support the view that force is the only remedy, and that reforms of government and administration can only come by strong pressure from without, and by the subsequent control of the Transvaal by Outlanders, with the support of the British Empire. Now two undeniable facts give a semblance of truth to this view. Paul Kruger, a man of narrow, deep-set political convictions, who has helped to make the entire history of his nation, is strongly hostile to the threatened political dominance of Outlanders, and the entire people support him in his resistance to the menaces of British arms. But this uniformity is but a momentary phase of patriotic feeling—that brief cessation of intestine quarrels which always occurs in facing a common enemy. It is part of the Jingo case to say that progress from inside is impossible; that the Boer is wholly and hopelessly reactionary in his thoughts and ways. Now this is not so, and a crude narration of selected legal enactments of the last ten years does not prove it. The franchise policy since 1890 may indeed be regarded as reactionary and foolish, though not so foolish as at first sight it seems. The ultra-Liberal franchise before 1890 required modification in view of the tremendous pace of the new immigration of mixed foreigners. That this restrictive policy was being driven too far was recognised from the beginning by a minority of the more intelligent and enlightened burghers. Those who represent the nation as a mass of stolid and ignorant Conservatives are not aware that from 1890 right on to the present there has been conducted, both among the people and in the Raad, a vigorous campaign of education and reform by a progressive section of the burghers. Mr. Esselen, an Afrikander of British education, formerly a Judge of the High Court, headed a vigorous attack on the franchise law of 1890, and, with a powerful body of young burghers, stoutly opposed the policy of restriction which alarm rather than definite reactionary principle led the Raad to sanction. I have read speech after speech of Mr. Esselen, delivered as far back as 1892, which present the legitimate claims of the Outlander and the interests of the Republic in assimilating the new population. If Mr. Kruger be taken as the champion of reaction, history shows that he has not exercised the complete and unquestioned sway that is attributed to him. So far from this being so, the violent cleavage of parties under Mr. Kruger and General Joubert has more than once been carried to the verge of civil war. In 1893 General Joubert's friends claim that he was actually elected by a majority of votes in the election for President, but that Mr. Kruger's friends manipulated the returns, and that sooner than break the State by open strife General Joubert resigned his claim. The support of the Liberals was given at this time to the General, who was a man of generous sympathies and open to many of the new ideas.

It is only at moments of critical danger to the State that the strong will of Mr. Kruger has been allowed to assume a sort of dictatorial power; it is not because he normally represents the entire views and feelings of the people. The Dutch trekkers of the Transvaal differ in no real respect from their brethren of the Orange Free State, whose policy is admittedly most liberal and enlightened. Why is it that the Transvaal policy has been so different, and yet that the Free State burghers are standing to a man shoulder to shoulder by the Transvaalers in their fight against external compulsion? Mr. Fischer, of the Free State Executive, one of the most far-sighted and genuinely progressive men in South Africa, put the case to me in the plainest and most uncompromising way. He described how educative influences were at work undermining the sullen suspicions of the British which had been branded by experience upon the early Voortrekkers; how the slow-moving forces received a check when the foreign flood poured in after 1886; how at the very time that the Raad, under President Kruger, was tightening the restrictions, there was a new vigorous rising of internal progressive forces working towards the assimilation of the new blood and the new ideas in industry and politics. Even Mr. Kruger has not been the stolid stumbling-block that he has been represented. In 1895, before the Reform movement in Johannesburg took serious shape, he had plans of franchise reform; he saw the necessity of doing something, and his friends were urging changes in the franchise law. The Jameson Raid not unnaturally hardened his heart and drove him back on ancient prejudice. Recovering from this shock, he and his Conservative burghers were soon confronted with a renewed agitation, conducted in Johannesburg, not by friends of constitutional reform, but by foreigners, strangers to Boer life and character, who urged claims of an alarming kind, who assailed every legislative and administrative act of the Government which gave them shelter and enabled them to amass wealth, and who called, in notes of ever-growing clearness, for a British army of conquest and occupation to secure for them a controlling voice in the State.

But though the Liberal party among the burghers had its organisation broken and its political hopes dashed to the ground by the Jameson Raid, it is distinctly incorrect to assert that no concessions and no progress have been made during the last three years. Much is made of the alleged failure of the Government to carry out the recommendations of the Industrial Commission appointed by it in 1897 to examine burdens and grievances. Mr. Fitzpatrick would have his readers believe that "nothing" was done to carry out the liberal recommendations of that body, and even many well-informed and well-disposed critics, like Mr. Bryce and Mr. Garrett Fisher, have in effect endorsed this view. In point of fact, while the Raad Committee, appointed to consider the report of the Commission, rejected some of its recommendations, those which it approved and which were carried out were not inconsiderable. Taking the chief economic grievances, we find that a reduction of 10s. per case in the price of dynamite was effected; the special custom dues were taken off most of the staple foods, and so far from this reduction being compensated, as is alleged, by an increased tariff upon luxuries, a net reduction, estimated last year to amount to about £700,000, was achieved. The rates of the Netherland South African Railway Company were likewise reduced to the extent of some £200,000 per annum.

The administration of the Liquor Pass, and Gold Thefts Laws were made more stringent, and ample testimony exists to prove that the mine-owners themselves admit a great improvement in the administration of these laws, which were specially designed to secure the interests of the mines. Much is made of the refusal of the Government to grant full self-government to Johannesburg and the Rand, a proposal which Mr. Chamberlain urged in 1896. If the establishment of powers equivalent to those possessed by an English municipality had been sought, this proposal would have been eminently reasonable, but no such powers were sought or would have been acceptable to the mining industry. Good local government, though a real, was a secondary object of this proposal, the first object being to mark off the Rand, the treasure-house of all South Africa, as a special preserve of the mining magnates, to save it from bearing that burden of taxation which rightly and reasonably is imposed upon the natural resources of the country, and to give the control of the laws affecting native labour to the mining managers. It was utterly unreasonable to expect that the Government should quietly consent to such a scheme, which virtually meant the alienation of the Rand, though the scheme of municipal government they did devise was far from commendable.

Those who fairly investigate the facts will acknowledge that, even under the spell of reaction imposed by the Jameson Raid and the threats which followed, some substantial progress in better government was made. The pace was certainly slow, far too slow to suit the hasty ambitions of the gold-seeker, but it was all that the circumstances rendered feasible. A little longer time to wear down the suspicions and the ignorance of the old Boer mind and the pace might have been quickened.

I found in Pretoria many men of most liberal mind, not a few trained in the traditions of English Liberalism, recognising fully the need and the gain of identifying the new inhabitants with the old burgher population. But their mouths have been absolutely shut since the Jameson Raid and the appeals to English force which ensued; they could not plead the cause of progress without appearing traitors who were seeking to divide the people by factions in face of an outside force. Had there been no Jameson Raid, and no subsequent appeals to England, the inner spirit of reform would have shown worthy fruits ere this, the dangerous personal ascendency of Mr. Kruger would have been checked, if it had not been overthrown, and the peace of South Africa would not have been destroyed as it has been. This, it may be said, is highly speculative, but it is legitimate hypothesis based upon historic fact and knowledge of human nature. There did exist a genuine though slowly growing Liberal party in the Transvaal, penetrated, moreover, by views and sentiments definitely British, working towards an enlightened policy and seeking a peaceable solution of racial and political problems. External force has displaced natural growth; revolutionary methods with an appeal to arms have been preferred to the evolutionary method which Nature imposes. Ignorant men tell us that the Boer is unteachable, the permanent prey of brutal prejudice and inveterate selfishness. But are these the radical, unchangeable properties of the Frisian blood which we have in common with these Boers? If so, shall we judge them? If not, if these Dutchmen really belong to a race shown by history in Europe, and even in Africa, to be amply capable of economic, political, and

PERSONAGES AND PARTIES

social progress, is it not the part of true statesmanship to give the educative forces of inward growth time to operate upon their political forms rather than to hammer them by brute force into shapes of mechanical correctness? I do not pretend that the Volksraad is a very enlightened body of statesmen. The hopeless *impasse* of recent years has kept out of it not a few of the best and finest men. Yet this Raad came in with a majority of what may rightly be called Moderate Progressives, men pledged to check those concessions and corruptions which have been eating away the honesty of the official class. At their opening they elected a progressive chairman and vice-chairman; schemes of political and economic reform were freely canvassed. Many hopes were founded on this Raad. The common charge of corruption requires closer analysis than can be given here. I can only say that I find no reason whatever to endorse those widespread and general charges of direct dishonesty which have been freely made both in England and South Africa. On the contrary, there is reason to believe that this Raad contains many honest and fairly able men determined to cleanse the corruption of the State and to force the pace of progress. But this they would not do at the dictate of England; the disclosure of the policy of Mr. Chamberlain and Sir Alfred Milner, the dictatorial assumption of suzerainty, the charges of duplicity brought by a Power whose interference is in their view a flagrant breach of the Convention, have made all these men set their teeth and grip their guns as Englishmen themselves have always done and always will do when a foreigner attempts to drive them.

CHAPTER IV

THE PERSONALITY OF PRESIDENT KRUGER

To many people there is only one personality in the Transvaal, one all-powerful will. Hero or villain, Paul Kruger is taken to be the embodiment of Boer nature, the man whose force, experience, and craft dominate Boer policy. How far is Mr. Kruger personally responsible for the present trouble? It is hardly possible for a casual visitor to get beneath the outer husk of this grim old man, with the massive, furrowed face, who sits upon his stoep puffing a huge meerschaum pipe and growling out disconnected sentences between the spits. You ask yourself as you sit waiting for his Dutch to be put into English (Mr. Kruger speaks no English), What manner of man is this? A pious patriot, soldier, hunter, farmer, driven by sheer circumstances into high politics and adapting some natural bucolic cunning to the purposes of diplomacy in the defence of his country, or a scheming old hypocrite, who has richly feathered his nest by every art of political corruption, and who employs every trick of evasion and falsehood in defence of his monopoly of the public power and purse, using for these purposes the single genuine passion of his life—hatred of the English? Even those who have associated intimately with the old man for many years differ widely in their estimate of his nature and his political power; indeed, this inscrutability is itself a strong factor in the situation. There are even those who, upholding Mr. Kruger's personal and political honesty, yet think he is prepared to wreck his country by war, in order to maintain the supremacy which might fall from his hands under reform. A brief personal impression of such a man is not worth much; even corrected and filled out by the freely expressed opinions of many of his friends and enemies, it only warrants some general conjecture. To strangers Mr. Kruger is not often communicative; the State Secretary, Mr. Reitz, who took me to him, told how he had a few days before introduced a well-known member of the British Parliament, but could extract nothing but an occasional grunt and a "Yes" or "No" from the old man, who buried himself behind a cloud of tobacco-smoke. Sometimes, however, he dilates and opens out in free narrative. Olive Schreiner told me of a talk she had with him a short time ago, in which he warmed up with a long, animated, and wonderfully picturesque account of the hunting and fighting of his adventurous youth. Even now his reserve of physical force is immense; by his sheer power of voice and presence he cows the Opposition in the Raad. In ordinary talk he exercises little self-restraint; if any point of controversy rises, he will bring his big fist down upon the table with alarming force.

I was somewhat fortunate in my reception. After I had been introduced to the old man, he himself expressed the desire to make a statement to the English people upon the matter of the broken promises imputed to him. He evidently feels very keenly on this matter, for, if I remember right, Captain Younghusband tells how he harked back to this topic in the two interviews he had with him. The allusion is to the promises of "equal treatment" which he made in the negotiations previous to the Convention of 1881. He passionately insisted that he had given equal treatment so far as all civil rights were concerned, and that, as regards the rights of burghership, he had all along sought to practise the same policy, but the foreigners who came in refused to accept the duties of burghership while seeking to gain its privileges. He cited to me several instances where, instead of helping the burghers to defend the country, settlers had preferred to register themselves as British subjects or to make an appeal to the power of Great Britain so as to escape the commando. "I have," he said, "always striven to bring these people into the full rights of citizenship by inviting them to help our citizens to bear the burdens, but they always refused; they wanted the rights without the duties." He then went on to tell how those who fought in the Malaboch campaign and in other Kaffir wars had burghership conferred on them by an edict of the Raad. Historically there is some substance in this defence, though it is far from being logically complete, for when appeals have been made to Outlanders to take up arms under commando or as volunteers, they have never been promised burghership as a reward. But the real interest lies in the light it throws upon Kruger's conception of politics; fighting has played so essential a part in the making of the nation, that it seems to him that such personal service is the only basis of burgher rights. "How," he would ask himself, "can these Johannesburg people become true and worthy citizens? Even were they well disposed, they would be incapable of fulfilling the first duty of a burgher, that of fighting against our foes." Animated by such feelings, one can understand how he regards the agitation of the speculators and tradesmen of the Rand, who look on the burghership not as linking them with the destinies of a country for which they are prepared at twelve hours' notice to mount their horse and fight till death, but rather as a means of helping them to develop the industrial resources of the country and make a pile. I do not say this position is ultimately tenable, but it is inevitably the position which such a man as Mr. Kruger was bound to take.

Such a view expresses the whole dramatic antithesis of the situation; the old seventeenth-century countryman, with his crude, belated politics and his stern Old Testament direction, is brought all of a sudden face to face with a culminating type of modern capitalist civilisation in the luxurious, speculative, cosmopolitan life of Johannesburg. If to a Londoner this golden city fairly staggers the imagination with its dizzy artificialism and the rapid transformation of its life, how must it appear to Mr. Kruger and his following of inexperienced Boers? Is it any wonder that they have thought these brilliant, tricky strangers intend to take from them the control of their country, and that they view an extended franchise as a political and moral cataclysm? "Yes," it may be said; "but this assumes Paul Kruger to be the honest, simple-minded peasant which he is not." It is idle to shirk the accusations brought against the President; they are not merely the vague whispers of agitators on the Rand. Many Transvaalers not hostile to the general policy of Mr. Kruger are evidently staggered and perplexed by certain aspects of that policy and certain incidents in his career. Enemies boldly cast in his teeth personal corruption, insisting that he has taken large sums of money, not merely for the dynamite, but for other concessions and dealings; that he has allowed some members of his family and a little clique of personal friends to enrich themselves by abuse of official power and by lobbying. Upon this matter I have probed many well-informed persons, and can get no sure conclusion. One thing is certain, that Kruger has not what we should call a "nice sense of honour" in these matters. The case of the Salati Railway is conclusive on this point. It is admitted that on this occasion, in 1890, when Mr. Oppenheim's agent was actively engaged in pushing through the Raad this railway, connecting the Rand with Portuguese territory, presents of "spiders" were made to and accepted by a number of Raad members who voted the concession. When the matter was afterwards brought up for criticism, Mr. Kruger defended the innocence of their conduct, insisting that there was no harm in accepting such "presents," which he regarded as tokens of friendship, not as bribes. The most specific charge, however, that has been made against him is in the dynamite affair, when even in the Raad it was plainly insinuated that certain shares entered in a fictitious name were really owned by the President, who had received them as a consideration for giving favourable terms to the concessionaire. The recent *volte face* of several members of the Dynamite Commission who were previously committed to cancellation is commonly attributed to the pressure of the President, who is alleged to have threatened resignation if any course was taken which would make public the nature of a certain secret contract. A study of the entire history of the dynamite concession indisputably supports some *prima facie* suspicion.[1] On the other hand, high officers of State, whose honour no one impeaches, and who alone have direct access to the documentary evidence, assure me that there is absolutely no founda-

[1] See Chapter XII.

tion for this charge. They freely admit that when the concession was first granted, the State, being urgently in need of ammunition, made a bad bargain; that later on it negligently allowed the Dynamite Company to evade its obligations; that when the earlier concession was cancelled and a new company formed in 1891, a large batch of shares was given in compensation to parties interested in the cancelled concession, and these are the very shares Mr. Kruger has been charged with holding. Such statements, however correct, of course do not solve the dynamite mystery nor explain why members of the Commission turned round in the Raad. Still, it must be allowed that the allegation of corruption against the President is based on purely hypothetical evidence, and those who are aware of the reckless way in which such imputations of fraud are launched by South African politicians will be slow to accept this charge.

Other accusations of "feathering his nest" are lavishly made—how he has zig-zagged a certain railway so as to make it go through property he owned, and how otherwise he has used politics to assist his business interests. But though, as I shall show later, there is too much reason to believe that corruption eats far into Transvaal officialism, I can find no definite evidence in support of these direct imputations against the honour of the President. In large measure they seem to be based on the admitted fact that Mr. Kruger has grown rich during these later years, and enemies trace these riches to a foul source. Yet it is certain that a perfectly sound explanation of his wealth is afforded by the land operations by which, in common with many leading citizens, he has made money. For instance, not long ago he sold his Geduld estate for £120,000, which was at once disposed of to a company for half a million, and was recently worth between two and three millions. A shrewd business man owning land in mining districts has these chances. General Joubert, against whose honour no whisper has ever been heard, is considerably richer than the President, and has made his money by similar dealings. Mr. Kruger's lax notions about "presents" and a disposition to screen certain friends who have indisputably yielded to corruption, coupled with a good deal of nepotism, have not unnaturally brought grave suspicions upon his personal honour. But under cross-examination these charges are found to rest upon mere conjecture.

The strongly religious character of Mr. Kruger spells hypocrisy to those unaccustomed to analysis of character. That religiosity is consistent with certain curious ethical perversities is a commonplace of which perhaps Mr. Kruger and the Boers furnish some instructive illustrations. But the deep, passionate genuineness of his belief in the Bible and an inner light derived from its study can only be questioned by inveterate "malignants." Paul Kruger is a fanatic, a narrow-minded bigot, if you will, but no hypocrite. His obtrusively uncompromising attitude towards other religions than his own is illustrated by several quaint incidents. A few years ago he was induced to take part in the opening ceremony at a Jewish synagogue. On entering and taking his place, he removed his hat, and paid no heed whatever to the suggestion of his secretary, who explained the Jewish custom of covering the head. When the time came for the President's address, he ejaculated a few brief sentences, and amazed his congregation by concluding thus, "I declare this synagogue open in the name of our Lord Jesus Christ." On another occasion, shortly after he had presented on behalf of the

State a piece of land (an erf) for the building of a Dutch Reform Church, he was approached by an influential Jew who tendered a similar request on behalf of a Jewish congregation. The President promised to consider the request, and soon afterwards announced that he had granted it. Shortly after, however, he was waited on by his Jewish friend, who complained that the piece of land they had received was only half the size of that given for the Dutch Reform Church. "Well," retorted Kruger, "what fault have you to find? They believe the whole Bible, so they get an erf; you only believe half the Bible, and you get half an erf."

In politics, as in religion, Paul Kruger is governed by a few simple, deeply-rooted notions. The notion that he is a far-sighted, foxy politician seeking his own ends seems to me quite unwarranted, and arises from the situation, which often forces him to give reasons and arguments for actions which are really based upon sentiment, intuitive caution, or set prejudices. Mr. Kruger has continually been fighting for the independence of his country, as he conceives it, warding off the danger of an overwhelming rush of alien influences. When called upon suddenly for a set defence of his position, he has no ready dialectic, but often blurts out reasons which are not the real actuating forces. His evasions and dilatory bargaining are not really a conscious statecraft so much as a rude instinctive fence which has been successful against a "politician" like Mr. Chamberlain, because the latter, by a characteristic fallacy, supposes his antagonist to be the same manner of a man as himself. At the same time, able men that know him well tell me Mr. Kruger is a powerful thinker, who drives right down to the bed-rock of an issue, has a keen nose for fallacy in argument, and is even willing to admit an error when it is clearly pointed out to him. There is, however, one weakness in his position which deserves notice. He reads nothing except the Bible, neither books nor newspapers, though extracts from the latter are read to him. The result is that he has to depend upon the friends around him for all his knowledge of the larger world. Even as regards the most material facts which reach his mind, there is thus a constant danger of unfair selection and misrepresentation. Mr. Kruger is not the self-sufficing man he is sometimes painted. Dominated by certain passions and experiences, he is never shaken by threats or by violence, but he is very amenable to the influence of friends. This, too, is a characteristic of his race which England has foolishly ignored. The concessions which seemed to them to have been wrested by threats of force were really made under the urgent pressure of friendly representations. Of Mr. Kruger's actual power it is hard to judge. The Boer is a suspicious man, and, until England's open menaces closed all discussion and hushed all dissensions, he was not prepared to give absolute discretion even to the President. The dynamite vote and the proposed concession of a five-year franchise evoked a storm of indignation which by no means spared the President. Many persons, indeed, insisted to me that Mr. Kruger and his Government could in no case have forced the adoption of a five-year franchise. But I am not convinced of this. There is no strong man in or out of the Raad who could really stand up against the President or could rally a powerful party against him in a national emergency. Boers do not like the notion of dictatorship, and are strenuous in their insistence on extreme forms of democracy. But my conviction is that Kruger's power in

PERSONALITY OF PRESIDENT KRUGER 31

a grave emergency like that which the country has entered is that of a virtual dictator; that his hold upon the minds of the great majority is such that they would have acquiesced in almost any decision, and have endorsed, however reluctantly, almost any concessions he might have made. To this extent the Transvaal may be regarded as a one-man State; but it must ever be kept in mind that this power of Mr. Kruger is due to an abnormal stress of circumstances, that it is not created by his sole will and authority, but is the half-conscious recognition by the people that he is the true repository of the ancient Boer spirit and traditions, and that he will fight with all his mind and all his might for the independence of his country.

CHAPTER V

OTHER FORCES IN TRANSVAAL POLITICS

THAT Mr. Kruger dwarfs the other public men of the Transvaal is a commonplace. In studying the politics of Pretoria, it must be remembered that we are not dealing with a capital which contains a large body of trained diplomatists. The brains of the Transvaal are for the most part applied to industry; higher education has hardly made a start; the older men in politics and business have no culture. I am told, and I can well believe it, that there is only one member of the First Raad who would be termed highly educated according to European standards. The Government of course has access to better education and more talent in some of its higher officers, but the inadequacy of its present resources for the difficult functions of government, in a country where new and complex problems are constantly appearing on the political horizon, is manifest. Several of the leading politicians are indisputably men of sound business ability and of perfect honour, but they can hardly rank in intellectual calibre or training with the experts of a European State. The result of this has been to throw upon a few young men of brains and energy an amount of work and responsibility in the conduct of high politics which severely taxes their capacity.

Among the older men there is no one who can be termed a statesman except Mr. Kruger. The Vice-Presi-

OTHER FORCES IN TRANSVAAL POLITICS

dent and Commander-in-Chief, Joubert, is a man who has played a prominent part in making Transvaal history. Of a softer, more plastic, and more liberal temperament than Kruger, he has for many years been a keen opponent of the latter. There was, as I have shown, a time when the younger and more enlightened Boers of Pretoria thought General Joubert might lead them along a path of victorious progress. But though a brave soldier, General Joubert is by nature a man of peace, without the force or stubbornness of Mr. Kruger for action in the political arena. Moreover, while more liberal in feeling, he is distinctly limited in his political outlook, and possesses few definite constructive ideas of progress outside the realm of administrative reforms, to which he is genuinely attached.

The evil genius of Transvaal politics has undoubtedly been Dr. Leyds. The notion of an unqualified Dutch political supremacy, with a complete dominance of Dutch language and ideas, which this imported Hollander sought to impress upon Transvaal politics and administration, has been a chief source of such Outlander grievances as possess a real foundation. His personal influence was persistently used to harden the heart of Paul Kruger against conceding political power or any considerable measure of self-government to the Outlander. Born in Java, and trained in the atmosphere of Roman-Dutch law, which, though in some respects an excellent administrative system, is hostile to British notions of liberty, he strove to impose this rigid Hollander character on the laws and public institutions of the Transvaal, which for a time became a perfect nest of Hollander officials, mostly men who came for what they could get, and who, having got it, drifted back to Holland. The language and education grievances, which have some real substance, are largely

Dr. Leyds' creations. His appointment of Dr. Mansvelt as Director of Education is responsible for a certain amount of genuine discontent, though, as the facts recorded in the Appendix show, this grievance like others has been gravely exaggerated.

The influence of this able but narrow-minded Hollander has been everywhere perceptible. It is, however, weaker than it was; and if the land had only been allowed the boon of rest, there are genuine reformers even in the present Government. Mr. Reitz, who two years ago replaced Dr. Leyds as State Secretary, is a man of courteous manners and patient, thoughtful mind, a moderate reformer, willing to purchase peace by all reasonable concessions. He is a lover of literature and a keen student of history and archæology, more fitted for a leisurely intellectual career than for the "Sturm und Drang" of South African politics. South Africa is constantly engaged in fitting square pegs into round holes. Mr. Reitz resembles the better type of public man in an English municipality of middling size; but no one would suppose that he had been a President of the Orange Free State and a Judge of the High Court. Most of the men managing high affairs of State are young men, one or two with an English training, like the State Attorney, Mr. Smuts, a brilliant young lawyer.

Of the pressure of family influence in public life there is, however, far too much. The President, in particular, has been a most unblushing practitioner of nepotism. His relations fill many of the most important posts. Piet Grobler, a grandson, a man of great energy but of no wide experience, occupies the important post of Under-Secretary of State, and exercises no small influence in high politics. Another grandson, Piet Kruger, was appointed over the heads of many senior men to the place of Master of the High Court, though possessed of no legal training or experience whatever. One of Mr. Kruger's younger sons, a notorious "wastrel," also destitute of education and official experience, has been in control of the Secret Service Fund; while a son-in-law, Mr. Frickie Eloff, has notoriously been involved in shady financial transactions. Another grandson, Mr. Hans Malan, is Chief Inspector of Roads, and yet another is in command of the fort at Johannesburg. The husband of one of his grand-daughters is Assistant State Attorney. The list might be greatly extended if notice were taken of remoter family connections.

A little State like this, with some 30,000 burghers needs to select and use its very best talent; but the Executive Council, the most important body after the President, has been quite inadequately furnished with men of culture and experience in politics. This fact gives a dangerous power into the hands of any man of determined character. The Raads are almost wholly composed of farmers, some of them possessed of wealth and trained in the arts of business, but by no means well equipped with ordinary knowledge of the world. This should be borne in mind in reviewing the negotiations that have taken place. It is most unfair to expect more ability or a higher standard of efficiency and honesty from the Boer Government than could be got out of the native population of similar size in an English provincial town. If one of these boroughs were called upon to create and control the entire government of a large new State, with a Rand population thrown in, out of their native resources, would they have succeeded so much better? "Yes," it will be retorted; "but precisely for that reason ought they to have availed themselves of the superior ability of the Outlander." And there can be no question that the State would have been immensely strengthened in its capacity for legislation and administration by the enlargement of the field from which State officials and politicians could be drawn. A simple population of farmers could be governed tolerably well by the rude methods that have hitherto prevailed; but a complex industrial society, working the largest goldfields of the world, demands wider and keener business ability. Such ability exists and is accessible in plenty, if only it can be found conjoined with common honesty and some measure of public spirit.

APPENDIX

THE EDUCATION GRIEVANCE

THE following is the statement given to me by an English Church clergyman who has for several years had charge of a Church school in Johannesburg. "The Mansvelt policy has been to get in Hollanders as headmasters even to the exclusion of Cape Dutch. His policy has always been restricted and illiberal, but the Volksraad partially kept him in order, and he has been unpopular with the Dutch community. . . . The whole policy was largely influenced by what the Boers considered an improper and agitating policy of Outlanders, not simply on educational, but on general politics. The latest condition for grants was a diminishing quantity of English and increasing quantity of Dutch, from the first to the fourth Standard, when Dutch alone was used. Grants were refused to Afrikanders with Dutch names (*e.g.* Auret), unless they were in a Dutch school. In the best days it was difficult to get grants without perpetual visits to Pretoria. Mansvelt always had to be 'squared'—not bribed, but talked to. I think it used to please him that we had to go across to Pretoria and see him. When seen, he could usually be made to do anything." My informant has a very bad opinion of the tactics of the Educational Council which the Outlanders formed in order to deal with the education of their children. "The Volksraad," he writes, "generally was not illiberal, but the Educational Council got their backs up badly. The Educational Council may be abused *ad lib*. Practically it did nothing except pay Robinson £1000 a year, get him to write incorrect things to the *Times*, and make things generally uncomfortable. They had no desire to work with Government; they were unpopular with the Outlanders. In Jeppestown they spent a lot of money on a school, and the Jeppestown people gave them a cheque and cleared them out. In Braamfontein the Wesleyans starved them out by co-operating with Government and starting a school which cut out the others. I tried to work with them, so did my predecessor—it was impracticable. He and I commenced dealings with Government, and were on the point of making our Church school a Government school. This was partly because with Government we had free entry to the school—with the Council we were excluded. Educational policy was on a line with general policy—that is, it grew more restrictive as time went on, as a response to more imperative demands and increased agitation.

"In spite of all, the Government was preferable to the Council, the exasperating part of the former rather being that one was forced upon one's knees to get anything."

To the statement, commonly reported, that the Government refused to make any provision for the needs of Outlander children, so far as instruction by the medium of the English language is concerned, the following letter, stating facts which are undeniable, is the best answer.

SPEECH AT PRESIDENT SCHOOL.

"The Rev. J. T. Lloyd also made a few remarks."—Transvaal Leader, Aug. 22, 1899.

To THE EDITOR OF THE LEADER.

SIR,—I quote above your report of the Rev. Mr. Lloyd's speech at the President School prize distribution. In view of the importance of the reverend gentleman's address, rightly appreciated by your contemporaries, both of which supply their readers with a very full report, it is extremely unfortunate that exigencies of space (no doubt) forbade you from giving Mr. Lloyd's "remarks" the publicity and prominence which they undoubtedly deserve. It would be surprising if such statements as those made by Mr. Lloyd yesterday should be thought unworthy not only of comment or criticism, but even of record.

Mr. Lloyd made four statements which distinctly call for attention :—

1. That the Government of this Republic has established four State schools in which the sole medium of education is English.

2. That the Government of this Republic has established

APPENDIX TO CHAPTER V

eight State schools in which the medium for English children is English and for Dutch children Dutch.

3. That the Government of this Republic grants yearly subsidies to six other schools in this country, not State schools, in which the sole medium is English.

4. That the Government of this Republic is at all times willing, through the Education Department, to provide English education on the proclaimed goldfields to any community that makes application for it.

Having also, like Mr. Lloyd, made inquiries on this subject, I beg leave to supplement the four statements recorded above with the following details:—

1. The four State schools in which English is the sole medium of instruction are (1) Barberton State School, opened in January 1897; (2) Union Grounds State School, opened in September 1897; (3) President State School, opened in August 1898; (4) Randfontein State School, opened in December 1898.

2. The eight State schools in which English is the medium for English children, and Dutch for Dutch children, are (1) Klerksdorp State School, opened in August 1897; (2) Maraisburg State School, opened in January 1898; (3) Market Street State School, opened in April 1899; (4) Vrededorp State School, opened in May 1899; (5) Krugersdorp State School, opened in May 1899; (6) Kaapsche Hoop State School, English section, opened in January 1899; (7) Pilgrimsrust State School, opened in February 1899; (8) Nigel State School, opened in July 1899.

3. The six English schools which are not State schools, but subsidised schools are: (1) Diocesan College, Pretoria; (2) St. Mary's College, Jeppestown; (3) Wesleyan Day School, Jeppestown; (4) High School for Girls, Doornfontein; (5) High School for Girls, Langlaagte; (6) The City and Suburban School.

4. Applications for English, or English and Dutch, State schools, have been received from the following places, and are still under consideration: (1) Roodepoort; (2) Ophirton; (3) City and Suburban; (4) Lorentzville.

Hoping that you will be able to find room for this communication.—I am, &c.,

HUGH J. EVANS.

August 22, 1899.

CHAPTER VI

THE WAR SPIRIT IN PRETORIA

PRETORIA is a quiet, leisurely little city, laid out with wide streets and ample gardens, where, at the time when I came there, the spring sun was bringing out a wealth of blossoms on the fruit trees and restoring the first tinge of verdure to the faded grass. There is little of the formal State capital about it; business is virtually contained within the limits of the single large square which contains the post-office, the branches of the large African banks, and the two costly and really imposing piles of the Government buildings and the Law Courts. Round this square the lawyers and other professional men have their chambers, and radiating from it are half-a-dozen short roads containing the hotels and shops. The tram service carries one in about three minutes to the suburbs or residential parts, chiefly composed of middle-sized white bungalows, with a very few large, handsome single or double storeyed modern houses. Everywhere is a sense of incompleteness; the roads, if you follow them, soon leave you in the open veldt. There is little attempt at elegance in architecture; everything is new, and even the startling fecundity of Nature does not enable the Pretorians to raise noble and imposing gardens in a single decade. Yet, crude though everything is, there is none of the scurry and noise of the mushroom industrial town; a spirit of ease and cheerfulness pervades the place. It was difficult to realise that this bright, peaceful little town was, during my visit last August, the theatre of a terrible drama which threatened to play havoc with the fortunes of all South Africa.

As I sat writing in the lobby of the Government buildings, in an inner hall the First Raad was debating the issue peace or war. That day would probably determine whether this little State, with a burgher population less than that of Nottingham, would by itself dare the greatest and most populous empire the world has ever known to do its worst. It is no easy matter to understand or to describe the many cross-currents of passion and conviction which played through the heated atmosphere. There was none of that loud, open expression of excited views by public meetings, by street demonstrations, by eager groups of café frequenters with which we are familiar in European crises. A stranger might wander for hours through the town without finding the faintest sign of any excitement, unless he entered the club or bar and listened to the growl of the conversation there. Even in these places there was a curious self-restraint and absence of personal animosity. At night, when the hostility of Boer and English might have been supposed to break all amicable intercourse, I sat in the smoke-room of the club amidst a group composed about equally of Boers and Englishmen, both sides expressing themselves with the utmost vigour and freedom, applauding and denouncing the course of the President and his Government, and yet there was not the slightest personal resentment exhibited by Boer to Englishman, or the faintest danger of such a fracas as in France or Germany would have been quite inevitable. It cannot, of course, be pretended that the political and racial conflict was not straining social intercourse here, as indeed throughout South Africa. It would be a miracle if this were not so. For it must be kept in mind that these political differences did not stand at merely verbal controversy; in not a few instances these club members would shortly find themselves in arms against each other. Not only from the Transvaal, but all over South Africa young English Afrikanders were volunteering; many were leaving Johannesburg with the intention of re-entering with the British troops. While in Pretoria I met a large handful of young Transvaalers who have been to the English universities, or have been trained in the medical and legal schools of London, whose dearest associations outside those of their own country are English, who have lived for many years in closest habitual familiarity with English Outlanders. This is less the case in Johannesburg, where society is entirely Outlander; but here Boer and Briton were bound by countless ties of friendship and of social interest. It may be imagined what was the stress of political discussion under such conditions. And yet these men freely and amicably bandied arguments likely within a few weeks to be referred to the brutal arbitrament of the Mauser and the Maxim. To listen to them talking, one would never have realised what was at stake, never have imagined that these very men at home were polishing their new Government rifles.

The self-restraint of the ordinary Boer is marvellous. It is not sheer ignorance or brutish callousness, as some represent, but the mental aspect of that racial endurance which has set them where they stand and made them what they are. It is only by entering many houses and talking to many men that the powerful pent-up or half-articulate spirit of a people who believe they will be called on in the near future to engage in a death-struggle for their independence becomes manifest. All the men and women were keen politicians. They had followed as well as they could the play of motives in diplomacy; but the game had been too intricate for most, and they had fallen back upon a sort of instinctive inspiration for their interpretation. Underneath the claims and counter-claims, proposals and counter-proposals, they seemed to discern one solid kernel of lamentable truth, namely, that England was seeking to destroy the independence of their country. They bitterly remembered the treacherous Raid of Jameson and the virtual whitewash by the British Government in the Committee and its sequel. This present assault, masquerading as a demand for a redress of grievances, they regarded as the next act in the same drama—a political raid. "England wants our country"—the exact meaning of this constantly reiterated phrase was difficult to grasp; it varied widely according to the intelligence of him who used it. The most ignorant of the remoter farmers seemed to have a notion that the English would take away their farms, but the more prevalent idea was that England had determined to make the Transvaal a colony or vassal State, or else to fasten upon it the virtual supremacy of the Outlander population of the Rand. The majority of those who had followed more closely the issues readily distinguished between the British people and the British Government. It was for the Government that they reserved their animosity, and naturally the Government was personified in Mr. Chamberlain. Sir Alfred Milner was hardly named excepting as a tool. Some of them had a clear-cut explanation of what had happened, to the following effect. Mr.

Rhodes they knew to be a large holder of shares in the Consolidated Goldfields; this man, their ancient enemy, they said had gone to Mr. Chamberlain and handed over a number of these shares, in return for which the Colonial Secretary had undertaken his political raid. A curious feature of Boer feeling was the respect and veneration with which they spoke of the Queen. " The Queen, she is a good and a pious woman, who means no evil to us; it is only that *verdomde* Kimberlain " (the common pronunciation of the Colonial Secretary's name) " that has led astray the British people." So an old farmer, a pioneer and voortrekker, put it to me.

These people did not want to fight; the Boer is not by nature a warlike animal; he wants to be left alone and to lead a leisurely and somewhat lazy life upon his farm. But he can and will fight for what he calls independence, and, rightly or wrongly, he was persuaded that " Kimberlain " was goading him on by constant demands for concessions which would in the near future mean either British sovereignty or, what is worse to many of them, the rule of the foreigner upon the Rand. These notions had been slowly growing in their minds, and the distrust and dismay with which many of them regarded the rapid climb-down of their Government in conceding nine years, then seven, then five as the qualifying term for burghership was a really serious factor in the situation. It is true that when President Kruger and the Raad went to the burghers after the Bloemfontein Conference, they received what might be termed "a free hand " to deal with the franchise, but in the case of a stubborn and suspicious people that does not mean what it sounds. Only a small number of the young bloods, who had never tasted war, clamoured for it; the older men would mount their horse,

THE WAR SPIRIT IN PRETORIA 45

with their Mauser and their slice of " biltong " hanging to their saddle, when they were " commandeered," but they would do it without enthusiasm or sanguine hope. The notion that the mass of Boers imagined they could beat the British nation is in the main a falsehood, fabricated to feed the animosity of Englishmen and to revive memories of Majuba. No doubt there was a certain contempt for Tommy Atkins, with his red uniform, as they remembered him. There was also among some of them a fanatical religious spirit, an Old Testament Puritanic conviction that the Lord, fighting with them, would cancel all advantages of science and numbers. But taken as a whole, the people had no desire to fight with another white race unless they were driven into it by a conviction of its necessity for self-defence.

CHAPTER VII

THE RACE CONFLICT IN SOUTH AFRICA

THE horrible meaning of the "domestic fury and fierce civil strife" threatening South Africa was first brought home to me in the fulness of its meaning by a week-end visit to the little country town of Potchefstroom. This place, large village rather than town, is illustrative of the ups and downs of this rapidly eventful country. Before Pretoria came into being it served as a sort of capital of the Transvaal, and in the war of independence in 1881 lay in the thick of the fighting, and was the scene of a stubborn resistance by a small body of English troops entrenched just outside the town, who were driven by starvation to surrender after Majuba. When the gold fever set in, Potchefstroom had some years of bright promise; capital flowed in, and the population doubled and trebled. But no large quantity of payable gold was found, and when the entire energy of industry settled on the Witwatersrand, the promise of Potchefstroom fizzled out, its population declined, and its trade languished. But, for all that, Potchefstroom has merits which will assert themselves when the country is settled on a firmer basis than that of the single gold industry. Eighty miles from Johannesburg, it lies in one of the richest and most fertile parts of South Africa, and enjoys to a marvellous extent the boon, which most of South Africa vainly craves, of abundance of water. The elder and the oak flourish wonderfully, and even now, before summer rains had begun to fall, the country was bright and green. A great agricultural future should lie before this little district; the soil is magnificently rich, and shrubs and fruit trees grow at a wonderful pace, while there is splendid grazing for cattle all round. One great drawback (Africa is full of drawbacks) retards its agriculture—the swarms of locusts which for the last eight years have come every spring and devoured all the greenness of the earth. There are other incidental evils too—the rinderpest, which, however, has been got under, and the storms of hail, which not infrequently ravage whole districts, stripping every leaf from the trees and battering stout shrubs to the earth. But, making all due allowances, we have a district which in climate, soil, and, I would add, in inhabitants, is beyond praise. The village itself, already the centre of a considerable outlying farm population, will probably become a fashionable pleasure resort in time to come. At present it is a simple, easy-going, unpretentious village; its people live a quiet and, it must be admitted, a somewhat idle life. But what struck me most, and what bore most directly upon the issue of to-day, was the intimate union or combination of Dutch and English everywhere apparent. The terrible folly of this violent upheaval came home when one perceived how British influence had been quietly and quickly making way by peaceful methods of industry and social intercourse all over the country. Did Great Britain seek to thrust the English language at the sword's point on the Boers? What need? The conveniences and the merits of our tongue need no such championing. There in the streets of Potchefstroom, though the vast majority are of Dutch descent, one heard far more English than Dutch. The shop fronts, with their advertisements of goods for sale, are a continual education in English. There is an English church, with a real live archdeacon resident in the place; there are English schools, and every inoffensive sign of English influence, and even dominance. Even now, though racial feeling had been fanned to its intensest heat, I saw no evidence of that personal incivility which is imputed to the ruling race. Among themselves, doubtless, these feelings find free vent in detestation of the "red-necked" Englishman, but there is wonderful self-restraint in public.

But only by visiting the people in their homes is the "civil" nature of this war made manifest. Dutch and British are at each other's throats in Africa, but there is scarcely a single family where the races do not in some way meet. Everywhere men of British descent have married Boer girls, and many of them have taken burghership and have grown sons who are by upbringing and by sympathy full Boers. Enter any of these farms, and you would find that there are relatives living in the Colony or in Natal, British subjects, divided in feeling between loyalty to the Empire and affection for their Republican kin. Remember that here it is no mere sympathy with the success of a professional fighting class, the hired defenders of their country. Well-to-do England supplies a minute fraction of its manhood for such a combat. The Transvaal is a nation in arms; every peaceable occupation in the land is stripped of its workers and entirely stopped. Each one of these farmhouses has sent its three or four soldiers, some mere lads of fifteen, just strong enough to handle a Mauser, some grey-headed old men of sixty, who have already earned their rest after a good life's work. Near Potchefstroom I saw an old man, one of the first party to cross the Vaal nearly seventy years ago—then a lad, now a man of over eighty-five—whose old eyes blazed with excitement as he spoke of the coming fray. "I have written to my son," he said (this son was an officer in the Staats Artillerie at Pretoria), "to tell him there must be no nonsense about my remaining here; I shall demand to go to the front." The people of England have little notion what it means to wake this demon of war in an entire nation, every man of whom must fight and risk his life. Out of the 30,000 burghers on the Field Cornets' books, upwards of 25,000 certainly turned out—probably a larger number. The President himself is said to have put seven sons and over forty grandsons in the field (these Boer families run large); the civil officers from highest to lowest will fight; and almost all civil administration, with the exception of the postal and telegraph system, has been entirely suspended. My host took me to visit an old English officer, who had lived for a quarter of a century a rough farming life, preferring it to the more stately life of a country gentleman in Leicestershire, a burgher who fully expected to be commandeered and to be called to face in mortal conflict the British troops from Natal, amongst whom one of his own sons is an officer. Nor is this horrible contingency so exceptional as it may be thought. I personally came across a dozen families or more, the burgher sons of which are liable to be confronted in combat by brothers or cousins volunteering in Cape Colony or Natal.

The oneness of South Africa comes out most powerfully at such a time. Among the better educated classes, particularly of the towns, there has been an immense amount of intermarriage going on between British and Dutch, with constant migration between the colonies and the Republics. If, as seems quite possible, the area of conflict spreads from the Republics to the whole of South Africa, and a general race war ensues, the tragical horror of the situation may be well imagined. It must be kept in mind that a large proportion of the younger men risk nothing but their lives in such a cause. Over a large portion of the colony land is worked by a sort of patriarchal system, the father or head of the family being legal owner of the land and allotting portions to his sons to work. Large numbers of these sons of the soil have quitted their land, taken to the saddle, and ridden over the border. Months before the outbreak of hostilities it was quite evident that when the British forces confronted the Boers, many thousands of these young colonists would be there, pointing their rifles, treason though it be, against the soldiers of their Queen. Should the British troops suffer a reverse at the outset, it was then fully recognised that the number of these colonists would be doubled or trebled, and every obstacle would be set against the march of British troops through the colonies by the country population. How far things might go in the direction of civil strife over the continent it was unsafe to predict; but it was impossible to watch the gathering wrath of the phlegmatic Dutch farmers in the colony without a feeling of the gravest apprehension lest the whole of South Africa become a battlefield. These men had not generally followed the *finesse* of the diplomatic sparring, but their plain, shrewd sense had struck down to the bed-rock of the situation, and they knew many of the sort of facts which are hidden from London, and even from Cape Town. They knew perfectly-well that the Outlander of Johannesburg was not grievously oppressed, but that, on the contrary, he enjoyed a licence of practical freedom and luxury, and, in an economic way, was "cock of the walk."

They remembered how the Free State was forced to surrender the Diamond Fields, and they believed the same game was being played for the goldfields of the Rand; they had a good working comprehension of the ways of Mr. Rhodes and of the ways in which Capitalism was handling British Imperialism, though they saw the history not in abstract "isms," but in hard, concrete deeds and persons. Of the power and policy of Great Britain these folk, of course, had little inkling, but the Dutch farmer in South Africa has always had a strong grip of the facts and forces on the spot, and what has taken place this winter has probably surprised him far less than it has surprised the British nation.

CHAPTER VIII

THE HELOTS IN JOHANNESBURG

I TAKE it that the motive which has led the majority of English people to approve, so far as they have approved, the policy of their Government, is not their convictions on the merits of the franchise or the suzerainty issues, but a deep and genuine belief that British subjects were grievously oppressed by the Boer Government, and were without security of life, liberty, and property. A recent issue of the *Nineteenth Century* contains a statement from Sir Sidney Sheppard that "neither their persons nor their property can be held safe during the present *régime*." Those who are responsible for working public opinion have been wisely aware that the most effective means of rousing British anger against the Transvaal was to reiterate the statement that English people in Johannesburg were subject to brutal ill-treatment and went about in fear of their lives. I found it very difficult to persuade people upon the spot of the prevalence of this English view of their grievances; and no wonder, for the audacity of the misrepresentation is almost incredible. When I left England, filled with the atrocities of Mr. Chamberlain's Blue-book and Canon Knox Little's commentary upon Boer character, I looked forward to my sojourn in Johannesburg with deep apprehension. I pictured in my mind the oppressed helot of Sir Alfred Milner's famous telegram, continually harried in the peaceful pursuit of his calling by extortionate officials, subject to the personal violence of the brutal "Zarp" in the public streets, and liable to have the privacy of his domestic hearth invaded by blackmailing detectives. The slightest breach of arbitrary and vexatious regulations would, I was assured, be seized upon as a pretext for arrest and fine, while an appeal to the justice of the courts would only add insult to injury. The first doubts of the accuracy of this picture were instilled into my mind on the voyage out in the good ship the *Carisbrook Castle*, by a fellow-passenger who had for some years played an active part in the Outlander movement of Johannesburg. On questioning him respecting the reign of terror on the Rand, he smilingly explained to me that these outrages and sensational grievances were only designed for British consumption; that Britishers got what they wanted and did as they liked in Johannesburg; that the one real grievance which they suffered and resented was the "cocky" and insolent tone of the Boers with whom they came into contact. These people despised the British, and lost no opportunity of showing that they regarded them as inferiors and as cowards. This, in his eyes, was intolerable, and was only to be cured by giving the Boer a downright good thrashing, that he might know his place.

After a month's close inquiry on the spot, I became convinced that this view correctly represented the feeling of the great majority of Outlanders of British birth, or did so before they had been lashed into a brief enthusiasm for franchise and other reforms by a handful of politicians. I am not condemning these demands for reform, many, if not most, of which were both desirable and feasible; but I am convinced that, until the agitation of the last year, the concrete grievances which arouse the sympathy and indignation of the British public lay very lightly on the soul of the average Outlander. When I began to examine upon the spot, I found plenty of men at the Rand Club and elsewhere who told me startling tales of police brutality and miscarriages of justice, and launched into wholesale denunciations of Boer misgovernment. But two things soon struck me. My informants either confined themselves to generalities unbacked by specific cases, or more commonly narrated wrongs inflicted upon some friend of theirs. When I asked a man to give me instances of injuries or indignities which he himself had experienced, he generally allowed that he had been fortunately immune. Again, I soon observed the same stories coming up with insignificant variations; the story of the detectives who, seeing a man engaged in a harmless game of cards in his own house, forced their way in and hauled him to the charge-house under the Gambling Act; the police who came to the manager of an insurance business, and informed him that a building heavily insured was about to be attacked by incendiaries, and that, unless they were well paid for protecting it, it would certainly be destroyed. I soon became aware that these tales of wrong formed a stage army, the paucity of which was tricked out by continual reiteration. Again, it was nearly always the politician, the member of the League or the Outlander Council, who was so anxious to impress upon me the perils of the streets, the brutality of the "Zarp," the injustice of the courts. As I came more freely into contact with all sorts and conditions of men—the quiet professional man, the shop assistant, the mining overseer—I found these things played no part whatever in his life. Grumblers they were one and all, as healthy Britishers always are; many of them hated the

Boer, and believed him corrupt and incompetent; some of them exhibited a certain fervour on the franchise issue; but none of them had undergone any serious personal trouble with police or other officers of State. Several young men told me they had been for years in the habit of knocking about Johannesburg at night and returning home to the suburbs early in the morning, but that they had never been subjected to any interference. This view was certainly borne out by my personal experience. During the weeks I spent there, public feeling ran high, and then, if at any time, it would seem reasonable to expect scenes of disorder and even riot. But never have I seen a large English town more quiet or more orderly at night than Johannesburg. Though a great deal of drinking goes on at the bars, where the company (Outlanders almost to a man) has often a most disreputable aspect, there was scarcely any of the street-brawling which I saw in Cape Town. Where occasionally a noisy tippler staggered by, the neighbouring "Zarp," with orthodox official delicacy, generally looked the other way, though the delinquent was in most instances one of the Britishers who wanted his country. I have no desire to whitewash Johannesburg or its administration; there is much reason to suppose its police to be more bribable than those of London, and more ignorant and incapable; but I saw literally no indication of the prevailing terrorism and oppression, the insecurity of person and property, charged against it, nor did my cross-examination of many Outlanders elicit any material support for such accusations.

That the machinery for the detection and punishment of crime has reached any high standard of excellence may certainly be doubted. When the rapid growth of this huge cosmopolitan city, with its environment of gold mines, peopled by ten thousand white and nearly a hundred thousand black miners, is taken into consideration, it will be recognised as most unfair to compare the order and government of Johannesburg with those of Manchester or Glasgow. On this matter the testimony of Sir William Butler is more to the point, who compared the condition of the Rand with that of the Californian and Australian goldfields, which he knew well, and who considered the former incomparably superior in all the elements of orderly government. But what about the Edgar case, the Appelbe case, the Cape "boy" cases, and the other villanies? The answer is a simple one. The very hubbub created by these matters, and the monopoly of public interest they aroused, are sufficient to mark their exceptional character. Is there any large town in Europe where one could not cull from the police courts and the nightly streets a crop of similar charges? Assuming all these charges to be true, what did they prove? Nothing, unless they were shown to be indicative of a general condition of misgovernment. No such thing has been shown of Johannesburg. Sir Alfred Milner, prompted by his advisers from the Rand, has literally scooped together every specious example of injustice or tyranny that could be obtained. I make bold to say that he is quite unable to show that these cases are indicative of any general conditions. Indeed, at least one of them may be turned against him. If the Transvaal were really the semi-barbarous country which it is sometimes described as being, is it likely that a policeman shooting a criminal caught red-handed and in violent resistance would be promptly charged with manslaughter and brought to trial? It is very doubtful whether a policeman in one of the Western States of America shooting an Outlander under similar circumstances would even be put upon his trial. In Johannesburg he was charged, tried, and, in the judgment of any one who takes the trouble to read the evidence, fairly acquitted.[1] In the treatment of Cape

---

[1] In his Birmingham speech Mr. Chamberlain spoke of "the murder of Edgar," and in his despatch of May 10 he thus characterises the case: "But perhaps the most striking instance of arbitrary action by officials, and of the support of such action by the State, is the well-known Edgar case. The effect of the verdict of the jury, warmly endorsed by the judge, is that four policemen, breaking into a man's house at night, without a warrant, on the mere statement of one person, which subsequently turned out to be untrue, that the man had committed a crime, are justified in killing him there and then, because, according to their own account, he hits one of them with a stick." Now when Mr. Chamberlain wrote these lines he had in his possession a full report of the trial of this case. Any one who reads that report will perceive that the above-quoted account completely misrepresents the evidence. The proved facts are briefly these. Edgar, a British workman, addicted to drink, but not drunk at the time, was coming home late at night to a yard where he and other Outlanders lived. As he was coming down the yard another Outlander, Forster, said something to his dog which Edgar took as an insult addressed to him. Although the man explained that the word was not applied to him, and a third Outlander, Sheppard, coming out, pointed out that Forster was drunk, Edgar, a big powerful man, struck Forster a violent blow, and left him senseless on the ground. Bystanders thought him dead, and his friend called loudly for the police. Four policemen came at once, saw Forster lying on the ground, and heard Sheppard say, "The man that ran into that room killed him." They proceeded at once to Edgar's window, and saw him standing with a weapon in his hand. They then paused a little to consider whether without a warrant they should break in the door. The Outlanders urged them to do so, and the police then pushed in the door, one of them, Jones, entering first. The police case is to the effect that Edgar stood just in the entrance with a sort of life-preserver, a tough stick with an iron nut screwed on one end, and a loop of cord to fit the hand upon the other, and that with this he struck Jones twice. Thereupon Jones, expecting another blow and unable to retire by pressure of the others from behind, drew his revolver and fired, killing Edgar. The resistance of Edgar was disputed at the trial, though the weapon described was produced in court, and two surgeons, one an Outlander, who examined Jones on his return to the police office, attested to the fresh wounds upon him. In reality the violent resistance of Edgar is clearly proved, not merely by police testimony, but by the sworn evidence of two Outlander witnesses. Even the *Star* in its report admits that "Edgar actively resisted his arrest." The policeman Jones

"boys" under the Pass Law and the commando there was undoubtedly good ground for complaint. But even here it must be remembered that the law of the country, as also in the neighbouring British colonies, enjoins harsh and often brutal interference with natives; and though British subjects from the colony or from India are technically exempt from some of these laws, the difficulty of distinguishing these cases from those where the law is applicable must necessarily lead to many mistakes. The notion that Englishmen or white British subjects have commonly been made the victims of oppression and terrorism is grotesquely and utterly false. No Johannesburger, however militant, pretended seriously to defend such an assertion upon the spot; he reserved such tales for British audiences and British newspapers. On the contrary, Johannesburg was a place where liberty prevailed in its extremest form—with the single exception of the franchise. So far as practical freedom of action, speech, and publication are concerned, there was no place upon the Continent of Europe which could for a moment compare with it.

But what about the tyrannical laws against the freedom of the press and the right of public meeting, which bulk so big in the parade of grievances? The Outlander politician sometimes sought to persuade me that he had been robbed by law of the very elements of liberty of expression. But on examining these laws, I did not find them differ in form or spirit from the laws which stand upon the statute book of England and other European

was charged at first with murder; subsequently the State prosecutor reduced the charge, on his own initiative, to culpable homicide. Upon this charge he was tried; the judge's charge, fully given, is scrupulously non-committal, and the jury, after a long retirement, gave a verdict of not guilty, which the judge approved.

States. The Press Law of 1896, against which so loud an outcry was raised when it was used for the temporary suppression of the *Critic* and the *Star*, contains no more oppressive powers than are contained and have been enforced within the last few years in the English law. In Ireland and in India during recent years many prosecutions have been instituted for offences which were venial as compared with those habitually committed by the Johannesburg press. Day after day, in defiance of the Press Law, the *Leader* and the *Star* continued to urge the grossest charges against the President, the Executive, and the Judiciary of the land, and to call on the hostile arms of England to cleanse the Augean stable. One cannot read the language of this press, some examples of which I give in a later chapter, without wondering at the apathy of a Government which could tolerate such abuse.

The Law of Public Meeting (No. 6 of 1894) is a close copy of the English law in its general regulations regarding the limitations of the right of public meeting. It acknowledges the general right of meeting, but limits that right in the interest of public order, refusing it in cases of meetings "which have for their object disobedience or breach of the law or any legal enactment, disturbance of the rights of any one, the use of forcible means whereby public peace and safety are or may be endangered, or whereby the authority of constituted powers and officials is attacked, or whereby good morals are assailed," &c. It differs from the English law, and is assimilated to the special law for Ireland, in vesting in the police the right to be present at every public meeting, to decide whether it is illegal, and to disperse illegal meetings.

Until last autumn, upon the eve of war, no prosecution under this law had taken place: it was then applied in the case of a disorderly street meeting.

In the Transvaal, as in England, there are laws upon the statute book which, when quoted, sound like terrible restrictions upon liberty, but which as administered, or rather not administered, are harmless. Let me mention one or two crucial facts. Last summer you could stand at any street corner in Johannesburg, within hearing of the "Zarp," and hear Englishmen loudly and bitterly lamenting the sluggishness of the British arms they had invoked to invade the country which had given them shelter and gold; in any bar or other public place you might hear the most vehement denunciations of the Boer Government, and meetings were freely held to advocate the destruction of "the corrupt oligarchy at Pretoria." In front of the stationers' shops of Commissioner Street were displayed the most insulting caricatures of President Kruger, accompanied by letterpress which would not be tolerated by the officials or the public of any European city.

This license was at last carried so far as to stir the Government into active interference, and in September the "freedom of the press" was violated by the arrest of the editor of the *Leader* and the attempted arrest of the editor of the *Star*, though even then the publication of the papers was not stopped.

This interference, as also the earlier stoppage of the *Star* and the *Critic*, was I think unnecessary and unwise. I believe that the mendacity of the Outlander press, balanced by similar propensities in the Hollander press, would far better have been left to run its evil course unchecked. But it is hardly possible to feel strong resentment against a Government when it makes tardy attempts to regulate the press which, by its systematic misrepresentation, had already brought the hostile forces of England to the borders of the Transvaal.

As for general liberty and even license of conduct, it existed nowhere if not in Johannesburg. Every luxury of life, every extravagance of behaviour, every form of private vice flourished unchecked; every man and woman (except Kaffirs, who do the work and don't count) said and did what seemed good in his or her own eyes. The helot wore his golden chains with insolent composure of demeanour, as he feasted in the sumptuous rooms of the Rand and the New Clubs, or lolled in the rickshaw which, drawn by the toiling Kaffir, bore him to his luxurious home. The entire wealth of the country, drawn from the bowels of the earth by Kaffir labour, passed easily into his hands, with the exception of a toll taken by the Government, which he resented as if it were the fruits of the toil of his own hands; in a land of simple-mannered, plain-living farmers he alone had material luxury and the leisure to enjoy it.

As for the official insolence upon which my ship-companion fell back as the solid grievance, nothing of it was observable. People sometimes told me that the "Zarp" answered Englishmen uncivilly, and that other officials put impediments in the way of Englishmen transacting business unless their palms were greased. This may have been so; the country Boer drafted into the police force was certainly ignorant, probably rude in manner, and more than possibly corrupt; but to suggest that out of such matters intolerable grievances could be constituted is a bold defiance of common sense. So far as the evidence of a visitor is permissible, I may say that I experienced none of that incivility of matter or manner in dealing with postal and other civil officials which English people expect in France or Germany. My sober judgment, formed upon careful consideration of the kind of Englishman who was working up these grievances, is that this insolence imputed to the Boer simply consisted in his assumption of equality and refusal of that deference or recognition of superiority which the British have come to expect in other parts of South Africa. Britishers coming from the colonies had been accustomed to despise "the dirty Boer," and to regard him as a social inferior; in the Transvaal they found him in power and refusing to accept the rôle of inferior; hence their indignation.

To this one ought to add the fact that the average Johannesburger had virtually no contact with the Boers, and that his assumed knowledge of the character and feelings of the burgher population has no substantial basis of personal experience.

CHAPTER IX

THE DEMAND FOR THE FRANCHISE

THOUGH the tempest has swept the franchise issue from the land of live politics, and few any longer care to ask, "Did the Outlanders want the franchise? How many would have taken it?" a certain value still attaches to these questions, for the future of the Transvaal is not so entirely sundered from the past as the fevered imagination of catastrophic politicians seems to think. It is still worth while asking, "How many of the Outlanders in the year 1899 would have been willing to renounce their citizenship in some European State in order to become citizens of the South African Republic?" Now no safe answer to such a question was possible without experiment. The British Government, in insisting upon a franchise which should give immediate and substantial representation, placed itself in the predicament of proposing tests which were impossible of application. It might be possible to ascertain how many Outlanders would be competent to take a franchise with a seven or five years' residence and a given property qualification, but how many of them would actually take it there could be no sure means of ascertaining beforehand. How Sir Alfred Milner was able to satisfy himself that the Seven Years' Franchise Law, actually passed, did not satisfy the proposed tests, is a mystery which still waits solution. Everything turned upon the question, How far was the demand or the franchise genuine? There were no data for a satisfactory answer. The political agitators of the South African League, though admitting that prior to 1895 very few troubled their heads about political rights, insisted that the great majority of Outlanders were now alive to the importance of political rights, and were eager and earnest in their desire to possess them. The conservative Boer, backed by a large amount of Outlander opinion, regarded the whole movement as of artificial origin, the product of professional grievance-mongers, and affirmed that very few Outlanders really wanted the franchise and were prepared to renounce their British or other nationality to get it.

Now it seems at first sight as if the genuineness of the demand were a matter of present wish or desire—distinctively subjective conditions. This no doubt has a bearing on the issue, and many of my first inquiries in Johannesburg were devoted to trying to gauge the width and depth of this desire for the franchise. I came to the conclusion that two sets of people were really keen about the matter, both of them belonging to the well-to-do professional and commercial middle classes. There was first the Afrikander, chiefly of British origin, drawn from the Cape or from Natal, accustomed in these colonies to exercise the franchise and to regard himself as in every way at least the equal of the Boer. Many of these men, recognising the essential unity of South Africa and the need of solidarity among the white races, had long chafed against the political exclusiveness of the Transvaal Dutch. Not a few of them had come to stay, and though they would have sincerely preferred to remain British subjects, they were not so quixotically British as to be willing for this sentiment to forego all the solid advantages of citizenship in the land of their adoption. Even if they did not intend to bind themselves to permanent settlement in the Transvaal, they entertained the view that a white man should not anywhere in Africa be placed in a position of inferiority in face of the native population which it was his chief business to rule. The second class consisted of Englishmen, Scotchmen (quite as many of the latter), and Jews of mixed nationality, who had come to the Transvaal to "hustle" in business, who were conscious of possessing brains and energy, and were annoyed by the slow and clumsy methods of the Government; they wanted to get politics into their hands so as to impart speed and security to industrial development. Many of these men, as I shall show, were chiefly prompted by purely selfish motives, which would ultimately lead them to use politics against the common weal; but some were moved by a genuine interest in the cause of good government, quickened by the irritation which a sharp-witted business man feels when he sees incompetent people round him muddling things and wasting the public resources. When Sir A. Milner and the South African League described the Reform movement as distinctively belonging to the intelligent, educated middle classes, it is these people that they meant, and there is this amount of truth in the description. How far the few big men known as the capitalists were genuine politicians, and sought the franchise in order to improve the government, I need not here inquire; it suffices to say that they had never openly clamoured for the franchise, preferring to press against the Government those grievances relating to dynamite, liquor, and pass laws, railway rates, &c., which bore directly upon the mining industry.

The feelings of the working classes—miners, mechanics, clerks, shopmen—were most difficult to gauge. At least half of those I talked with wished to have no concern with politics, had been earning good money, and objected to any political disturbance : most of the miners held this view. But a good many, perhaps a large minority, had been stirred by the League and other politicians into a conviction that the franchise was a right, and the absence of it a grievance. Few exhibited any keen desire to get it, but many could be induced to shout for it at a public meeting. When I put to them point-blank the question, "Would you be willing to abandon now your British rights and become a burgher of the Transvaal, liable to be commandeered?" I seldom received a confident affirmative reply. Indeed, many of the leading men in the Reform movement fenced with the question, requiring all sorts of guarantees, and, in particular, the right of reverting at any time to their abandoned British status. Their hesitancy was curiously illustrated at the preliminary meeting of prominent reformers summoned to plan the formation of the Outlander Council, when an earnest man got up and proposed that those present should show their *bona fides* by each man personally declaring his willingness to accept the franchise. This proposal was strongly opposed by various members, who objected to pledge themselves, and the division of opinion was so strong that the proposer of the resolution was induced to withdraw it. My opinion is that only a small minority of British Outlanders would have been willing definitely to accept the franchise upon the conditions indicated by Sir A. Milner at Bloemfontein, and afterwards at Cape Town, that they should in the future not look to the British Government to redress their

THE DEMAND FOR THE FRANCHISE

grievances, but to themselves and the burghership they had acquired.

But in reality the issue did not chiefly hinge upon the present intensity or extent of desire for the franchise. The important matter was not how many earnestly desired to become burghers in five or seven years' time, but how many would, in fact, have taken and used the burgher rights. This was far less a matter of desire and inclination than of economic and social circumstances. Let me put it thus. The vast majority of those who came to the Transvaal, as business men or as manual workers, did not come to stay, but to make money and take it away; they had no intention of settling down for good in a new country and of bringing up families. But some of these men did actually stay (or, if they left, returned), some because they had fared badly and could not leave, others because they had done well, and wished to do better. The capitalist who made his fortune and cleared with it to Europe, scarcely counts numerically; it is to the average business or working man that we must rightly look. Those who took for their criterion the recent turn of events and the current temper of the Outlander population, could make a strong *prima facie* case for the view that the franchise was entirely a sham grievance. A large proportion of the business men in Johannesburg were not confined in their operations to the Transvaal, but had interests in other parts of South Africa; the financial and professional classes in South Africa are peculiarly nomadic; the shopkeepers, whose local attachment is somewhat closer, had not that firm confidence in the permanent prospects of Johannesburg which would make them eager to obtain a fixed political status in the country. Extreme and unforeseen fluctuation is a law of South African life; the example of Kimberley was ever before the mind of the Johannesburger, and he feared lest his city might fall into the same decadence and decay. The white wage-earners of Johannesburg, shop-assistant or mechanic, had certainly no firm grip upon the place, and the recent crisis has probably shaken off most of them.

The miners were the only large solid section of the population who were distinctively English. The great majority of these were single men, or married men with families in England: no large proportion of them had come to regard the Rand as their permanent abode. The Jameson Raid and the recent crisis illustrate the slender attachment which bound them to the country upon whose citizenship they were supposed to set so high a value that England must fight to win it for them. I do not blame them or call them cowards for always "clearing" at the first scare, but merely adduce the fact to show how slight an actual hold the Transvaal had upon them. But the best available evidence of the unsettled and transitory character of the mining population is afforded by the figures which Mr. C. S. Goldmann presented before the Industrial Commission in 1897, which dealt with the white miners of 53 companies employing 3620 men, or considerably more than one-third of the total number of miners employed upon the Rand. Of these men, only 470, or 12.9 per cent., were married men with families on the property; 1195, or 33.1 per cent., were married men with families abroad; while 1955, or 54 per cent., were single men. Still more significant is the statement that, during the six weeks preceding the inquiry, which was a period of normal industrial and political condition, no fewer than 827 miners, or about 27 per cent. of the whole number, threw up their employment at the mines. Of these 827, about 380, or 46 per cent., were ascertained to have left the country, while 447, or 54 per cent., remained, finding presumably some other work.

So far as the mining population is concerned, it is evident that only a small number have hitherto looked to the Transvaal as their settled home: most lived there for a time, and, saving money out of their high money wage of £25 to £30 per month, sent their savings home, or stayed long enough to make sufficient to set up in some little business elsewhere, and disappeared. If this was to be the normal condition of affairs in the Transvaal, it seemed idle to clamour and criminal to fight for the franchise and the rights of burghership on behalf of a population which did not value them and could not use them properly. This is the Boer contention: "These gilded butterflies and their parasites are here for a brief day to snatch what gain they can and pass away: they have no solid footing in the country and no desire to link their lives with its well-being; they have no affection for it. How then can they make good citizens?"

If the experience of the few years that have passed since the discovery of gold be taken as final, there is no sufficient answer to this plea. The theories about inherent rights of the governed to participate in government, the iniquity of taxation without representation, have no clearly rightful application to a fluctuating population, however large, of mere temporary sojourners. Even the fact that they are already owners of the greater part of the land and other property in the country is no sufficient argument for giving them that citizenship which in every country implies personal interests and obligations, and not mere investments. If a property stake is in itself a right basis of a claim to burghership, then all the European holders of any considerable stock in Rand mines might have fairly claimed the franchise. No; the real and only solid ground for securing the franchise for the present and prospective Outlanders was a belief that the future would not be as the past; that the industrial resources of the country afforded a firm foundation for secure and progressive material prosperity, and that the political and social problems which had imparted so stormy a character to the past years admitted of a tolerable settlement. If such economic and political security could be obtained, a growing proportion of Outlanders would, in fact, establish themselves permanently in the Transvaal, making homes, rearing families, and identifying themselves in human interests and sympathies with the nation.

Now, for economic reasons stated hereafter, I do not believe in the permanent settlement of a large British population in the Transvaal. But for the next few decades, at any rate, a certain number of Britons will make their home in this country, and a larger number of non-British Outlanders, mostly Russian, Polish, and German Jews, with roving propensities and no strongly rooted attachment to an old country, will dwell in Johannesburg and on the Rand. A prospect of successful business for a tolerably long future, with full personal, civil, and political liberty, will keep the bulk of these people in the country, and inspire them with such patriotism as they are capable of entertaining.

Among them will be a certain number—not nearly so large as is supposed—of British miners, earning higher wages than they can get elsewhere, and willing to settle down in the Transvaal, instead of consuming a large proportion of their wages, as now, in flying visits to England.

THE DEMAND FOR THE FRANCHISE

Improved government and industrial confidence would induce many of these classes to make a permanent settlement in the Transvaal.

Now it was most desirable that these people should be attached to the country of their adoption as closely as possible, and that they should have been encouraged, upon reasonable terms, to take the rights and duties of citizenship. It was important not merely for these persons, but for the State, that they should have the franchise and should use it. This was the firm conviction not only of the Dutch politicians of the Cape, but of all the educated people in Pretoria. But for the disastrous consequences of the Raid, and the consequent fear that a quick enfranchisement of a large class might revolutionise the government and run the country entirely in the interests of the Rand, a liberal franchise would have been voluntarily accorded by the burghers. Even among the more conservative and unenlightened classes there was a growing disposition to accept the inevitable. This is well put by a gold-mining expert who knows the people well, and whose judgment I quote because he is no politician.[1] "A few more years will see the government of the country, and that with the consent and co-operation of the Boers, pass into the hands of more enlightened and progressive rulers." The rooted reluctance of Kruger and his stalwarts would certainly have given way before a tactful handling by conciliatory diplomatists. If the demand for a reasonable franchise had been dissociated from other demands, which seemed to threaten the independence of the country as defined by the London Convention, such franchise could undoubtedly have been obtained. Even had the obstinacy of Kruger not yielded to the importunities of the more

[1] Curle, "Gold Mines of the World," p. 28.

liberal members of his Government, several of whom notoriously favoured a liberal franchise, the representations of the Free State politicians would have been effectual. Many close conversations and inquiries at Pretoria and Bloemfontein justify me in registering my firm conviction that a clean and satisfactory five years' franchise, moulded, if required, on the model of the English law, could have been obtained without war or the menace of war, provided that British diplomatists had genuinely sought a settlement upon this basis.

CHAPTER X

OFFICIAL CORRUPTION AND INCOMPETENCY

THAT certain grave faults existed in the administration of government in the Transvaal cannot seriously be disputed. Most of these were not in any special sense Outlander grievances, for they were injuries to the entire body politic, but all the more on this account they demanded recognition and remedy. First and chief among these defects I should place the incompetency and corruption of a considerable part of the officials and the maladministration of the finances of the country.

The faults of officialism arose naturally from the circumstances of the Boer Government, and were undoubtedly enhanced by the policy of exclusion which prevailed. There are probably not more than 29,000 adult male Boers in the Transvaal, the vast majority bred on outlying farms, with no education to speak of and no knowledge of affairs. Even with the best process of selection, it is evident that a full complement of capable officials competent to deal with the social and industrial problems of life in Johannesburg and the goldfields could not have been obtained from such a source. The Government offices at Pretoria, the Netherlands Railway, the regulation of the natives, the administration of the Gold, Pass, and Liquor Laws in the Rand, the provision of municipal government for the quick-growing towns with their heterogeneous population, could not be properly under taken by this small community of farmers. The old semi-military system under commandants and field-cornets could not be adapted to fit the new circumstances of a large industrial population. There was no proper means of training officials, or even for securing for them a decent business education, since the Boers took no direct part whatever in the development of the goldfields and the subsidiary industrial life. Counting in the police (no less than 800 are required for Johannesburg and district) there were probably not fewer than 3000 men in direct Government employ, an enormous proportion of the entire burgher population. Even allowing that the less skilled and routine work could be properly done, it was evident that the more highly skilled work of the Government must suffer. This to some extent the Boers had recognised. Naturally enough, though most unfortunately, they looked to Holland to assist them, thus introducing the Hollander factor, which has been the root-cause of much serious mischief. For technical work in Government offices the Hollander was doubtless a convenience; from Holland a readier supply of educated lawyers and officials competent to handle the High Dutch language was obtainable than from the Colony. Unfortunately, the kind of Hollander who came, and the temper and aspirations which he introduced and fostered in the Boer, were most damaging influences.

To Dr. Leyds and the compatriots whom he set in certain most important offices, particularly in the department of education, both the policy and the spirit of racial antagonism are largely due. One might almost go as far as to say that had there been no Dr. Leyds there would have been no Transvaal crisis to-day. The Hollander taught the Government of this country the art of red-tape qualified by corruption. Set in many of the most important and lucrative places, having no intention to live permanently in the country, they acted as officials have always acted in such circumstances—they sought at once to satisfy a lust for power and to feather their nests. There were of course exceptions, but such was notoriously the rule. It is right, however, to remark that the Transvaal had of recent years discovered and done much to rectify this evil: the number of Hollanders in high places had greatly diminished, being replaced either by Afrikanders from the Colony, or by Transvaalers themselves, educated in the Colony and in Europe. Last year out of 1958 officials in the country no less than 1452, or about three-fourths, were of South African birth, 478 of these being Cape Afrikanders, as compared with 306 drawn from Holland. Moreover, if we take the high posts in the State, we scarcely find any Hollanders now in possession—President, Vice-President, Commandant-General, Auditor-General, Treasurer-General, State-Attorney, Commissioner of Railways, nearly every head of department is a born Afrikander. Even the judicial bench, once a monopoly of the Hollander, has now been nearly purged of him, for at the present time only one acting judge is a Hollander. With this change, and the freer drawing upon Afrikander sources during the last three years, a decided improvement both in the intellectual calibre and the character of the higher State officials is admitted to have taken place. This is an important reform for which due credit should be given. For instance, the administration of justice has been greatly benefited during the last two years by the appointment of an English-trained lawyer, Mr. Smuts, to the post of State Attorney, and by the presence of Dr. Krause as Public Prosecutor in Johannesburg. Both these men belong to a young progressive school which has other able representatives in various State departments. Nepotism has certainly to some extent retarded these reforms, a recent notorious case being the appointment to a judgeship of a young barrister, Mr. Kock, son of a member of the Executive Council, a young man of no known ability and no experience. Such cases, however, occasionally happen elsewhere. Regarding the higher officials, the opinion of all, save the blind Boer-hater, is that they are a fairly competent and fairly honest body of men. There were many who told me that the whole of Boer officialism from the ordinary Zarp in the street to the President, and including the judges of the High Court, were corrupt almost to a man, habitually taking money bribes and abusing their offices. Now I took much trouble to sift these charges of corruption, not of course by detailed investigation of instances, obviously impossible, but by a careful comparison of testimony of various kinds of witnesses. There is, I think, some *prima facie* ground for suspecting that certain high officers of State have indulged in "shady practices" relating to concessions and land speculation, using their public powers to assist their private purses, though none of these charges have been proven. I found no reason for accepting the charges of common bribery freely brought against the President and high officers of State, which were almost universally received as facts by Englishmen in the Transvaal.

Mr. Winston Churchill's description of South Africa as "a land of lies" is not quite the reckless generalisation it sounds. Whether it be a subtle psychical reaction of certain deceptive qualities of the country, its illusive distances, mirages, the incalculable tricks of nature in this "land of surprises," or contact with "the treacherous

CORRUPTION AND INCOMPETENCY 77

Kaffirs," or whether it be a "natural selection" leading to the survival of mendacity for use in speculative business, I am unable to decide.

But about the fact there can be no doubt. "There are liars and credulous folk in every land"; but for minute detailed mendacity and the wanton acceptance of the same, South Africa stands pre-eminent. It took me some time to adjust my inexperienced mind to this focus. For some time I was disposed to accept readily the circumstantial statements made, apparently in all good faith, by sober intelligent business and professional men. But I soon learned the need of severe scepticism. In the art of which I speak it is scarcely necessary to add that politicians were the greatest adepts; and when the business man becomes politician, he brings his business talent for detail into his politics, with marvellous results.

The case of the Selati Railway will serve as an example of what I mean. Baron Oppenheim, wishing to obtain a profitable concession, alleges that he employed an agent to pay bribes to Transvaal officials and Raad members, and in a plea filed in a case against the Government for unjustly depriving them of their rights and seeking to cancel the contract, he placed certain sums of money against the names of these officials and members, alleging they had received them. Upon the strength of this *ex parte* statement, made by a man guilty upon his own confession of gross corruption, Mr. Fitzpatrick evidently considers the charge has been proved, and speaks of "the indisputable fact of bribes having been taken wholesale,"[1] though he has just before admitted that the charge is denied by all of those incriminated

---

[1] "The Transvaal from Within," p. 321.

who have condescended to answer it, and that no impartial investigation has taken place.

What is still more curious is the fact that many English readers of Mr. Fitzpatrick's book are convinced that the case of money bribery is proved in the matter of the Selati Railway. They have seen the exact sums of money which the Vice-President, and various specified members of the Executive and the Volksraad are stated to have received, and when Mr. Fitzpatrick audaciously assumes that this *ex parte* evidence from incriminated witnesses is proof, they are taken off their guard and swallow it.

Similar charges were sometimes launched against the judiciary; but, except in one case, there has been no attempt to substantiate such charges, which it is fair to say were never made by those brought into professional contact with the judiciary. I am convinced that whatever may be thought of the competence of some of the judges, these insinuations of dishonesty were the mere inventions of reckless malice.

But that a widespread practice, and even system of corruption, largely by direct money bribes and blackmail, prevailed among minor officials could not be questioned. The difficulty was to discover how widespread it is. On this head the evidence I got was not vague but perfectly definite, and given in many instances by men whose statements I did not doubt. I am inclined to believe that among the officials on the Rand, the secretaries and clerks in offices concerned with legal documents, the inspectors connected with mining and other industries, the police and detective services, and others, there was a wide prevalence of corruption. A good deal of this was of a comparatively venial character. For instance, a business man often told me that he could not get a matter of legal form pushed through without bribing at every turn; but on closer examination it appeared that the payment of money was to induce celerity, or, in most instances, priority of attention, not to procure such official assistance or assent as ought not to be given at all. The Johannesburg business man was in a hurry, had plenty of money, and was wont to spend it freely in getting what he wanted; the Boer official was naturally, and, after due education, purposely slow; hence a practice grew up of quickening the pace of official business by private presents.

// There is reason to believe that this form of habitual corruption was confined to the mining businesses of the Rand. To those who indict in general terms the officialism of the Transvaal I would oppose the testimony of a lawyer of strong Outlander sympathies with a large conveyancing and general practice in Pretoria./ This man had for nine years done business which had constantly obliged him to seek the service of officials in the Mining Commissioner's office, and in various other departments. In no single instance had he ever paid a sou, nor had he been asked for payment. He did not consider that his business had suffered from this policy, and he did not personally know any case in which irregular payment was made to officials in Pretoria and Krugersdorp offices, where most of his business lay.

Such douceurs for encouragement of despatch are not, however, the worst form of corruption on the Rand. There was a wide prevalence of pernicious bribery which consisted in paying inspectors to neglect their duty or to wink at breaches of the law. Here is an instance given me first hand by a mine manager. When the boiler inspector comes round this man says he hands him a £10 note in order to save trouble. The inspector takes it, and does not stay to examine the boilers. "But why do you pay him this money?" said I; "surely your boilers will stand inspection?" "Yes, the boilers are all right," he replied, "but if he didn't get the money he would quite unnecessarily have every fire out for the day in order to inspect, and that would cost us nearer £1000 than £10." The same informant told me he also bribed the "Pass Inspectors," whose business it was to see natives had proper passes. This also he did to avoid trouble. There is little doubt that this is a common practice in the mines. The mine managers and other business men of the Rand coming into contact with ignorant, greedy, and not well-paid officials, set to administer a complex machinery of State restrictions, have had no scruple in easing matters for themselves by bribery, which as soon as it has become custom they denounce as blackmail. That these very men who have caused the corruption should assume a tone of moral denunciation, and should place it in the front of the catalogue of grievances, is a piece of humorous effrontery. From the standpoint of individual ethics it may be a nice point to distribute the blame between the briber and the receiver, but for the former to appeal to a third party to put down a practice which he has caused, and he can stop, is surely the height of impudence.

Johannesburg was the seat of all the corruption: its capitalists had undoubtedly debauched the morals of a large section of the official world, just as its liquor-sellers and its bawdy-house keepers had debauched the morals of the police. I learned on good authority that until lately a system of bribery or blackmail (the concave and convex of the same fact) was practised by the Johannesburg police in dealing with illicit bars and disorderly houses, resembling that which the Tammany police established in New York, and that which even now prevails in some parts of the West End of London. It is, however, admitted that since the deposition of a notorious Chief of Police and the restriction of police power brought about by Messrs. Smuts and Krause, many of the evils had diminished. In particular, the drastic Liquor Law of 1896 prohibiting the sale of liquor to natives, the systematic breaches of which had been a constant complaint of mine owners, was recently admitted to be so well administered as to have virtually suppressed the illicit liquor trade over a large portion of the Rand.

So far as the police grievance is genuine, the worst scandals were chiefly due to an imperfection of the system which gave excessive power to the common uneducated Zarp. Until 1896 a policeman charging a man with a breach of the law brought his charge before another policeman, who had the power to take the accused into custody, and he had virtually no chance of escape until such time as he was placed on trial. This power is now taken from the police, who make their charge before justices of the peace, one of whom is continually present at the charge office. These justices are trained and educated officials, entirely removed from police influence. The charge made before them is next investigated by one of the four assistant-prosecutors under Dr. Krause, who conducts a preliminary inquiry similar to that made before a stipendiary magistrate in England, and upon his order the matter is referred to judge and jury. The machinery of justice in Johannesburg is excellent in principle, and, so far as I could discover, works well in practice. I attended the Criminal Court, whose proceedings were conducted with complete dignity and order upon lines having the closest resemblance to an English court. I happened upon a case where, under strongly suspicious circumstances, two Englishmen were charged with attempting burglary; the chief evidence was that of the police, and the men charged could, in addition to their own sworn evidence, only call witnesses to character. The Boer jury, however, without retiring, gave an acquittal which the judge approved. This was, of course, a single instance, and could not justify any general judgment, but it served to show that the Boer is not the consistent monster of oppression he is sometimes made out to be.

I have, however, deviated somewhat from my main topic—that of corruption. Apart from official corruption, the gravest charges are frequently made against the legislators. Mr. Lionel Phillips, it will be remembered, wrote in one of the letters disclosed in the inquiry on the Jameson Raid, that he had set aside a large sum to "improve" the Raad. Many men told me that the Raad was purchasable almost to a man. Whilst at Pretoria I talked with an official of the Chamber of Mines, who came there to resist certain proposed changes in the Liquor Law. He pointed out a group of men in the hotel who, he said, represented the Illicit Liquor Syndicate, and who had brought with them £12,000 to buy votes in the Raad. I heard other similar stories from men claiming to be well informed; but when sifted these stories were never conclusive. That money was paid out by capitalists seeking concessions, by the Liquor Syndicate and other parties, with the object of influencing legislation, there is little doubt. That some members of the Raad have taken money, though not proved, is highly probable, and three or four members of the present Raad are suspected by well-informed Boers of being bribable. But that the entire Raad or any considerable proportion have been prepared to sell themselves is a quite unfounded calumny. Indeed, it may be reasonably urged that if corruption were so generally prevalent as is alleged the capitalists would have found it cheaper and safer to buy the Boer Government than to enter a troublesome political campaign for its reformation or its overthrow.

There does, however, exist a " corrupt gang at Pretoria," not chiefly officials or Raad members, to whom payments have been made to influence legislation. These men are often called in mockery " the third Raad"; they consist of some half-dozen hangers-on of Kruger and his Government, lobbyists or legislative middlemen, who have acquired a reputation for being able to influence the President or the Raad. Several of these were freely named, though the personnel of the "third Raad" naturally shifts with circumstances. Money was certainly given to these men, who alleged that they could use it to get votes; but the best-informed persons told me that this money, though supposed to be disbursed, remained mostly in the hands of these middlemen. But truth is difficult to get in such matters. This third Raad constituted, however, a real and a grave scandal, though the actual amount of bribery and the influence it exercised was probably exaggerated.

CHAPTER XI

THE NEED OF FINANCIAL REFORM

THE maladministration of finance has been a great and a growing evil, because the funds capable of maladministration have increased with the industrial development of the country. In 1885 the total revenue of the State was £177,876, and in twelve years later it had reached £4,480,217, the expenditure keeping pace with this increase of revenue.

The following statement of revenue and expenditure after 1889, when the Rand industries were fairly established, indicates the rapid progress that has been made:—

Year.	Revenue.	Expenditure.
1889	£1,577,445	£1,201,135
1890	1,229,060	1,386,461
1891	967,191	1,350,073
1892	1,255,829	1,188,765
1893	1,702,684	1,302,054
1894	2,247,728	1,734,728
1895	3,539,955	2,679,095
1896	4,807,513	4,671,393
1897	4,480,217	4,394,066

There is no shadow of a doubt that much of this expenditure was wasteful. It is with a State as with an individual—easily got, badly spent. Exactly how much was ill-spent, and in what ways, we have no means of ascertaining: secrecy and defective auditing of public

THE NEED OF FINANCIAL REFORM 85

accounts were among the most serious vices of the financial disorder. Mr. Loveday, the only Englishman at present sitting on the first Raad, told me that a few years ago, being appointed a member of the finance committee, he tried to challenge various accounts in order to get the vouchers for the expenditure, but that he was unable to carry the committee, and that he had never been put on that committee since. It is indeed admitted that the heads of the treasury and the auditing departments were incompetent to undertake the elaborate finance of the State, and the Raad had accepted the proposal that an expert financier should be appointed to undertake full control. The most casual examination of the figures of the Budget statements for recent years shows the necessity of such a step. Since 1891 the Special Expenditure (commonly styled Secret Service Fund) rose by leaps and bounds from a little over £50,000 to £682,000 in 1896, while another equally vague fund, entitled Sundry Services Account, grew from £76,000 to £129,000. War expenditure is of necessity a highly fluctuating quantity, especially when no large money payment is made for a standing army, but an advance from £87,000 in 1885 to £496,000 in 1896, however justifiable as a defensive operation, certainly demanded careful financial management.

The hasty assumption that such an income and expenditure are in themselves excessive, however, has no warrant in fact. When Mr. Conynghame Greene maintained that there were two really substantial grievances, over-taxation and maladministration, he confused his issue. His language is characteristic of the slipshod thought which pervades the whole statement of grievances. "It is unnatural that a State whose white population consists, according to official statistics, of 250,000 people, should have an annual expenditure of from four to five millions sterling, more especially when the newer population have to pay nearly the whole of it" (C. 9345, p. 28). Why it is unnatural that the Transvaal should spend as much per white head as Cape Colony or Natal (the expenditure being in fact considerably less than in either colony) Mr. Greene does not explain, nor, assuming the expenditure justified, does he explain why it is unnatural that the bulk of the taxation should be defrayed by those who own the bulk of the property and income of the country. Personally I am a strong advocate of direct taxation, and condemn the indirect and protective system which prevails in the Transvaal; but whatever system be adopted, it is eminently "natural" that those who have the means to pay should pay rather than those who have not the means. There is the gravest reason to believe that much of the income of the State was wastefully used; there is no reason to suppose that the sum raised was in excess of what the State could profitably expend in sound public services, or of what the great Rand industry could well afford to pay.

The incidence of certain indirect taxes was certainly vexatious, as, for instance, the price of dynamite and railway rates; but no fault can be reasonably found with the general design that the gold-reef, in which the natural wealth of the country consists, should, through the agency of those who work it, defray the bulk of the expenses of government and public works.

A radical financial reformer with a free hand would certainly have abolished the dynamite and other concessions, or, if the State chose itself to work them, would have charged more reasonable terms; he would probably have lowered many of the railway rates. On the other hand, he would have greatly raised the taxation imposed directly upon the gold industry and the incomes made from it, well aware, from the profitable nature of this industry, how much it could bear without an excessive check upon development. The Gold Law of the Transvaal is the most liberal in the world, taking no more than 5 per cent. out of the admitted profits of mining, or, if we look at the output of 1898, taking $\frac{1}{70}$ of the total value of the gold got in the year. Compare this with the Gold Law of Rhodesia, where the Chartered Company has been accorded the right of taking as much as 50 per cent. of the net profit of any prospector who finds a purchaser for his claim. In Rhodesia the shareholders of a company thus wield a taxing power for their private benefit vastly in excess of the power which the Transvaal Government exercises for the public good. Sound finance requires that this defect should be rectified, and that a substantial tax upon the profits of Rand gold-mining should be substituted for the foolish and wasteful methods of indirect taxation employed at present.

Bearing in mind the exigencies of a growing State, and the general prevalence of high prices for all goods and services, there was no just reason to denounce the overtaxation of the Transvaal. But there was every reason for the burghers of that country to insist that its methods of taxation and its methods of expenditure shall be subjected to rigid scrutiny and radical reform.

CHAPTER XII

THE DYNAMITE MONOPOLY

How far the dynamite affair falls under corruption, how far under financial maladministration, it is difficult to determine. In either case it constitutes a grave scandal. Into the intricacies of this purposely involved affair it is impossible to penetrate; it is not even easy to piece together a completely intelligible outline history. The main facts, however, appear to be as follows. In 1888, when the mining industry was yet an infant, the sole right to make and sell explosives in the Transvaal was granted to one Lippert, who made over the concession to a French company. This form of "monopoly" was, in fact, a breach of the London Convention, but no serious exception was taken to it on this ground. An agitation, however, was directed against the mode of conducting the business, which, instead of building up a local industry, as was intended, imported explosives and sold them at an enormous profit. An official investigation was followed by cancelment of this monopoly in 1893.

Shortly afterwards a new monopoly was established. In form this was a Government monopoly, an agent being appointed by the Government to purchase and, as far as necessary, to import materials and to form a business which should "produce dynamite and other explosive materials in such quantities as the needs and demands within the South African Republic require." The agent appointed was one Vorstman, a partner of Lippert in the expropriated company, and the new company he formed absorbed Lippert's former company, assigning as compensation for the cancelment of the concession a large number of shares in the new company, registered in June 1894 as the South African Explosives Company. This new company was formed with a nominal capital of £450,000 in £1 shares: of this sum 220,000 shares were subscribed and fully paid up by Nobel's Dynamite Trust, a European company, who floated the concern; 25,000 shares were granted to Lippert in terms of a prior contract; 182,000 shares were granted to the French company as indemnification for the cancellation of its contract; and 22,500 shares were granted to Dr. Gobert, a German lawyer, "for services rendered."

Mr. Phillip, managing director of the Company, when examined before the Industrial Commission, refused all information as to the disposal of other shares than those held by Nobel, but the above-named allotment is given by the State Attorney. I understand that the large compensation given to the expropriated company was forced upon the Government by threats from the French and German Governments, whose subjects were shareholders of the old concession. Those who accuse the President of being actuated by personal interest in defending the dynamite monopoly have asserted that the shares standing in the name of Dr. Gobert, an unknown, are really owned by the President. There seems, however, no direct evidence to support such an allegation, which is floated upon an *à priori* supposition that there must be some corrupt motive for the President's attitude.

The real suspicion attaching to the Government arises from the fact that a so-called Government monopoly has operated so as to give to a private firm a far larger share of the gain of the monopoly than accrued to the State. Although exact computation of the profits of the Company was rendered almost impossible by the reluctance of its directors to answer questions, a Volksraad Dynamite Commission agreed with the report of the Industrial Commission (itself appointed by the Transvaal Government) that a profit of quite 40s. per case was made by the Company, only 5s. of which went to the State as its share. The total profits of the Company were estimated by the Volksraad Commission at £580,000 for the years 1897 and 1898.

The sum taken by the State had been 10s. before 1897, but as a concession to the mining industry, upon the advice of the Industrial Commission, a reduction of 10s. was imposed upon the prices of the Company, the Government consenting to bear half of this reduction by taking 5s. per case instead of 10s. Why the Government thus reduced the public income from the State monopoly, instead of taking the whole 10s. from the admittedly exorbitant profits of the Company, is one of the several mysteries in this dark business.

The closer the matter is investigated, the more unsatisfactory does it seem. In the first place, it is absolutely clear that the so-called agent of the Government, the Nobel Trust, from whom all the "materials" are bought, and the South African Explosives Company, are the same persons.

The directors of the South African Explosives Company at Pretoria were Mr. Wolmarans (a member of the State Executive), Mr. Vorstman the agent, Mr. Wolff, Mr. Phillip, senior, and Mr. Phillip, junior. The elder Mr. Phillip, being chairman of the Pretoria Company, was a director of

THE DYNAMITE MONOPOLY 91

Nobel's at Hamburg, and Mr. Phillip, junior, is also a director of the European company. The personnel of the Board of the Company in Europe is virtually identical with that of Nobel's Trust,[1] the general manager of the latter serving likewise as secretary of the former.

The evidence makes it clear that the "monopoly," though nominally a "State" affair, is really in the main a private business. The Government agent is not an independent official to guard the interest of the State, but a private profit-monger buying and selling in the interests of two related companies, each of which makes a huge profit out of the affair. Mr. Albu's concise statement admits of no dispute. "Nobel's sells dynamite to the Government, the Government sells it to the dynamite factory, selling it back again to Nobel's; so that Nobel's sells it to Nobel's, and they try to make a profit on both sides."[2]

It is true that the Government has not left the dynamite monopoly wholly uncontrolled. In 1895–96 enormous profits were made by simply importing ready-made dynamite instead of manufacturing it according to the concession. This was stopped, and an expensive factory for converting the material into dynamite suitable for mining purposes has been established. So likewise the illegal writing off of capital, by which the Company hocussed its accounts, has been stopped.

On the face of it sufficient reasons seem to exist for cancelling this concession, and this course was strongly urged not only by the mining industry, but by the Industrial Commission and a Committee of the Volksraad. The concession has been long unpopular among the body of Transvaal burghers, and strong representations in

---

[1] *Cf.* "Report of Industrial Commission," p. 409.
[2] Industrial Commission, p. 391.

favour of cancelment have been made. So far as legal authorities are concerned, the preponderance of advice has favoured the legality of such a course, the present legal adviser of the Government standing almost unsupported in his contrary opinion. When this pressure, strongly backed by the representatives of the Free State, was applied in vain, and President Kruger and Mr. Wolmarans were believed to have used all their personal influence to save the concession, a strong and pretty general indignation was aroused, which seemed likely to force the hands of the Government, had not the menaces of the British Government saved the monopoly by enabling its friends to represent the proposed cancelment as a concession to a British interference, which all burghers were united in resenting.

This statement of the dynamite matter justifies grave suspicions of corrupt administration, but it cannot be said that any of the charges made are supported by direct evidence. So far, moreover, as the complaints of the mining industry are concerned, it is not clear that their grievance is so intolerable as they make out. They undoubtedly paid a heavy price for dynamite, and the Company made a handsome profit. But apart from State support, Nobel's Trust would occupy a very strong position in dealing with the mining companies. Although Nobel's has competitors, they are comparatively small producers, and the Transvaal, which takes half the world's supply of dynamite, could not obtain what it needs from other sources without great delay. It would take years for other firms to raise their output to the required extent, or, as has been proposed, for the mining companies themselves to produce the dynamite they use. If the dynamite monopoly were cancelled, it is by no means evident that the mines would get their dynamite much cheaper. Mr. Fitzpatrick boasts, indeed, that the gold industry would be strong enough "to break the greatest monopoly in the world." But a well-informed critic casts doubt upon this confident statement. "As a matter of fact it might be that the Dynamite Trust could break the combination of the heads of the gold industry for the reason that, pending the erection or equipment of any factory or factories which the latter might undertake, Nobel, otherwise the Dynamite Trust, could refuse to supply the African market unless under the conditions of a contract extending over a number of years." No doubt it is a delicate question how far the economic monopoly of Nobel can stand without State aid, but it is by no means certain that the mines can get rid of it so easily as they assume.

Moreover, if the concession were abolished, there is good reason to believe that the mining industry as a whole would not be gainers, but that a ring would be formed for working the dynamite and charging prices to the mines which would not be materially lower than those now paid. This is no idle surmise, for the De Beers Company had formed a definite plan for the establishment of a dynamite factory which would have enabled them to further the consolidation which has been taking place by the close co-operation of Wernher Beit and Co. with the Consolidated Goldfields. With the dynamite business in their hands, De Beers would have taken one further step towards the establishment in Johannesburg of that supremacy which they have long held at Kimberley, squeezing out refractory competitors, or compelling them to "come in" upon terms dictated to them by a "higher power."

That the high price of dynamite is to be regarded as an intolerable burden on the mining industry cannot be maintained. In his evidence before the Industrial Commission, and again in his book, Mr. Fitzpatrick admits that the Chamber of Mines was ready in 1893 to enter into a contract for no less a period than sixteen years with Nobel for the delivery of No. 1 dynamite at 90s. per case.[1] Now since 1897 the price of this dynamite has been 75s. per case, and this year an offer was made which, had it proved acceptable to the mining interest and the British Government, would have secured dynamite for the mines at the price of 70s. per case.

The State Attorney's argument against the legality of cancellation[2] in view of the current obligations of the Government is undoubtedly a powerful one. But its validity implies a recognition of gross negligence of its own plain interests by the Government in its past relations with the Dynamite Company.

The grievance of the dynamite monopoly from the standpoint of the Outlanders is one of no serious magnitude. But the whole history of the matter shows a culpable mismanagement from the public standpoint. Whether corruption has been used or not, the bargains between the State and the Dynamite Company have exhibited an incapacity in the former to safeguard and advance the public interest which merits the severest criticism.

The fact is that finance is always the weakest point of a Government like that of the Transvaal, suddenly called upon to tackle the intricacies of industrial politics.

[1] Report Industrial Commission, p. 50, and "The Transvaal from Within," p. 309.
[2] Quoted in full, C. 9317, p. 10.

Less educated and prepared than any other nation in the world for such a task, the bucolic statesmen have been ignominiously worsted in their dealings with the race of astute financiers which has obtained the economic mastery in their country. This public bargaining has been so bad that, on looking back on it, one finds it easiest to assume that some base forces of direct corruption are responsible. But though there is certainly no reason to claim for the Transvaal immunity from the vices which are prevalent in the oldest and best established Governments of the world, it is quite unwarrantable to assume that every failure to safeguard the public interest is attributable to official bribery. Maladministration, with some considerable measure of corruption, are genuine grievances of the Transvaal. But they are not specifically or chiefly Outlander grievances; they are rather to be looked upon as diseases of the entire body politic, and impartial inquiries will disclose the fact of a growing disposition among the burghers and in the official ranks to recognise this grave evil and to seek means of genuine redress.

CHAPTER XIII

A GENERAL ESTIMATE OF GRIEVANCES

In the last few chapters I have given a detailed examination of some of the leading "grievances" which led to British pressure being brought to bear upon the Transvaal Government. Those who consider that England was justified in carrying this pressure as far as war, generally maintain three connected positions—first, that the misgovernment of the Outlander population was so oppressive that armed interference with the internal affairs of the Transvaal, though expressly excluded by Convention, was justified as a last resort; secondly, that no adequate redress could have been obtained either by voluntary concessions, or by the moral influence of diplomatic representations; thirdly, that a successful war will be followed by a peaceful settlement, which will speedily restore political and social tranquillity to the Transvaal and to the rest of South Africa.

Leaving for future consideration this third position, we are now in a position to form a judgment on the other two.

The examination of specific grievances, while disclosing a misgovernment which is serious in some of its aspects, does not indicate a condition of affairs so grave or so intolerable as to justify England in transgressing her obligations under the Convention to leave to the Transvaal

A GENERAL ESTIMATE OF GRIEVANCES

independence in the management of her internal affairs. Some of the alleged grievances I have found quite unsubstantial, as, for example, the dangers to person, liberty, and property upon the Rand, and the charge of excessive as distinct from unwise taxation. Other grievances though substantial, had neither the bulk nor the aggravated character imputed to them. To this class belong the charges of official corruptness and of maladministration, especially of laws affecting the labour in the mines, the abuse of coloured British subjects, and the education issue. A third class is attributable to the conservatism or slow adaptability of the Boer character, and is represented by defects of the political constitution and of finance, and by a reluctance to face the inevitable progress of the British race and language. The accumulation of these grievances did not weigh heavily upon the Outlander population. Certain classes of individuals were annoyed, but not oppressed; the average dweller on the Rand was not subjected to any serious inconvenience through Government action or inaction from one year's end to the other. That serious scandals did exist in the Government was evident, but taken neither individually nor collectively did they constitute the intolerable burden which has been pretended.

The Outlander grievances did not rightly furnish any *casus belli* by warranting armed interference in accordance with international usage, where the subjects of one State are denied ordinary security of life and property in a foreign State. They did warrant peaceable and tactful negotiations on the part of the British Government, with the view of obtaining for these Outlanders the opportunity which they claimed to become burghers of the State upon reasonable conditions of residence. The main position assumed by Sir A. Milner in his earlier negotiations, which sought a franchise upon terms enabling the Outlanders to effect a redress of specific grievances by ordinary constitutional means, was a sound one, and could have been carried, if the negotiations had been conducted in an amicable spirit. Instead of this, unfortunately, a tone of menace, an abrupt refusal of the "give and take" which is the essence of diplomacy, and a denial of any finality to future demands, were allowed to appear in the negotiations which Mr. Chamberlain and Sir A. Milner were conducting nominally with a view to a reform in the franchise.

No one carefully and fairly examining the details of this part of the negotiations, an analysis of which I have presented in a later chapter, can arrive at any other conclusion than that the redress of Outlanders' grievances by the means deliberately suggested by Sir A. Milner, namely, by a reform of the franchise, was not very seriously pursued. The conclusion imposed by a perusal of despatches is that the franchise was a pretext, an object so little desired that, when offered in a form to which no further exception could be taken, it had to be accepted in a fashion which could only be understood as a refusal. The unreality of the demand for redress of Outlanders' grievances, and of the demand for a franchise as the means of this redress, stands out in strong relief as we follow the course of events from early summer into autumn, and watch the deposition of the Outlanders' grievances in favour of the larger real issue which was all the time assuming shape and vigour in the background—the issue of a British empire over South Africa south of the Zambesi—and north too, as soon and as far as is desired.

CHAPTER XIV

THE ALLEGED DUTCH CONSPIRACY

THE condition of feeling among the Afrikanders of the Colony on the eve of war could I think be fairly gauged. Promiscuous charges of disloyalty and treason were of course freely launched by part of the British press, implicating the entire Dutch population, their representatives in the Assembly, and the "Bond" Ministry in some big vague conspiracy for the overthrow of British power in the Colony, and the establishment of Dutch domination over South Africa. But better-informed persons confined their attack upon the Ministry (who are in fact chiefly British in race and sympathies) to charges of passive resistance to the Transvaal policy of the British Government, and of a wilful and mischievous resolve to blink the danger of invasion and rebellion within the Colony. Mr. Schreiner and his colleagues were violently assailed for forwarding arms to the Free State, for not calling out the volunteers, for refusing leave to Civil servants at Kimberley to take arms, for delay in issuing a proclamation against treason, and, more broadly, for neglecting to defend the Colony at a time when Natal and most other British colonies had expressed active sympathy with the war policy of Great Britain against the Republics. It was not, however, pretended by the hottest-headed politicians that men like Mr. Schreiner, Mr. Merriman, or Mr. Sauer would carry this "treason" beyond the point of placing obstacles in the path of the Imperial policy and maintaining the strict neutrality of the Colony. They were distrusted because they were known to condemn the war policy of the Imperial Government, and were the visible heads of the political power which the Dutch party won at the polls last year. Against the body of their followers in the House open charges of more positive disloyalty were often made. Not a few of them, it was more than hinted, were prepared for open rebellion when the time came. But these sinister suggestions bore no probing. Even the boldest organ of the South African press seldom accused the Dutch members of recent inflammatory speeches or of other incitements to join hands with the Republics.

It was, indeed, admitted that their present attitude was one of extreme caution, and that they were doing their utmost to keep the discontent among their constituents from coming to a head. The strongest supporters of the Imperial policy, men like Captain Brabant and Mr. R. P. Fuller, chief organisers of the South African League, informed me that they did not impute directly rebellious designs to the Bond members in the House; these were mostly men of substance, and knew what they had to lose by treason. Such was the generous interpretation put upon their abstinence. But I talked long and closely with many of those Dutchmen, and I am convinced that their loyalty to the Imperial Government was genuine and substantial. They simply deplored the fatal policy of coercion upon which her Majesty's Government had embarked, with its terrible legacy of race hatred and domestic tragedy. It is hardly too much to say that this war has come home to each one of these men in his own family; there can hardly be one of them without a son or other close relative, in the Transvaal or the Free

State, fighting for his country against British troops; every one of them has innumerable ties of friendship with his Dutch kindred there. Not one of these men is a blind supporter of the Transvaal. All admit and deplore its faults of misgovernment, but every one of them is convinced that these faults have been made the cloak of aggression, and sympathises deeply, passionately, with the Republics in their struggle to defend the rights of self-government. Of any other "disloyalty" I found no trace; the language and the conduct of these men were a continual refutation of such a charge. Take the recent behaviour of the Afrikander Bond, denounced as the special instrument of this "Pan-Afrikander conspiracy," and its leaders. Were men like Mr. Hofmeyr and Mr. Theron going about the country uttering inflammatory speeches, inciting the public to take up arms for the defence of the Republics, or in any way utilising the heat of this crisis for revolutionary energy? Not at all. It was allowed even by their enemies that their self-restraint was exemplary, that they exerted all their influence to prevent public meetings from being held in disaffected regions, and that they and their powerful organ, *Ons Land*, strained every nerve to keep the public quiet. "Yes," sneers the Jingo; "they were afraid to move just now; the time was not yet ripe for the disclosure and fulfilment of their real designs." The value of this sneer I need not here investigate; it is sufficient at this stage to record the general admission that the Bond leaders not merely were not inciting their followers, but that they were persistently occupied in checking attempts at organisation or demonstration. "Yes, these people speak fairly with their lips, but they harbour evil thoughts," is the answer I received a score of times when I asked for some concrete evidence of the treason imputed to these men. Such an accusation merits no reply, and, in the nature of the case, admits of none.

But possibly I may be allowed to quote a recent incident. At a meeting of the Dutch members specially convened to consider the petition for a peaceful settlement presented to and rejected by the British Government, the chairman, Mr. Theron, began by reading, with tears in his eyes, a letter he had just received from his son, a young burgher of the Transvaal, to whom he had written asking what he proposed to do. "You ask me what I intend to do. I intend to do my duty as a burgher towards the country of my adoption, and leave to God the care of my wife and child." Reading this letter, the chairman turned to his fellow-members: "This teaches us a true lesson. As my boy rightly determines to be loyal to his country, so shall we be loyal to ours"—a remark which was received with loud murmurs of assent and sympathy. I am told that Mr. Theron forwarded this letter to the High Commissioner, with the brief pathetic comment, "This is my only son." This is no single instance. I hardly entered any house occupied by one of the older Colonial families which was not shadowed by some such impending tragedy: here a daughter recently came down whose husband had left his office to do his duty as a Transvaal or Free State burgher; there the father, a strong British Jingo, lamented the infatuation of his sons who had cast in their lot with the Republic under whose protection they had lived and worked, while the mother tearfully tried to check the fierce war-talk which was ever harrowing her heart. These people harboured no treason against the British Government. They were simply grieved, astonished, and indignant at the almost incredible success of a policy

THE ALLEGED DUTCH CONSPIRACY

which, by persistent misrepresentation and concealment of essential facts, had brought about a catastrophe the fatal effects of which are swiftly coming home to the hearts and lives of every one of them.

But is there no substance at all in the charges of active disaffection that are brought? A certain considerable section of the Colony was seething with anger against the attack on the Republics, and, if the Afrikander Bond were the treasonable body it is represented as being, it could have evoked a most dangerous rebellion. It was well known that, whereas in the western and southern districts, which are generally more settled, where there is a larger admixture of British farmers, and where there is less sport and less scope for roving and adventure, the Dutch could not be roused to any active co-operation with the defiant Republics, the condition of the northern border districts was very dangerous. The districts where large definite disaffection existed were those bordering on the southern boundary of the Free State and portions of counties, such as Middleburg and Craddock, which adjoin these. Long before the outbreak of hostilities fears of disturbance in this part of the Colony were entertained by responsible Ministers and members of Assembly. Many of the latter expressly left their post at Cape Town before the session was over, in order to exert their personal influence among their constituents in preventing popular meetings from being held, and other demonstrations which might give colour to the charges of treason. The South African League and the Progressives openly charged these districts with long-planned rebellion. For years, it was said, they had been arming, and during the last year emissaries from the Transvaal had brought large quantities of Mausers, some of which had been freely and openly distributed among the farmers, while others had been sold by dealers below cost price. Organised recruiting of volunteers to fight with the Republics was alleged to have been going on as part of a general propaganda of sedition. How much, if any, truth exists in these charges it is not easy to ascertain. They are denied outright and *in toto* by most of the Bond members and by Messrs. Schreiner and Hofmeyr. Both the latter gentlemen told me that they had repeatedly challenged these statements, and asked for any single concrete case to be proved, and that their challenge had never been met. Bond members for these very counties in question most positively asserted that they had made close inquiries, and found no tittle of evidence for these statements. The kind of evidence I could get from the officials of the South African League and other Progressive politicians was certainly not what lawyers would consider as "good evidence." I am disposed to think they would have great difficulty in bringing home any single case to support their general charges. Indeed, many of those who strongly held this doctrine of the Dutch conspiracy in the Colony, frankly admitted that specific charges were difficult or impossible of proof, appearing to think that a large quantity of inferior and dubious evidence was equivalent to a smaller quantity of superior and certain evidence. What they did not sufficiently consider was the common interested source of this accumulation of hearsay evidence, which completely annuls the value of mere quantity.

But while this sort of evidence entirely failed to sustain the allegation of a set conspiracy, there is no reason to doubt that attempts have recently been made, successful in some measure, to stir parts of the Colony. Dutch members admitted that a circulation of seditious

THE ALLEGED DUTCH CONSPIRACY 105

leaflets, probably issuing from the Transvaal, had taken place. Moreover, there can be no question but that a canvass had been made by Transvaalers to ascertain the probability of assistance from the Colony, and, on the eve of war, attempts were made to enlist actual support and to furnish arms to those who appeared willing to render aid. Though I do not believe, as is often suggested, that this has been an integral part of a long conscious policy of the Transvaal Government, I think it quite probable that individual energetic agents of that Government, endowed with a fairly free hand, and possibly with money, may have done these things. But whether these specific charges be true or not, it is certain that a deep, wide-spread resentment existed among the Dutch of these districts, which has already led to a considerable defection of the younger colonial frontiersmen, and which in certain events will lead to a wide-spread and dangerous rebellion. The forces which hitherto have held these people within bounds are the Ministry, the Afrikander Bond, the personal and extraordinary influence of Mr. Hofmeyr, and the powerful paper *Ons Land*.

The soothing doctrine that this war was inevitable is explicitly adopted by some of our leading statesmen. When challenged, it takes its stand upon the idea conveyed in the striking sentence attributed to Sir A. Milner, the necessity of crushing "the dominion of Afrikanderdom." The great majority of the British colonists of the towns have firmly persuaded themselves that the perverse and defiant attitude of the Republics, which has now blossomed into war, is the first open expression of a general revolutionary movement which has for a long time been gathering force among the Dutch inhabitants of South Africa. Even those who think war might have been averted by diplomacy, and who are not enthusiastic admirers of the Johannesburgers, defend the drastic policy of Great Britain on the ground that a present settlement could have had no permanency, and would have merely given time for the Dutch conspiracy to have attained more formidable dimensions. It is not easy to gather any very definite idea of the nature and growth of this "conspiracy." The Progressive politicians are, however, fairly agreed in dating the definite formulation of the notion of an independent Dutch South Africa, as an object of political agitation, back to 1881, when the Transvaal was given back, or to 1883, when Mr. Hofmeyr organised the Afrikander Bond. Ever since then, I was informed, the idea of overthrowing the British power and of establishing Dutch supremacy has been secretly growing in the minds of the Dutch. The Afrikander Bond, as an insignificant revolutionary faction, came into being in 1880, under the leadership of Mr. Du Toit; it professed to aim at the establishment of a political union of the South African States under an independent flag. Mr. Du Toit, however, was a man of small account, and when Mr. J. H. Hofmeyr, already recognised as the leading Dutch politician, effected a fusion between this body and the Farmers' Protection Association, the "independent flag" was expressly knocked out of the constitution of the Bond, which henceforth avowed its object to be "the formation of a South African nationality by means of union and co-operation, as a preparation for the ultimate object, a United South Africa." The notion, sedulously fostered by those who seek to prove the disloyalty of the majority of Cape colonists, that something treasonable lurks in this pronouncement of South African nationality, is most mischievously false. The true consistency between British

Imperial control and South African nationality is excellently stated by Dr. Beck, one of the ablest members of the Bond party in the Cape Assembly: "The British notion of the broad and true Imperialist of to-day is something far wider than a mere English empire; it is in the widest sense an empire made up of a group of nations which have been evolving through the wise statesmanship that has hitherto mainly guided the Imperial destinies. These notions, developing each along its lines of least resistance, have been gradually reaching a point where they could demonstrate to the world that, although they were individually distinct and far apart as the poles, collectively they stood together, constituting through community of interests and aspirations one compact body. Gradually these notions were reaching a condition to show to the world that 'John Bull & Co.' was an unlimited liability concern, with John Bull as senior partner, and all manner of nationalities as junior partners. But is all this to be changed now? The Canadian Prime Minister, speaking in England at the time of the Jubilee celebration, said, and he prided himself on the loyalty of his sentiments, that he was proud to remind England that Canada was no longer a colony; it was a strong, self-reliant nation.

> 'Daughter am I in my mother's house,
> But mistress in my own.'

Only to poor distracted South Africa is this natural aspiration, this desire to be 'mistress in her own house,' to be denied; only the Dutch-descended South African, who, because Nature wills it so, cannot be English, and who is not allowed to be an Afrikander, is to be relegated to a position where he has no corner of the world to call his own, no place to call home; and all this is proposed to be done in the name of Imperialism."

There is surely no Imperial gain in checking this legitimate and wholesome growth of an Afrikander nation, which comprises, as it was always intended to comprise, all those racial factors of South African life which make their permanent home in that country.

It is difficult for any one who follows the part played by the Bond in politics to recognise it as the revolutionary instrument it is charged with being. After its early and successful efforts to get the Dutch language released from the embargo placed upon it, and to obtain equal treatment for the Dutch and English tongues, most of its political work has been directed to questions relating to the agricultural and native labour questions, which chiefly affect the Dutch farmers. The tactics of their leaders have always been plainly constitutional; they have worked mostly with English statesmen — recently with Mr. Rhodes, now with the Schreiner Ministry—for an openhanded, concrete policy, often narrowly conservative or even retrogressive, but with no tincture of revolution in it. The larger purpose of its programme, the establishment of a South African nationality, has certainly never obtruded itself on the political arena. Neither in Parliament nor outside has the Bond ever devoted itself to the formation of a great Dutch nationalist party seeking to throw off British control and to establish an independent Dutch South Africa.

Those who depict the Afrikander Bond as a vast party or race organisation like the Irish National League, to which every Dutch politician belongs as a matter of course, and which by a great network of propagandism is constantly stimulating the people to the active realisation

THE ALLEGED DUTCH CONSPIRACY 109

of separatist aspirations, completely miss the truth. The members of the Bond, counting branches all over South Africa, have never amounted to more than a few thousand; among these are a considerable minority of colonists of British or other non-Dutch descent. The great secret fanatical associations with which we are familiar in Italy, Russia, France, and Ireland are utterly alien from the character and circumstances of the scattered Dutch colonists, who are essentially individualistic in feelings and in methods of action, and who neither for social, industrial, nor political purposes have shown any real capacity of powerful close co-operation. The Bond is a substantial and effective organisation of small groups of farmers and professional men in the small towns and country districts, for the purpose of urging practical schemes of reform upon the Legislature, and of protecting the local interests of the inhabitants. There is nothing whatever in the constitution of the Bond about Dutch nationality or about a union which shall exclude British control or supremacy.

Those who charge the Bond with harbouring and propagating these designs have been challenged repeatedly to make good their charges from speeches of Mr. Hofmeyr and the leading Dutch politicians, and they have never taken up the challenge. It is likely enough that the idea of South Africa for the Dutch has been entertained by some speculators on the future destiny of the country, men who realise the more tenacious grip upon the country which agriculture gives the Dutch as compared with those gold and diamond industries which, outside the Cape Peninsula, are the chief British interests in the country. Here and there an agitating spirit may have sought personal influence among his fellow-Dutch by foolish appeals to race feeling as a basis of political, or even of revolutionary activity; but though this is an issue upon which documentary evidence might be expected to be available, there is a singular dearth of it. In the press the paper which for circulation and influence holds a unique position in the colony is *Ons Land*, but no one accuses it of preaching sedition or of advocating revolutionary methods. When Sir A. Milner can find no popular press from which to illustrate his charges of disloyalty against the people whom he is set to govern, and is driven to quotations from papers so insignificant as the *Rand Post* and the *Stellalander*, he surely gives away his case. Here, according to Sir Alfred and his British Imperialists, is an organised revolutionary movement, with ample means at its disposal, confronted by a powerful omnipresent Rhodesian press, which nevertheless has utterly neglected to use the most potent engine of sedition which our century has produced.

Again, we should expect to find in the reports of Bond meetings ample testimony of the Dutch conspiracy. Do we find this? No such thing. When I consulted prominent Progressive politicians, they referred me with confidence to a branch meeting of the Bond held last May at Burgersdorp, a place spoken of to-day with bated breath as a hotbed of rebellion. A careful perusal of the report of this meeting, as given by the *Cape Times*, yielded but a single sentence which could be twisted into treason. A certain Mr. Van der Walt "prayed the Almighty that the day would yet come when the whole of Afrikanderdom would be freed from the foreign yoke." But Mr. Van der Walt was a Transvaal burgher, and this imprecation of his, however regretable, could hardly justify the wholesale charge of treason brought against the meeting. The only really important personage at this gathering was Professor J. C. Cachet, head of the Reformed Church of South Africa, whose speech consisted of a powerful appeal against the methods adopted by the Rand agitators and their press to prejudice the mind of the Imperial Government and to fan the flame of race hostility. There was indignation, even invective, in his address, but no single word which carried a suggestion of disloyalty. Instead of being an incentive to revolution, it was a powerful plea for peace, and the following passage, received with great applause, points a most important lesson which Sir A. Milner and some of the more inflammatory journalists who support him might digest with advantage :—" There were the Englishmen born and resident in the country. He knew that if the majority of them were asked, 'Do you wish to make an end of the Boer?' they would say, 'No; we live here and are quite satisfied. We have no grievances.' The Englishmen in their midst were not the mischief-makers; it was the new-comers, who knew nothing about the country, except to be continually making an uproar and keeping the fire of race hatred alight."

But suppose that here and there there were dreamers of a Dutch South African Republic, and loose-tongued orators who gave voice to the notion, what of that? Surely between this feeble sporadic speculation or agitation, and the organised conspiracy charged against the Dutch by Progressive politicians, and endorsed by Sir A. Milner, the widest possible difference exists. The one belongs to those innumerable little currents of thought and feeling which abound everywhere in every country where race factors are in slow progress of fusion, and where differences of economic function are conterminous with race; the other is the offspring only of persistent personal oppression or of grievously oppressed sentiments of nationality. Why should the Dutch in Cape Colony conspire? For many years they have exercised a preponderating influence in practical politics, even out of proportion to their numbers, and every important British politician has sought to ingratiate himself with them. If they seriously desired to realise the larger object of the Bond, there has been, except perhaps in Natal, where the British are relatively stronger, nothing to prevent them from working in a regular constitutional way towards rendering effective the idea of South African nationality by achieving a growing union between the colonies and the Republics. Indeed, in spite of "set-backs" incident on ill-advised and premature attempts at mechanical union, the feeling and fact of African nationality has been growing apace both among British and Dutch inhabitants, and were it not for recent unhappy appeals to race hatred, most satisfactory progress towards an end in itself highly desirable might have been attained.

There never has existed in Cape Colony any desire to expel British control, or any conspiracy to achieve such an object. All the direct evidence goes to prove the contrary. As for Mr. Hofmeyr and the Dutch Afrikander leaders of the Colony, they have constantly and strongly delivered themselves in favour of the maintenance of the British flag and the control which it implies. I have had long conversations with Mr. Hofmeyr and with leading Bond members of Assembly, and I am firmly convinced of the sincerity of the feeling with which they deplore and denounce the imputations of disloyalty. If any man voices the true inwardness of Dutch sentiment and Bond politics, it is Mr. Hofmeyr. Yet it was this man, not many

THE ALLEGED DUTCH CONSPIRACY 113

years ago, who strongly urged in England a scheme of Imperial federation, by which England's colonies might be more closely bound to her and to one another. Subsequent experience may have modified his views as to the feasibility of such a project, but Mr. Hofmeyr is as far as ever from desiring to weaken the bond which unites to England the destinies of South Africa.

But suppose it were otherwise, as it is with some. It may well be admitted that there are thoughtful Dutch, and not a few British Afrikanders, who look forward to a diminution of direct Imperial control over the domestic affairs of South Africa, who distrust government from Downing Street, and even contemplate a time when they may elect freely their own Governor, and England's control may be confined to a general protective influence and a control over foreign affairs. I am convinced that there is no organised movement in the direction of such a change. But suppose there were, and that an active educational propaganda were on foot with such an aim. If it were sought to promote such an object by education and by peaceful representation to England, and not by an appeal to arms, would that be treason, would that justify the adoption of brutal measures of coercion? I ask these questions because, from what I have seen and heard in South Africa, I feel confident that, sooner or later (if, indeed, British South Africa survives the present conflict), the time will come when some such requests, hardening into demands, will actually be made for complete internal self-government, and that these requests or demands will proceed at least as largely from the British colonists as from the Dutch. But if a few thoughtful men entertain this notion (I heard it oftener from British than from Dutch), it belongs at present to the region of speculation or remote aspiration,

H

and has certainly no place in current politics, though the new turn of events may well ripen it more rapidly towards fulfilment. I am convinced that not the closest Commission of Inquiry could fasten on the Bond or upon their British associates the charge of aiming at any political changes of such a magnitude; still less could it bring home the charges of treason which malicious slander associates with their name. Numerous utterances of these men are extant showing them to be supporters of the British Imperial power. Would the leaders of a party pledged to rapidly ripening revolutionary action have voted with enthusiastic unanimity the sum of £30,000 towards the Imperial navy last year, and have handed over Simonstown to the possession of Great Britain for a coaling station? These are in themselves perhaps slight incidents, but to any one acquainted with politics they are of conclusive significance.

In the face of such facts, how is the idea of an organised conspiracy to found a Dutch Republic defended? By an argument of dazzling impudence. "Yes," it is said, "these men speak fair with their lips; their conduct is also beyond reproach; but then we must remember that among conspirators, the arts of simulation and concealment are necessary to the success of their cause." So, too, with the lack of convincing evidence regarding revolutionary action; "such a movement is essentially secret and does not admit that sort of proof which is accessible and is required for the acceptance of ordinary statements of fact." So the hypothesis built in the air is sustained by imputed motives and suggestions equally aërial in origin. "Your speech and action are substantially loyal; but then we know you are disloyal. So you must be meaning something different from what you say and do." Let me give one or two samples

THE ALLEGED DUTCH CONSPIRACY 115

of the sort of evidence I got. Take the case of the Mausers said to be distributed among the Colonial people on the Free State frontier. There was no real evidence that large numbers of these men possessed either Mausers or other non-sporting arms; but let that pass. Suppose they had, how did they obtain them? The stories about waggons full of guns coming across from the Free State crumbled to pieces directly one examined them; the name of the informant was withheld, place and date were invariably absent, there were generally several links between the narrator and the avowed eye-witness, who had never presented himself for cross-examination, and who never seemed to have taken the ordinary precaution to inform the local magistracy of the proceedings in time to get a thorough investigation. But generally it was admitted that the guns were bought, and the charge simply amounted to a statement that many men too poor to have paid the full price for a Mauser were found to be possessed of one. These guns, it was alleged, were bought in large numbers at small shops in the towns by Dutchmen, but an Englishman who wished to buy one could never find one nearer than Port Elizabeth; and so on. The Rhodes organs in the Colonial press adopted the same method, poisoning the public mind by utterly unsubstantiated imputations. Take for instance an unsigned letter in the *Cape Argus* of October 7, published on the eve of war, in which the anonymous writer asserts that an unnamed Dutch member of Assembly had recently said to an unnamed business man of Cape Town, "The time has come when we must have our own flag and be a separate nation."

I am almost ashamed to repeat such trashy evidence, but it was the only sort of support for the allegation of a preconcerted Dutch conspiracy. Stay! One other evidential gem, fallen from the lips of a leading official of the South African League, comes to my recollection. I asked him how he knew the guns were supplied by the Transvaal Government. "Why," replied he, "in what other way can you account for the enormous secret service expenditure that has been going on?" There is no substantial evidence and no inherent probability in the treasonable relations with the Republican Governments charged against Dutch colonists. A handful of rabid utterances, vaguely reported, and a vast amount of thought-reading, form an utterly inadequate warranty for such a charge. The notion that Cape Colonists have deliberately conspired to purge Africa of British influence and to set up a separate Dutch domination, in which the Transvaal, by virtue of its wealth and growing population, would impose Krugerism upon South Africa, is too preposterous for serious discussion. Is such a policy even plausible in the case of a country where every important family has British connections and British sympathies? Is it likely that a faction with such an end in view would have put in power a Ministry in which there are only two members of pure Dutch blood, and where British race and avowed Imperial sympathies preponderate? No one acquainted with the views and feelings of such men as Mr. Schreiner, Mr. Merriman, and Mr. Solomon can suppose for a single moment that Dutch conspirators could hope either to win their connivance or to cajole them into becoming the unconscious instruments of a conspiracy. It is idle to disguise the fact that a strong, widespread sympathy exists among the Dutch of the colonies with their kinsmen of the Republics, whom they believe to be the victims of unjust aggression, the nature, object, and instruments of which they believe

THE ALLEGED DUTCH CONSPIRACY

they clearly understand. This sympathy implies a passionate detestation of the present Imperial policy, and beyond question must be understood to verify the warning uttered months ago by the petition of the Colonial Dutch Reformed Church, which stated that in case of war upon the Transvaal "the allegiance of your Majesty's loyal Dutch subjects would sustain the most formidable shock which it has ever received." But let it be clearly understood that this is an ebullition of feeling and not a development of policy. Many of the politicians and publicists, who have by constant reiteration forced upon the public mind a belief in the great Dutch conspiracy, must be fully aware of the emptiness of the charge. They must know that the Dutch colonists have no desire to disestablish the representative institutions under which they have lived, and which have given them a controlling voice in the government, in order to set in its place that Krugerism which all their leaders have reprobated in the strongest terms, and against whose manifestations they have more than once been upon the point of taking up arms. I am compelled to charge the Progressive party and politicians of the Colony with a reckless use of these charges of disloyalty. I further charge them with conspiring, in the heat of their patriotism, by press, public, and private utterances, to produce disloyalty by suggestion. These Dutch Afrikanders have never been disloyal; they have merely been grieved and indignant, as they have every right to be. But call them traitors in a thousand insulting ways, fabricate charges of incipient rebellion in every issue of the press, set spies among them and threaten them with troops, and you take the most effective way to turn honest opposition into treason. Then, when this persistent goading has attained its natural result and some open exhibition of disloyalty occurs, the "agents provocateurs" of this malign policy gleefully rub their hands and say, "We told you it was there, and out it comes." The armed co-operation which has already taken place in certain districts with the Boer forces may indeed be regarded as a direct product of the consistent policy of the Progressive party, who last year, fairly defeated at the polls, chose this disastrous and contemptible method of avenging their party failure. This language may sound strong, but it is feeble to express a policy which at the present time seems likely to shatter the foundations of political and social order throughout South Africa, and to cost Great Britain, in blood, money, and empire, a price the magnitude of which is not even yet within the focus of her vision.

CHAPTER XV

THE DUTCH FEELING IN THE COLONY: AN INTERVIEW WITH OLIVE SCHREINER

MR. and Mrs. Cronwright Schreiner had been spending a couple of months on a farm among the most primitive Boers of the colonial frontier near Hopetown when the war broke out, and they were among the last to find their way down to Cape Town. Knowing that Mrs. Cronwright Schreiner had for many years lived as teacher and as friend among these Dutch farmers, most of whom have kinsmen fighting in the Free State or the Transvaal, and who are accused of hating England and harbouring treasonous designs, I asked her if I might question her about the feelings of these people. I found her in the pleasant unpretentious house which her brother, the Premier, has just built for himself in Newlands, a delightful suburb lying under the shelter of Table Mountain, the only bit of South Africa which combines sea and mountain and rich old English oaks, pines, and beech trees, with a perceptible but not overpowering blend of the sub-tropical, giving it a novel piquancy to English eyes. Needless to say, Mrs. Schreiner suffers terribly from the pain and shame of the catastrophe which has come upon the South Africa she loves so passionately. "Some mornings I wake up here," she said, "in the brilliant sunshine and hear the birds singing in the trees, and I have forgotten what has happened; and then suddenly the appalling fact breaks in upon my heart, this torn and bleeding condition of my country." And then we talked of the war, and Mrs. Schreiner told me of the Boer farms round Orange River which she had been visiting during the last few weeks, where the real old primitive life is still lived in a farmhouse little more than a mud hut of two rooms, with a few miles of veldt round it on which to graze scant herds of sheep and cattle, by which the farmer wins his hard livelihood. These are the people suspected of disloyalty, of wishing to join hands with the Republics and to break away from the British flag. I asked Mrs. Schreiner what state of feeling she found among them.

"Ah," she said, "Sir A. Milner and this malicious press do not understand (or is it even possible they do understand?) what they have done in separating Dutch and British and in sowing these charges of disloyalty at such a time. These men and women are suffering a terrible strain. All of them have sons and relatives in the commandos of the Transvaal or Free State, and they learn that the soldiers of the Queen, the great Englishwoman whose portrait is nailed up on their wall, are marching to shoot them down. And on the top of all this they are being goaded to disloyalty by those suspicions and accusations."

"But is it true that these Boers have any genuine feeling for the Colony and the British Government?"

"Most certainly. Great Britain is the only country to which they have ever looked. They are proud of their Government; they have loved the Colony as a part of the British Empire, just as in America an inhabitant of Virginia or Ohio loves and backs his State as against the other States. Now they feel pain and bitter resentment that their fidelity should suddenly be questioned."

"How did they first come to this suspicion?"

"Well, it was perhaps the forts and the soldiers that were placed amongst them. They felt this deeply. 'Why are they building these forts at De Aar and other places? Why are these soldiers brought here? When have we been disloyal?' These are the questions they kept asking."

"But are these people not really anti-English?"

"You would not ask this if you had been among them. I could drive you to farm after farm where you would have found all the younger generation proud of learning to speak English and of dressing in English fashion and learning English ways. In most of these small Dutch cottages you would find a harmonium and a book of English songs, which the daughters spent their leisure time in practising—songs mostly glorifying the British army and navy! The girls would make a sort of apology for their mother, saying, 'My mother, she can really understand some English, though she does not speak it.' All of them have been anxious to be as English as possible."

"But I suppose this will not continue now?" I said.

"Why, naturally not. This is the very worst thing we are doing; we are killing the love of these people. England in her Imperial policy is losing her empire over their hearts. In twenty-five years there would have been no more Dutch and English in this colony, but a fused Afrikander people owning allegiance to Great Britain as their mother. But this hope is gone."

"But what are their thoughts on the present situation? Do they bring political analysis to bear on it?"

"Yes; they are tremendous politicians, most of them.

Whenever they meet at markets, fairs, or church gatherings they will lay out the whole of politics as they see it. Their bitterest feeling is that they are being kept from the Queen, for whom they have intense love and reverence. It seems strange to English people, but these primitive folk think the Queen must be accessible, like Paul Kruger, and they have a personal pride and belief in her."

"Is there any truth in what is said—that this sort of regard for the Queen does not prevent them from entertaining treason against the British Government?"

"No; that is sheer misunderstanding. They largely see the Government personified in the Queen and in the British Ministers of the Colony. They feel, 'This is our Government, our Queen;' and their charge against Chamberlain and Milner is that they have come between the people and their Queen. An old farmer a few weeks ago put the matter quaintly: 'There are two people we don't want to see dead; it is a pity they are old—one is the Queen, the other Paul Kruger: the young will never take their place.' I fear more than anything for the shock which will be felt when they come to realise that they cannot get to the Queen. 'Why don't you go to the Queen and speak for us?' more than one has said to me. Up to the last they often said to me, 'Our Queen won't allow our friends to be killed.'"

"And how do they account for what has happened? Whom do they blame?"

"First let me tell you a curious thing about them. They seem to have no vindictive feelings whatever against the English soldiers sent to fight their friends and relatives. Most commonly they speak of them with a certain pity. 'Die arme Rooibaatjes, poor chaps; what

DUTCH FEELING IN THE COLONY

have they done that they should be shot?' I verily believe there is not a Boer woman amongst them that would not open her heart to a wounded soldier, turn out of her bed to give it to him, and nurse him as tenderly as her own son."

"Whom, then, do they hold responsible for the trouble?"

"It is not Mr. Chamberlain, nor Sir A. Milner, though they say, 'He has blackened us.' Their anger is reserved for one man, whom they regard as the root of the evil. The whole face will harden at the name Rhodes—'the traitor,' as they always term him. Before the matter had fully ripened into war I was talking with an old Boer farmer, a man of substance and of great influence in his district. He put it in this way: 'When I think over the matter, it seems to me Rhodes and those men won't be able to make war; for "our old Lady" has always been good to us and loved justice, and she won't let it be.'"

"Was it altogether Rhodes they blamed?"

"Well, chiefly Rhodes; sometimes the capitalists. They would sum up the discussion thus: 'And the root of the matter is Naboth's vineyard—the gold, and the capitalists that want it.' They have very clearly grasped the kernel—the determination of the capitalists to control the whole country; not only the mines and the towns' wealth, but the land. And when they have got the land, where is our freedom? But 'the capitalists' is no vague Socialist catchword. These people always mean those who buy up land, buy up votes, and so try to get away their freedom."

"And tell me, what do you think will be the effect when these people realise fully the blow?"

"I would rather not answer; I cannot tell. Much depends upon the discretion of the Imperial Government. One touch upon the principle of responsible government in the Colony would rouse in them that fine free instinct for representative institutions brought from Holland and born and bred in the bones of these colonists. Then, again, press and politicians have a terrible responsibility. Let me read you a passage from a letter received this morning from an Englishman, a wealthy merchant, who has lived many years up-country: 'The people of this district are remaining quiet, although the papers are eagerly read. If they could only stop those lying, peace-disturbing upstarts who are spreading reports about, I should have no fear of disturbance. For instance, on Saturday a man told me he had been informed by Mr. —— that if the Transvaal Boers lost we should all become slaves, our Parliament would be taken from us, and Cape Colony taxed to pay the expenses of the war.' Lies of this sort are intentionally circulated over the country and have a very disturbing effect. The Rhodesites are impressing on them that they will lose their Government, so goading them to rise."

"How do these Dutch feel towards Sir A. Milner?"

"They simply feel that they have no relation at all to him; that he has never taken the trouble to comprehend them. 'Ah,' they would say to me, 'if we only had one of our old Governors back, the good old Governors we used to have, they would put everything right; they understood us. If Sir George Grey were still alive we could go to him.'"

"Then the common view that they hate Englishmen is false?"

"It is an utter misapprehension of Dutch feeling.

Much of the apparent hostility is wounded feeling. Treat the Dutchman kindly, win his affection and trust, and there is no limit to his confidence in you. It is false to say he has a natural antipathy towards Englishmen. I would rather say he waits with open arms, and if you stand off from him, as so many English do, he feels bitterly about it. 'You are my fellow-countryman and you won't be my brother.' The English new-comer starts too often with the notion that a Boer is a sort of inferior strange animal. The Boers themselves often laugh over these stories, but they feel them all the same. They were telling me a lot of anecdotes about Tommy Atkins. At Orange River one of the newly-arrived English soldiers went into a store and asked the Dutchman who kept it, 'Are there any Boers about, because I want to see what they look like?' 'Well, I'm a Boer.' 'What! You a Boer? Nonsense!' 'Well, but I am a Boer. 'Why, you look just like any other man!' It is a terrible mistake that is being made, the alienation of the hearts of these people. How easy they are to be governed by affection! There is nothing they won't do for a man who is true to them. As things go now, we are crushing and destroying this great true power of government. More than that, we are even causing them to lose their faith in God. They are religious folk of the old sort. 'God is still reigning; He will see to the right.' That has been their confidence. What will be their feeling after England's destruction of their fellow-Boers in South Africa?"

CHAPTER XVI

TRANSVAAL ARMAMENTS

MANY who reject the notion of a Pan-Afrikander conspiracy against Great Britain in which the Bond and the entire Dutch-Afrikander population of the colonies are implicated, are yet disposed to accept a narrower view of this same conspiracy which accredits the Republics with aggressive designs. Ever since the Transvaal was retroceded, we are told, it has cherished designs of South African empire; the amiable weakness of the British was mistaken for cowardice; the great resources which the discovery of gold placed at the disposal of the Transvaal Government made an aggressive policy possible; intrigues with Continental Governments were set on foot; a propagandist movement was actively conducted throughout South Africa; large sums of money were expended upon modern armaments, with which Kruger and Steyn intended, when a convenient occasion came, to invade British territory, to drive the British into the sea, and to establish a Boer dynasty over South Africa. Now, of propagandism in the colonies I have already spoken. There is no evidence of any organised attempt to shake the allegiance of Dutch colonists until the present war was imminent. The foreign intrigues with Germany and Holland imputed to Dr. Leyds and his Hollanders it is idle to discuss. No definite intelligible allegations are made, no tittle of evidence is adduced to show that the

Boer Republics have ever dreamed of ousting Great Britain from her paramountcy in South Africa in order to put Germany or any other power in her place. Such approaches, if any have been made, are of quite recent date, and are explicable as part of a legitimate defensive policy conceived when the Transvaal became convinced that an attack upon her independence was intended by the mining capitalists and would be extorted by them from the British Government.

Apart from the surprising strength which the Boers have shown in the field, the only piece of evidence adduced is the expenditure on armaments: all the rest is vague insinuation and unsupported conjecture.

Not only the man in the street, but responsible politicians have defended the inevitability of this war by asserting that the vast expenditure upon armaments of the Transvaal was proof of their aggressive intention. "Sooner or later they intended to attack: they would have chosen a time when we were in some other difficulty: we should have been fools to have waited for this emergency."

Now, this position is at least intelligible: it throws overboard the pretence that we are fighting about Outlanders' grievances, or for the empty word suzerainty, or because the Boers have actually invaded British territory: the real cause of war is the aggressive preparations of the Boers and the necessity of taking invasion by the forelock.

All that the advocates of this view are required to show is that the evidence of Boer expenditure on armaments is such as to make this aggressive intention manifest.

Do they show this? How many of those who flaunt this argument on public platforms or in the press have taken the ordinary trouble to ascertain what the Boer expenditure has been or when their warlike preparations were begun?

It is commonly believed that the Boers concealed from our eyes the war preparations which they have been engaged these many years in making, and it is this secrecy and the sudden discovery of these "vast armaments" which have persuaded many persons that war was inevitable. But what are the facts?

The following are the statistics of expenditure in the Transvaal upon the services in which portions of war expense may conceivably be included, dating from 1887, the year when mining development first made its impression on public finance, and the first year when a complete year's budget is obtainable:—

	Military.	Public Works.	Special Expenditure.	Sundry Services.	Total.
1887	£44,232	£194,116	£26,239	£86,786	£351,373
1888	53,508	165,906	48,201	91,923	359,538
1889	75,523	300,071	58,737	171,088	605,419
1890	42,999	507,579	58,160	133,701	742,439
1891	117,927	492,094	52,486	76,494	739,001
1892	29,739	361,670	40,276	93,410	525,095
1893	19,340	200,106	148,981	132,132	500,559
1894	28,158	260,962	75,859	163,547	528,526
1895	87,708	353,724	205,335	838,877	1,485,244
1896	495,618	701,022	682,008	128,724	2,007,372
1897	396,384	1,012,866	248,684	135,345	1,793,279
[1]1898	163,451	383,033	157,519	100,874	804,877

Now, in the first place, there has been no secret as to the main items of expenditure. The budget statements, containing this information, have been always published in the ordinary official way. Every one whose business it was to know, knew quite well the increasing

[1] First nine months only.

expenditure of the Transvaal Republic upon military and other services. The Outlanders' manifesto in the autumn of 1895 called express attention to the intentions of the Government to furnish increased armaments. A full statistical statement, dating as far back as 1882, was put in evidence before the Industrial Commission held early in 1897, and is printed in the Report. A despatch from Lord Rosmead to the Colonial Secretary, dated February 18, 1897, gives a full statement of the estimates for the current year.

No concealment was attempted, nor was there reason for concealment. Investigation of the statistics gives dramatic prominence to one single fact, viz., that military expenditure, which was kept within most moderate bounds until 1895, increased perceptibly in that year, but that the enormous expenditure on military preparation dates from 1896. A similar law of growth is manifested in the department of Public Works, which probably contains some expenditure on forts, barracks, &c., and in the department of Special Expenditure. Sundry Services, upon which fell a large expenditure on account of the Raid, showed a quite abnormal swelling in the year 1895. The total of this order of expenditure, which, of course, includes many other besides military items, marks 1895 as the year of financial change and increase of military expenditure.

It is said that the Boers began to arm long before 1895. And that is true. Why should they not? What is more reasonable than that this Republic, which from its beginning had been engaged in incessant warfare with bordering native tribes, which had, if you will, been engaged in frequent invasions of their territory, should use a portion of the increasing public income which it drew from the natural treasure of the country to improve its military strength? It is not, however, necessary to assume that the increased military expense, moderate enough before 1895, was incurred with exclusive regard to Kaffir warfare. The Boers, with the past experience of the continual encroachments of Great Britain to the north, the seizure of Natal, where they had first sought to settle, the annexation of the Kimberley diamond fields, the subsequent seizure of Bechuanaland, knew quite well that the independence of their country was endangered by the discovery of the Rand gold-mines. Their country, even when quite poor, had been annexed upon pretences afterwards admitted to be false by Great Britain. If it had been known to possess rich treasures of gold, would it have been given back in 1881? The Transvaal had every reason to suspect, from 1886 onwards, that some powerful attack would be made upon the Government, in order to secure the political control of the country for Great Britain or for the mining capitalists. Against this real danger they did prepare: they spent some share of their growing income upon weapons and ammunition.

In 1895 the threats and revolutionary agitation of the Outlanders and their outside friends took shape in the forcible assault of the Jameson Raid. It is not necessary to discuss the details of this miserable business, which made it evident to the Boer mind that this was only one attempt upon their Government, and that it would be followed by other more formidable attacks. The official position of Mr. Rhodes; the contemptible hush policy of the South African Committee, followed by the public whitewashing of Mr. Rhodes by Mr. Chamberlain; the appointment of Sir A. Milner, already regarded by many people as a somewhat aggressive Imperialist, to his post of High Commissioner; the incessant bickering with the

British Government, which, rightly or wrongly, they looked on as part of a provocative policy—consideration of these things surely obliges us to hold it reasonable for the Transvaal to expect some further attack and to make adequate provision against it. I am not arguing that the suspicions of the Transvaal were well grounded, but merely that, under the circumstances, they were natural, and afford a reasonable explanation of the largely increased expenditure on armaments which occurred. The Transvaal had some reason to suspect that her enemies, the resources and unscrupulous character of whom she well knew, would succeed in embroiling her in war with Great Britain. What has taken place now is what she feared, and against which she made this preparation.

The increased expenditure on arms before the Raid was substantial, but not in the least immoderate; it was not, in fact, so fast as the increase in other plainly peaceable services, as the following statistics of expenditure on Justice, Education, Police, and Hospitals will serve to show :—

	Justice.	Education.	Hospitals.	Police.
1887	£6,211	£11,781	£2,551	£13,263
1888	9,745	14,715	10,562	25,590
1889	17,152	24,987	20,647	33,602
1890	22,867	35,546	21,790	55,587
1891	22,822	43,823	19,174	53,697
1892	23,791	38,768	20,415	45,038
1893	25,968	34,145	34,089	57,645
1894	30,544	41,575	39,330	64,286
1895	37,774	56,800	55,466	59,092
1896	49,637	58,720	63,149	57,802

Both the increase of expenditure, and the new character of the armaments adopted, date from the year of the Raid, and are directly attributable to the alarm evoked by that enterprise. They constitute a defensive, not an offensive preparation. An overwhelming weight of positive testimony, from sources not favourable to the Boers, attests the fact that, prior to the Raid, none of the forts, artillery, and other armaments taken to indicate offensive policy existed. An article published in the *Times* in November 1890,[1] from a writer who had just completed a thorough investigation, says that the "standing army" consisted of "a single battery" of obsolete guns, and that "the military inefficiency in every detail was in 1889 beneath contempt." In 1895 Major Robert White made a similar investigation on behalf of the Chartered Company, and the record of his inquiry was picked up on the field at Krugersdorp, containing the following inventory of guns found in Pretoria: (1) Half-a-dozen very old pieces of ordnance, mortars, &c.; (2) one bronze gun of the date of the Second Empire; (3) a small Maxim-Nordenfelt; (4) a small muzzle-loader, in bad condition; and he sums up what he found thus: "None of the guns I saw were fit for much work." It may be suggested that Major White was deceived, but we can hardly be justified in believing that a large supply of modern guns were there because Major White did not see them. No one did see them; the assertion that they were there stands upon no evidence at all.

But this is not all. Positive evidence exists that it was in the year 1895, when the Raid was in visible preparation, that the Boer Government made up its mind to erect forts and to order modern guns. The language of the Manifesto issued by the Transvaal National Union at the end of 1895 cuts the entire ground from under the theory that the Transvaal had

---

[1] "Natal and the Transvaal in 1890" (*Times*, November 7, 1890).

been secretly arming itself for aggressive purposes years before the Raid. It states that "£250,000 *is to be* spent upon the completing of a fort at Pretoria; £100,000 *is to be* spent upon a fort to terrorise the inhabitants of Johannesburg; large *orders are sent* to Krupp's for big guns; Maxims *have been ordered*, and we are told that German officers are coming out to drill the burghers."[1] So far were they from having adopted an aggressive military policy, that they were notoriously deficient in ordinary means of defence, and the Outlanders were so well aware of this, that they planned to seize the fort and magazines at Pretoria with a handful of armed men. This fort is thus described by Mr. Fitzpatrick, who certainly knew what he was talking about: "The surrounding wall of the fort, a mere barrack, had been removed on one side in order to effect some additions; there were only about a hundred men stationed there, and all except half-a-dozen could be counted on as being asleep after 9 P.M. There never was a simpler sensational task in the world than that of seizing the Pretoria fort—fifty men could have done it."[2]

Mr. Selous, who knows South Africa as well as any living Englishman, roundly affirms that "there were no forts in the Transvaal before 1895, and, except that most of the burghers possessed a rifle of some kind, very little in the way of armaments."

At the time when the Raid took place, the Government was just awakening to the danger of their situation: the revolutionary movement in Johannesburg, aided and abetted by powerful outsiders, was beginning to alarm Mr. Kruger, and the building of the fort, together with the orders for machine-guns, were the first-fruits of the

[1] "The Transvaal from Within," p. 430.   [2] Ibid.

very natural alarm. Mr. Fitzpatrick and his Union rightly insisted that these measures were adopted to overawe the population of Johannesburg—in other words, to secure order by a display of force; but having adopted this explanation, it is not open to him to regard these same armaments as part of an aggressive policy to possess South Africa.

The Boers very rightly determined to strengthen themselves against the turbulent Outlanders, who, for some time past, openly threatened force, and were suspected of intriguing with British Ministers. The precautionary measures which they took are not to be twisted into evidence of Mr. Fitzpatrick's statement, that "many years before the Raid, Mr. Kruger had a well-defined policy to republicanise South Africa."

The most convincing testimony alike of the openness of the Boer preparations and of their cause is, however, furnished by Captain Younghusband, who, visiting Pretoria early in 1896 for the *Times*, thus stated what he found:—

"Orders for batteries of field-guns, quick-firing guns, and Maxims, and for sufficient rifles to arm every Dutchman in South Africa were being sent to Europe; European drill instructors and artillerymen were being imported, and forts were being constructed round Pretoria on the most approved designs. *One attempt had been made to take their country from them; they were thoroughly convinced that the attempt would be renewed at some future date; so the Boers were determined to be thoroughly on their guard the second time.*"[1]

The gist of the entire matter is contained in his pregnant sentences, "The Boers had very nearly been caught napping at the beginning of the year; they were

[1] "South Africa of To-Day," p. 101.

thoroughly convinced that the attempt would be renewed at some future date; so the Boers were determined to be thoroughly on their guard the second time."

Finally, we have the testimony of Lord Rosmead himself, the High Commissioner, who, when Mr. Chamberlain wrote complaining of the arming of Pretoria in 1896, expressed his conviction that the armaments were "defensive, not offensive."

This is surely a sufficient exposure of the theory of a Krugerite conspiracy. This theory rests entirely on the assertion that the Boers had been arming themselves for aggressive purposes. It has been proved that the great increase of military expenditure followed the Raid, and the fortifications and orders for big guns are attributed by hostile witnesses to this period and this cause. The Boers armed themselves in consequence of the Raid, to meet an attack upon their country which they anticipated would take place, and which is now taking place.

CHAPTER XVII

THE CASE OF THE FREE STATE

"BUT England has no quarrel with the Free State; why need you interfere when we are going to give our lesson to the Transvaal? Sir Alfred Milner has just wired to tell you that if you keep quiet, and guarantee that none of your people lend a hand to the Transvaalers, you shall not be touched. Why not take him at his word, keep quiet, and avoid trouble? As for your treaty with the sister Republic—well, surely there is some way out of that. Treaties and conventions are not now-a-days like the laws of the Medes and Persians." Such was the purport of the questions I put to the President, to Mr. Fischer, the energetic man of the Executive Council, who has played the chief *rôle* of peacemaker, and to other men of leading at Bloemfontein. The answer I got from all was identical in substance, and was the most convincing testimony to the *mala fides* of the British Government which I had yet received. Here is a little State, extolled as "a model Republic" by the very writers and politicians who are most unsparing in their condemnation of the Transvaal, with a franchise whose liberality verges upon license, whose treatment of foreigners is unimpeachable, against whose purity of justice and civil administration there is no breath of scandal, and which yet chooses to expose herself to the perils of war in support of her sister Republic. Can the sins of the latter have been so heinous as they have been represented? At any rate, they were not such as to cut her off from the enthusiastic support of the entire body of citizens in the Free State. This was not due to blind sentimental sympathy, based upon community of blood and adherence to a common form of government. There is no foundation for the view which represents the Free State as heroically sacrificing herself to a foolish, ill-considered treaty entered into with the Transvaal. That treaty, as well as the unanimous determination to abide by it, was the result of a clear perception by the shrewd statesmen of the Free State that the essential interests of the two Republics are identical, and that the danger and destruction of the one implies the danger and destruction of the other.

President Steyn put the matter forcibly before me in language of which the following is a close paraphrase:—

"Does England suppose that lightly and without good reason we contemplate breaking the friendly relations that have subsisted between us and Great Britain for the last twenty years? It is only because we are firmly convinced of the injustice of England's treatment of the Transvaal that we take our stand and link our fate with hers. Do not suppose that we are blind to her faults and shortcomings. Our friends at the Cape have been continually urging us to bring pressure on the Transvaal to give a more generous franchise and to rectify other grievances, and we have tried for years to do our best. Mr. Fischer and I have urged Mr. Kruger and his Government to make concessions, and they have made them, and would have made more if the British Government had not defeated our peaceful negotiations by threats of coercion. To these demands the Transvaal has given way even further than we had anticipated. We now agree that they cannot safely go further, as we are convinced that no concessions will avail to secure the independence of their country. When Sir Alfred Milner was here, he declared, both publicly and privately to me, that his policy was to secure a reasonable franchise, and that the enfranchised burghers should afterwards settle the other issues for themselves; but this position is now abandoned, other issues are put forward for immediate settlement, and just those issues are selected which he is convinced the Transvaal must refuse. Again, an inquiry into the seven-year franchise is proposed, but no sooner has the Transvaal accepted than the proposal is withdrawn. I have no option but to conclude that Mr. Kruger is right in thinking the English are aiming at his country."

Such was the substance of President Steyn's statement, and it was endorsed by the action of the Raad and the whole body of citizens. These men have shown themselves no blind sympathisers with the neighbouring State; they have been, and are still, outspoken in their condemnation of such evils as the dynamite monopoly and the corruption which prevails in certain State departments. They have had their quarrels with their neighbour time after time, but all these ill-feelings are now swallowed up by the sense of solidarity between the two Republics. It is said that England has no quarrel with the Free State, and we exhibit a mild surprise that the latter should choose to link her fate with that of the Transvaal and risk a common castigation. But those who say this are ignorant of past history and blind to the inevitable future. I asked President Steyn what he really feared, even if the Transvaal fell under British control. His reply, incomplete as it may seem, was full of significance. "Suppose," he said, "a valuable goldfield

THE CASE OF THE FREE STATE 139

were discovered in the Free State, how long should we keep our independence?" In common with all the thoughtful men of the Free State, brushing aside the minor temporary circumstances, he evidently interpreted our political raid as the endeavour of the gold-seekers to get the complete control of the gold-bearing country. Both he and Mr. Fischer spoke of the gold discoveries as the curse of the Transvaal, and no one who compares the two Republics can doubt the rightness of this judgment. All the maladies of Transvaal misgovernment, and all the dangers they have produced, have their origin in this fatal gift, which has corrupted all parties in the State and fed race hatred, now broken out into blood-guiltiness. Those who extol the Free State to the detriment of the Transvaal often forget that the nature of the two peoples and their history are identical. It may be that the Free State has been more fortunate in its leaders, particularly in the possession of the great and good President Brand, who moulded the character of its early institutions and wielded a personal influence which yet moves in the hearts of the Free State citizens. But the only substantial difference between the Free State and the Transvaal, the radical source of all recent divergences in character and history, is to be found in the one word "gold." Let a rich goldfield be discovered in the Free State, and the same corrupting influences would set in, with the same results. So long as the two Republics stand side by side, some resistance could be made to the political absorption, the destruction of independence, which is a mere incident of the march of modern Capitalism. But remove from the Free State the support of the Transvaal Republic, and resistance became impossible. It may be said that this was an idle fear. England had expressly repudiated the notion of destroying the independence of the Republics, and even were the Transvaal to be conquered the Free State had nothing to fear. But the statesmen of the Free State have longer memories and a firmer grip upon the situation than those who use this optimist language. When the President spoke of a possible goldfield and its consequences, he was not speaking in the air. He remembered the loss of the Diamond Fields, and the methods by which it was secured by the British Government from the Free State. Those who attempt to condemn this conduct by adducing the fact that £90,000 was paid to the Free State do not better their case, for this money was expressly paid, "not as recompense for any admitted wrong, but in consideration of the injury which the President and the people of the State represented they had sustained." Surely the palpable disingenuousness of this language convicts those who framed it. Did we, or did we not admit the injury done the Free State? If not, why did we pay money to them? A lawyer with a large conveyancing practice near Kimberley told me that even now the transfer of the most valuable lands shows that their ownership rests upon Free State titles—an absolutely convincing proof of Free State priority of claim. This "most discreditable transaction" was doubtless becoming dimmer in the national memory. But the Jameson Raid and its sequelæ have revived it, along with other instances of British fraud and force in South Africa.

Those who think this language vaguely strong are referred to the plain history told by the Chief-Justice of the Free State in the issue of the *Nineteenth Century* of March 1897, where they will find an unvarnished tale of British treachery and violence which will make their ears tingle with shame. They will then understand how the Free State regards England's indignant charges against the Transvaal of breaking Conventions. Chief-Justice de Villiers shows that the whole of England's northern conquests are founded upon deliberate breaches of Conventions, in particular of the Sand River Convention, which provides "that no encroachments shall be made by the said (British) Government on the territory beyond the north of the Vaal River," and that "all trade in ammunition with the native tribes is prohibited, both by the British Government and the emigrant farmers, on both sides of the Vaal River." His declaration that the annexation of Basutoland was a plain breach of definite pledges given by Great Britain, and that "every inch of ground subsequently acquired by her in that region was acquired in violation of solemn engagements," is proved up to the hilt.

The entire policy adopted by Sir P. Wodehouse as early as 1862 was a chronic manifold violation of our obligations. Sir Philip not merely intrigued to get Moshesh and the Basutos under British rule, but he directly contravened the Conventions by stopping a supply of ammunition coming through the colony to the Free State when the latter was at war with the Basutos, while on another occasion he went so far as to send Moshesh a present of gunpowder.

These incidents, however, are now of old date, nor did they deeply rankle in the breast of Free Staters. It was only the British demeanour of to-day, and her self-righteous trumpeting about respect for treaty obligations, which recalled this former misconduct.

The Free State feared not alone for the Transvaal, but for herself, and she saw certain facts which are at present kept conveniently in the background. She asked herself,

"If England assails the internal independence of the Transvaal by virtue of suzerainty or paramountcy, what is to prevent her from applying the same arguments to us if we have anything she wants?" England's demands are no longer made under the Conventions, and outside these the "paramountcy" of England is as applicable to the one Republic as to the other. New documentary evidence had recently been found by the Free State which makes even closer the analogy of her position to that of the Transvaal. On the signing of the 1884 Convention with the Transvaal in London, a telegram from the Secretary of State, communicated to the Transvaal and the Free State Governments, contains a summary of the essence of the Convention in the following terms:—"Same internal independence in Transvaal as in Orange Free State. Conduct and control diplomatic intercourse foreign Governments conceded. Queen's final approval treaties reserved." Reading such a statement alongside of the recent assertion by Mr. Chamberlain of British paramountcy over "the two Republics," it was not unnatural that Free Staters should regard their position as precarious. They had seen Great Britain, in plain contravention of her pledges, gradually absorbing the country to the north and east, so that the enclave of the two Republics became an eyesore to the ardent advocates of one British South Africa. They remembered the talk of Rhodes in 1893 about "the abolition of the two Republics," and Lord Salisbury's sneer about "nebulous Republics" had not been lost on them. Once let the Transvaal pass definitely under the unsympathetic sway of England, and the Free State lay at her mercy, not merely in a military, but also in an economic sense. The owners of the Transvaal could at any time ruin the Free State. The latter, a poor struggling agricultural commu-

THE CASE OF THE FREE STATE 143

nity, is absolutely dependent on the market which the Transvaal furnishes, sending nearly a million pounds' worth of goods per annum. Her public revenue, again, is chiefly dependent upon the railway and the trade it brings. In either of these two ways, by stopping the market for agriculture, or by diverting railway traffic on to the eastern lines, a hostile Government in the Transvaal might coerce the Free State. It is not, then, idly and without due consideration that the Free State decided to risk everything and stand by the Transvaal. She had watched the game of the last four years at close quarters, and understood how the British Government and people had been "worked" by the capitalists and speculators of the Rand. She understood the well-intentioned but futile pledges which English politicians continued to offer regarding the "independence" of the Republic. These soft words she compared with hard facts, and rated them accordingly.

The Free Staters knew what they were doing and what they wished. They are proud of their country, and have good reason for their pride. On a poor soil, unable to support its population except by assiduous toil, they have built up one of the most successful little nations the world has ever seen. The political and social structure of the State is admirable; its institutions are liberal and plastic; one-third of its little public income is spent on education, the rest upon public works, which form a valuable national asset. Bloemfontein, at great expense, has just secured an adequate water supply, and is establishing a municipal system of electric lighting. Its public offices are administered with that genuine combination of economy and efficiency which, even in England, figures only upon electoral addresses. I talked with many of their public men, and found them filled with a patriotic pride in the progress they had made. These people are lovers of their country, and they have a country worthy of their love. This is the secret of their willingness to fight and die for it. The more thoughtful among them admitted that in many ways they might gain by being absorbed into a British South Africa; but they believed that their independence, and the constant struggle it requires, were worth more to their national character than the security of British rule, and they will fight to the death to preserve this independence. English settlers, as a rule, thought and felt nothing of all this. Here in Bloemfontein I heard my countrymen, many of whom had lived and thriven for years as tradesmen under the hospitable protection of this State, expressing their gleeful confidence that British troops were coming to thrash the Boers of the Republics, and to set the flag of England in the place now occupied by the Free State flag. Whatever grievances the British had in the Transvaal, they neither had nor pretended to have any here, where the full civil and political status was freely given, and where they enjoyed the purest and, I am convinced, one of the most efficient governments in the world. And yet, obsessed by British Jingoism, they wished to see British troops at Bloemfontein. What was the reason? Legitimate motive there could be none. I can find no other explanation save the sheer lust of domination, which resents the claims of other people to freedom and equality with Englishmen. In the Transvaal this feeling is screened, for there are grievances, though much exaggerated, which seem to justify resentment. Here there are none, and yet the British population cherished the same resentment, the same desire to conquer the Boer.

THE CASE OF THE FREE STATE 145

But was not this spirit of hostility, this desire to domineer, common to Dutch as to English? Bitter hostility undoubtedly there was of late among the Free State Dutch. It would be strange were it otherwise. But I found no denial of equality, no desire to domineer among the Free Staters. The present English policy they hated and mistrusted, but against the English people and the English Empire there existed no strong or abiding hostility. I am convinced these people would have been serviceable friends if we had let them. An able young judge put this point most impressively to me. "Are these Republics really a thorn in the side of the British power in Africa? Surely not. We recognise the superiority of English rule to that of other Powers, and we value the security that Power can afford us. If we were left in our full present independence, and the time ever came when British supremacy were seriously threatened by Germany or any other nation, she would find her sturdiest and strongest defenders in these Republics, sturdier and stronger because of our independence and the spirit it maintains. But conquered and humbled by Great Britain, our respect will turn to rancour; we shall submit only because we must, and so long as we must; the spirit of freedom will not die, and the Republics, which might have been in friendly alliance with Great Britain, will remain permanent centres of disaffection, waiting an opportunity to strike a blow."

CHAPTER XVIII

THE SUZERAINTY ISSUE

IT is unprofitable to discuss the detailed niceties of the word or thing "suzerainty" and its application to the relations between Great Britain and the Transvaal, but two or three plain points still require to be enforced.

Why was the claim of suzerainty, never raised since the Pretoria Convention of 1884, reasserted by Mr. Chamberlain in 1897?

It is often said and supposed that this step was taken because Great Britain perceived a growing design in the Transvaal to wriggle itself out of the control retained by Great Britain under the Convention, and to issue forth as a completely independent State. Now whether the Transvaal entertained such an idea or not matters little here, for there is every reason to assign another motive for our revival of the claim to suzerainty.

Those who are still under the belief that England has all along desired and sought a peaceful settlement of our disputes with the Transvaal may be surprised to learn that the one and only object of the revival of a claim to suzerainty was the desire of our Government to avoid submitting her case to an impartial court of arbitration. This shameful fact is made manifest by the history of the way in which suzerainty came to be reaffirmed.

After the Jameson Raid the Transvaal had passed certain laws enabling dangerous individuals to be expelled

THE SUZERAINTY ISSUE 147

from the country, and enabling paupers and persons suffering from contagious diseases to be prohibited from entering —laws which not only independent countries, but our own colonies, have passed in their self-protection, and which are perhaps more needed by the Transvaal than by any other State. Great Britain complained that those laws contravened certain articles of the Convention. The Transvaal refused to admit that the laws were in contravention of the Convention, and urging their case, made an appeal to arbitration as the most suitable mode of settling the dispute.

I may here remind readers that at the recent Hague Conference, England, in common with all the other Powers, assented to the doctrine that the interpretation of treaties, conventions, and other written documents expressing international relations, are the proper subjects for a court of arbitration. But what did Mr. Chamberlain reply when invited to peaceful arbitration upon the interpretation of the London Convention? He raised from the grave, in which it had reposed since Lord Derby buried it in 1884, the doctrine of suzerainty; if not with the express object, at any rate with the inevitable result of rendering a peaceful mode of settlement impossible. This is so serious a charge that it is best to substantiate it by quoting in full the words of Mr. Chamberlain's despatch :—

"Finally, the Government of the South African Republic proposes that all points in dispute between Her Majesty's Government and themselves relating to the Convention should be referred to arbitration, the arbitrator to be nominated by the President of the Swiss Republic. In making this proposal the Government of the South African Republic appear to have overlooked the distinction between the Conventions of 1881 and

1884 and an ordinary treaty between two independent Powers, questions arising upon which may properly be the subject of arbitration. By the Pretoria Convention of 1881 Her Majesty, as sovereign of the Transvaal Territory, accorded to the inhabitants of that territory complete self-government, subject to the suzerainty of Her Majesty, her heirs and successors, upon certain terms and conditions, and subject to certain reservations and limitations set forth in thirty-three articles; and by the London Convention of 1884, Her Majesty, while maintaining the preamble of the earlier instrument, directed and declared that certain other articles embodied therein should be substituted for the article embodied in the Convention of 1881. The articles of the Convention of 1881 were accepted by the Volksraad of the Transvaal State, and those of the Convention of 1884 by the Volksraad of the South African Republic. Under these Conventions, therefore, Her Majesty holds towards the South African Republic the relation of a *suzerain* who has accorded to the people of that Republic self-government upon certain conditions, *and it would be incompatible with that position to submit to arbitration the construction of the conditions on which she accorded self-government to the Republic.*"[1]

Some people, whose attention was first drawn to South African affairs when the controversy took on a dangerous appearance last spring, expressed their astonishment that so much should be made of the suzerainty issue. It seemed to be a mere weapon of irritation—nothing more. No single demand, just or unjust, which England made or could make upon the Transvaal required the cover or support of suzerainty.

[1] Bluebook, C. 8721, No. 7 (October 1897).

THE SUZERAINTY ISSUE

England had the London Convention, the indisputable fact of paramountcy, and the general right of protecting her subjects accorded by international usage. Suzerainty added naught to this sphere of influence or interference It is true that the shifty term was sometimes applied in other historic instances so as to enable the suzerain power to levy taxes, control the army, determine peace or war, and regulate all external relations of the "subject" power. But these powers are neither *de facto* nor *de jure* applicable in the present case. On the contrary, the very articles of the Convention which, according to Mr. Chamberlain, contained or implied an assertion of suzerainty, explicitly assign to the Transvaal the free direction of all her internal affairs. Nor does this Convention impose any general control over her foreign relations. Article 4, the only one in which any concrete application of suzerain power can be pretended, merely provides a British right of veto in the case of treaties made by the Transvaal which are "in conflict with the interests of Great Britain, or of any of Her Majesty's possessions in South Africa."

If there is need of further witness, it is sufficient to quote the interpretation of "suzerainty" as set forth in the despatch of Lord Kimberley in March 1881 : "Entire freedom of action will be accorded to the Transvaal Government so far as is not inconsistent with the rights *expressly* reserved to the suzerain power. The term 'suzerainty' has been chosen as most conveniently describing superiority over a State possessing independent rights of government, subject to reservations with reference to certain *specified* matters." These "specified matters" are laid down in articles of the 1881 Convention, and, granting for the nonce the absurd contention that the preamble of this

Convention is carried over to the 1884 Convention, articles of that Convention limit suzerainty.

Why this trouble about a name which neither gives nor refuses any actual power?

The wisdom of the Transvaal Government in attaching to its offer of a five years' franchise an express condition that the further "assertion of the suzerainty" should be "dropped," is highly disputable; but those who say that this condition was inserted in order to ensure a refusal of a franchise never seriously intended, or that the Transvaal was actuated by merely sentimental considerations of dignity, do not understand the issue.

It was absolutely essential to the peace and security of the Transvaal that disputes which, quite apart from intentional offence, were bound to arise from time to time between her and Great Britain, should be capable of amicable settlement by reference to an impartial arbiter. Otherwise, she saw herself destined to be the victim of incessant new demands pressed upon her by *force majeure*, the merits of which were to be determined by the mere *ipse dixit* of Great Britain, or, in many instances, of influential British subjects in the Transvaal.

The continued assertion of suzerainty meant the continued refusal of a court of justice, the continued assertion of a reign of force.

For Mr. Chamberlain the assertion of suzerainty meant the "right" to make any demands he chose, in defiance of the London Convention or of the ordinary usages of nations, and to refuse to submit these demands to impartial arbitration. Under this condition of affairs the Transvaal rightly recognised that her "independence" was in constant danger.

That she was right in raising again a controversy which

THE SUZERAINTY ISSUE

Mr. Chamberlain himself had previously allowed to drop, is very doubtful, but that it was essential to her to repudiate the doctrine of suzerainty must be obvious to any one. So strongly did she realise this necessity, that in one despatch she took the much reprobated step of insisting upon her position as that of "a sovereign international State." To most Englishmen this seemed an utterly unwarranted and somewhat impudent assertion, but the circumstances under which that assertion was made and the real meaning of it ought not to be ignored. Mr. Chamberlain had said that if the "preamble" of the Pretoria Convention, containing the assertion of suzerainty, was not carried forward into the London Convention, then the independence guaranteed to the Transvaal in domestic government, which was contained in the same preamble, also lapsed. To this statement the Transvaal replied that the form of the Convention of London implied that the South African Republic was "a sovereign international State," and that "it was therefore superfluous in that Convention to specify or define its rights."

By this statement the Transvaal did not intend to repudiate any control secured to Great Britain by the London Convention, but merely to assert that the limitations upon her independence there contained were not such as to disqualify her from being a sovereign State. Mr. Reitz in a recent pamphlet puts the matter thus : " It would have been more correct to have said, that owing to the lapse of suzerainty, the South African Republic no longer fell under the head of a semi-suzerain State, but that it had become a free, independent, sovereign international State, the sovereignty of which was only limited by the restriction contained in Article 4 of the Convention. Sovereignty need not of necessity be absolute. Belgium is a sovereign international State, although it is bound to observe a condition of permanent neutrality. The South African Republic falls undoubtedly under the category of States the sovereignty of which is limited in one or other defined directions."[1]

But though the importance of securing a cessation of this assertion of suzerainty for the future peace of the Transvaal may be admitted, the correctness of her statement that such suzerainty had actually lapsed may be denied by those who have not followed the evidence.

It is therefore necessary briefly to review the absolutely conclusive evidence in favour of the contention of the Transvaal upon this particular point. To point out how the Transvaal deputation to Lord Derby in 1884 expressly sought abrogation of suzerainty and departed confident in having obtained it; how Mr. Kruger in his address to the Raad on his return announced the cancellation of suzerainty as the chief fruit of their mission; how the British Government abstained from all mention of suzerainty in correspondence with the Transvaal until Mr. Chamberlain's despatches of 1897—such evidence, however strong, may be considered circumstantial and inadequate. After all, it might be said, the fact of suzerainty remained, and the right of asserting it, though suspended in its exercise, was there. The absolutely crushing refutation of suzerainty consists in the direct evidence which exists of the intention of Lord Derby and the British Government to cancel it. A despatch of the Transvaal Government last year thus succinctly states this proof:—

"This Government has the written evidence in its archives that Lord Derby himself proposed that the preamble of the Convention of 1881 should be abolished.

[1] "A Century of Wrong," p. 24.

In Lord Derby's letter of the 15th February 1884 (Bluebook C. 3947, p. 43), his Lordship sends to the deputation a draft of the new Convention which Her Majesty's Government propose in substitution for the Convention of Pretoria. This draft was not published in the Blue-book, but the original is still in the possession of this Government. A true copy of the first page is affixed as an annexion to this letter. It is so clear in itself that it seems unnecessary to add one word thereto. Indeed, this page gives in printed form, in succession, first the preamble of 1881, and then the preamble of 1884. At the head is to be read the note:—'The words and paragraphs bracketed or printed in italics are proposed to be inserted; those within a black line are proposed to be omitted.' Now the preamble of 1881 is 'within a black line,' and is thus omitted. No conclusion can be clearer. There is still more. The last page of the draft sent by Lord Derby shows most distinctly that his Lordship meant to have suzerainty abolished. A true copy of this last page also accompanies this letter. That page, already referred to, indicates the concluding portion of the Convention of 1881, and the following words therein appearing, viz., 'subject to the suzerainty of Her Majesty, her heirs and successors,' have been crossed out by Lord Derby."

It is seldom that such convincing proof of intention can be supplied. Does Mr. Chamberlain now deny that it was the intention of Lord Derby and the Government of which he was Colonial Secretary to cancel suzerainty, or that that intention was fulfilled ? Not merely the Transvaal Government, but all lawyers in Europe and in South Africa to whom the case has been submitted, unanimously hold that no suzerainty has in fact existed since 1884. From this fact it would seem to be clear that Mr.

Chamberlain raised the suzerainty issue in order to avoid the necessity of arbitration, which was, in fact, the best chance of a pacific mode of settlement, and to enable Great Britain, a stronger Power, to enforce her will in a high-handed manner upon a smaller and a weaker State. It is equally clear that the suzerainty which he bases upon the Convention of Pretoria has no existence.

CHAPTER XIX

WHY DID THE BOERS ISSUE THE ULTIMATUM?

If neither the Government nor the people of the South African Republics desired to fight, how then did it come to pass that an ultimatum, amounting to a declaration of war, proceeded from them? To find an answer to this question we must first assume that there was a firm conviction in both Republics that war was intended by Great Britain. I had the opportunity of testing this conviction at Pretoria and at Bloemfontein within a month of the outbreak of hostilities. Not only the President and those who share most largely his stubborn and intolerant spirit, men like Messrs. Burger and Wolmarans, but milder and more enlightened officers of State like General Joubert, Mr. Reitz, and Mr. Smuts, were firmly persuaded that Great Britain did not genuinely desire a peaceful settlement, and was not really conducting her negotiations to that end. This conviction they supported by appeal to a series of crucial events dating from the Jameson Raid. The unsatisfactory inquiry of the Commission, with its perfunctory condemnation of Mr. Rhodes, followed by the eulogistic exculpation rendered by the Colonial Minister, and endorsed by nearly all the English public opinion which reaches South Africa, destroyed the belief of the Republics in the British sense of justice, and suggested suspicions of collusion or connivance on the part of Mr. Chamberlain, which, however groundless, was only a natural interpretation of events by a people unaccustomed to the niceties—(is that quite the word?)—of English politics and finance. Rightly or wrongly, these people are great believers in the personality of Mr. Rhodes, and when that gentleman, failing to get his end by private force, announced his intention to compass it by "constitutional means," they took him at his word. They soon seemed to see the operation of these constitutional means. A High Commissioner of pronounced Imperialist proclivities, chosen—so they believed —upon the express recommendation of Mr. Rhodes, was sent out, who soon signalised his reign by a policy, in their view, of diplomatic provocation. Making but little attempt to ingratiate himself with the Dutch, who form the white majority, or to win their confidence and affection, as other High Commissioners had done, Sir Alfred Milner chose for his chief advisers men whom the Transvaal had excellent reasons to believe their deadly enemies, and opened his mind to the stream of biassed evidence which flowed from a press and a party organisation financed and controlled by those very men who had conspired against the Transvaal three years ago. When the High Commissioner, who had never set foot in the Transvaal, was visibly captured by these hostile influences, and was induced to throw the full weight of his authority upon the British Cabinet, the constitutional raid definitely began. Knowing that the condition of the Outlander was not one of intolerable oppression, and that the demand for the franchise was not in a large sense genuine, they naturally disbelieved that a settlement of the ostensible grievances was the real end sought. In this conviction they were supported by the Outlander press, which, whenever signs of a peaceful settlement appeared, de-

WHY THE ULTIMATUM WAS ISSUED 157

nounced the proposed arrangement as unsatisfactory, and, as negotiations proceeded, threw off the mask and declared that nothing less than a complete and ignominious climbing down of the Boer Government ought to be accepted. Indeed, it was soon made obvious that even this climbing down was not really desired: the Rhodesite press and the average British Jingo in South Africa never concealed their distrust of any Boer concessions and promises which were not preceded by a thorough drubbing. So, while tedious and tortuous negotiations were proceeding between the Governments, a British press and people in South Africa were calling for war. Is it strange that the Transvaal should have believed that Sir Alfred Milner and Mr. Chamberlain also meant war? Not once or twice within the last few years the Transvaal had proposed a general submission to arbitration of all disputed issues, and Mr. Chamberlain refused. Throughout the whole course of the negotiations no *bona fide* proposal of arbitration was proposed or accepted by Great Britain; for the proposal to arbitrate, while refusing to name the issues reserved from arbitration, cannot be regarded as an offer. Add to this the strenuous and successful endeavour made by Great Britain's representatives at the Hague Conference to limit the use of arbitration so as to exclude the Transvaal. Did this look as if England desired a peaceful settlement?

But what weighed heaviest of all with the statesmen at Pretoria and Bloemfontein was the fact that the diplomatic demands of Great Britain all seemed expressly formulated so as to exclude finality. When the joint inquiry proposed by England, and accepted without unnecessary delay by the Transvaal, was withdrawn, when other issues kept until the last moment in the background were then thrust forward for immediate settlement, including the very coolie question which had already been decided by arbitration adversely to England, the Government of the Free State felt reluctantly compelled to admit that England meant war. The determinate motive of this unhappy war on the side of the Republics was the conviction that England, persistently refusing to formulate the clear limits of her demands, was not a *bona fide* negotiator.

This brings me close to the question, Why did the Republics issue the ultimatum? At first sight the question seems a curious one to ask. Believing that war was inevitable, it would be more natural to ask, "Why should the Republics wait for Great Britain to mass her troops upon their borders and to choose her time?" Yet, strange as it may seem, I am convinced it was the firm intention of both Governments to stay inside their country and abide the shock of invasion. President Kruger is credibly reported to have clung with superstitious persistence to the notion that the help of the Lord, to which he looked, was good for a defensive but not for an offensive attitude. But the policy of Mr. Chamberlain was to tempt him to the technical position of aggressor. This game was played skilfully and with success. The British despatch formulating *de novo* demands which would constitute an ultimatum was promised at an early date. Great Britain had all along complained of the dilatory method of Boer diplomacy. But what does Great Britain do? For weeks before the first Boer commandoes moved she had been moving troops into the country and towards the border, professedly for the defence of her colonies, though she had no reason to expect attack. It is of course now said that this action was justified by the fact that an attack was actually made. But such an argument is a plain inversion of the order of causation, for few people would seriously contend that, had not British troops been moved towards the frontiers, the Boer forces would have crossed.

Formally the Boers were the aggressors, actually the landing of British troops and the movement of them towards the frontiers, under a false pretext of self-defence, were the first acts of hostility. This indeed is virtually admitted in the reply made by Mr. Chamberlain and Sir A. Milner when they explained that the troops were there not only for defence but for "eventualities." The veiled menace of that phrase was substantially a declaration of war, and was gleefully welcomed as such by the Jingo press of the Transvaal and the colonies. Now mark what occurred with regard to the promised statement of final proposals. As a counter-move to the British massing of troops, the Republics took a number of their farmers from their homes and set them on the frontiers, awaiting the final proposals of Great Britain. Those proposals did not come. Days and weeks passed, still they did not come. Meanwhile they heard from England that the Privy Council meets, that Parliament was summoned to vote supplies, that the reserves were being called out, that British colonies, including Natal, were eagerly preparing to send volunteers; more troops were landed, and others were leaving England, while those already in South Africa were taking up threatening positions near their frontiers. The burghers, lying idle on the veldt, enduring days and nights of heavy rain, mostly without the shelter of a tent, began to grow restive; they thought of their neglected farms, where the sowing and ploughing season was beginning, of their wives and children. Capable of great physical endurance, these men are not trained to the implicit obedience of the professional soldier; individual will and the right of free judgment have not been ground out of them by military routine. Low grumbles gathered into open discontent. "We are here to fight, not to lie here as long as England chooses to keep us waiting while she strengthens her position and brings up her horse and artillery." This was the feeling which doubtless found expression upon every side. It is likely enough that many of these farmers threatened to leave and return to their homes unless their commandants took action. Could any one blame them for not waiting for the full forces of the greatest Empire in the world to enter their borders before they struck a blow? England maintains that she did not wish for war or intend it even to the last, that her final proposals were such as would have rendered an honourable peace possible. But that is not the point. The Republics could only judge British intentions from British speech and actions, and these, read as the Boers were bound to read them, carried no other meaning than that which they placed upon them.

CHAPTER XX

DIPLOMACY LEADING UP TO WAR

In the close of the year 1898, Sir A. Milner paid a brief visit to England. His return to South Africa in February 1899 was followed by a rapid and remarkable growth of the Outlander agitation. A series of alleged outrages upon persons and property, the most notorious of which were the killing of Edgar, the Amphitheatre incident, and the Appelbe murder, were communicated to Sir A. Milner, who, after making them the subject of hot protest and recrimination in his communications with the Transvaal Government, gave them large prominence in his despatches to the Colonial Office.

Concurrently with these events sprang up a fresh political activity in the press and on the platforms of the Rand. The South African League leapt from insignificance into an important political position, a new and violent political newspaper was founded in Johannesburg, the Outlander Council came into being, and a petition of grievances, purporting to be signed by 21,684 Outlanders, was presented to the Queen. This petition was followed by a number of political meetings organised by the South African League upon the mines, the resolutions and reports of which were fully transmitted by Sir A. Milner in order to fortify the petition. Reports and articles from the columns of the *Cape Times* and the Johannesburg *Star*, papers owned by great mining capitalists, are given as authoritative statements and largely figure in the Blue-book, "Complaints of British Subjects."

The growing pace of this agitation, and the close intercourse and strongly avowed sympathy disclosed in the relations between the High Commissioner and the leaders of the Outlander movement, cannot fail to impress readers with the certain feeling that an organised and critical attack was in preparation.

In pursuance of this design, Sir A. Milner transmitted to Mr. Chamberlain the long sensational telegram of May 5th, in which he supports the Outlanders' petition with the full weight of his authority, attesting "the absolute *bona fides* of its promoters," and the strength and genuineness of the political agitation which it expresses. In the most vigorous language he endorses the grievances, and urges the franchise as the proper remedy. The following are the most salient passages:—
"The right of Great Britain to intervene to secure fair treatment of the Outlanders is fully equal to her supreme interest in securing it. The majority of them are her subjects, whom she is bound to protect; but the enormous number of British subjects, the endless series of their grievances, and the nature of those grievances, which are not less serious because they are not individually sensational, makes protection by the ordinary diplomatic means impossible."

"The true remedy is to strike at the root of all these injuries—the political influence of the injured. What diplomatic protests will never accomplish, a fair measure of Outlander representation would gradually but surely bring about. It seems a paradox, but it is true that the only effective way of protecting our subjects is to help them to cease to be our subjects."

DIPLOMACY LEADING UP TO WAR

"The spectacle of thousands of British subjects kept permanently in the position of helots, constantly chafing under undoubted grievances, and calling vainly to Her Majesty's Government for redress, does steadily undermine the influence and reputation of Great Britain and the respect for the British Government within the Queen's dominions. A certain section of the press, not in the Transvaal only, preaches openly and constantly the doctrine of a republic embracing all South Africa, and supports it by menacing references to the armaments of the Transvaal, its alliance with the Orange Free State, and the active sympathy which, in case of war, it would receive from a section of Her Majesty's subjects. I regret to say that this doctrine, supported as it is by a ceaseless stream of malignant lies about the intention of the British Government, is producing a great effect upon a large number of our Dutch fellow-colonists. Language is frequently used which seems to imply that the Dutch have some superior right, even in this colony, to their fellow-subjects of British birth. Thousands of men peaceably disposed, and, if left alone, perfectly satisfied with their position as British subjects, are being drawn into disaffection, and there is a corresponding exasperation on the side of the British. I can see nothing which will put a stop to this mischievous propaganda but some striking proof of the intention of Her Majesty's Government not to be ousted from its position in South Africa; and the best proof alike of its power and its justice would be to obtain for the Outlanders in the Transvaal a fair share in the government of the country which owes everything to their exertions."

The amazing indiscretion of these vague general charges of disloyalty, launched against the people who form the majority of the British subjects he is set to govern, upon evidence which, so far as it has ever been disclosed, is of the flimsiest character, need not detain us.

The significance of this telegram as a diplomatic document lies in three points. First, it puts forward the franchise as the sole and sufficient object of present pressure, as a "radical" remedy. Secondly, it insists that we must exact this franchise from the Transvaal Government in such a manner as to make the concession a "striking proof" of our power. Thirdly, it assigns as the reason for this dramatic exhibition of power the existence of a Dutch conspiracy, involving "a section of Her Majesty's subjects." So early there is prepared the doctrine of the Dutch conspiracy as a second defence for our aggressive policy, when the first, viz., the intolerable nature of Outlander grievances, should break down.

At present, however, the franchise was to be the sole objective. If, in the early representations to the Transvaal Government, this had been clearly stated, some hope of settlement upon this basis might have been probable. But Mr. Chamberlain, in suggesting the conference between Sir A. Milner and Mr. Kruger, did not give the latter to understand that the franchise was to be the one, or even the chief, matter of discussion. His language in the despatch of May 10 was studiously vague, and suggested "that a meeting should be arranged between his Honour and yourself for the purpose of discussing the situation in a conciliatory spirit, and in the hope that you may arrive, in concert with the President, at such an arrangement as Her Majesty's Government could accept and recommend to the Outlander population as a reasonable concession to their just demands."

No clear definite understanding was ever sought by Sir A. Milner prior to the conference as a basis of discussion, and this utter disregard of the most ordinary business precaution ensured beforehand the futility of the debate. If Sir Alfred had desired the conference to be fruitless, he would have set about it and conducted it in precisely the way he did. President Kruger is blamed as a shifty politician for trying to evade "the issue," and to draw our astute representative into irrelevant side-issues, and Sir Alfred has been praised for his stubborn pertinacity in refusing to discuss the Swaziland question, the indemnity for the Raid, arbitration, and other points which Mr. Kruger introduced with the view of carrying out the object of Mr. Chamberlain by "discussing the situation in a conciliatory spirit."

Mr. Kruger, in his counter-proposals of June 2, stated that "his object in the conference was to remove existing grounds of difference, and to provide for friendly settlement of future difficulties by arbitration."

It was natural enough that, in default of any prior agreement, Mr. Kruger should have sought to settle other questions than the franchise, and that Sir A. Milner's hard declaration, " That I cannot agree to the basis which appears to have been laid down, that I should buy with something else the just settlement of the franchise question," should have caused surprise and given offence.

It was, of course, quite in keeping with Sir Alfred's intention of giving "a signal pooof" of British power that he should refuse to give anything, however reasonable, that might possibly have been represented as a *quid pro quo*. The franchise must be openly wrested from unwilling hands without conditions, to afford the "signal proof" desired. His attitude towards his opponent well illustrated this resolve. Instead of exhibiting the "conciliatory spirit" recommended by Mr. Chamberlain, he bombarded the President with dialectical artillery, bowling over in summary fashion his arguments, making debating scores off him, and eventually driving the old man to an attitude of obstinate despair.

The franchise issue did get discussed, but the temper of the two disputants was by this time such as to prohibit any possibility of close approach, or of that friendly attitude of "give-and-take" essential to a conference. The position and tone of Sir Alfred Milner were that of the man who came having plainly made up his mind to get all he asked and to give nothing. He presented his five years' scheme like a revolver at the head of Mr. Kruger. His request may have been perfectly reasonable, and Mr. Kruger would doubtless have acted discreetly in accepting it; but if Sir A. Milner has any of the ordinary knowledge of human nature required for a diplomatic post, and of Boer nature in particular, required by the special post he occupied, he must have known that the way he chose was the way how not to get it, and we must suppose him to have planned and contemplated failure.

The man who announces that he will not bargain, that he must have all he wants and will give nothing, is out of place in any conference designed "to discuss the situation in a conciliatory spirit."

The franchise offered by Mr. Kruger at Bloemfontein was not, as it stood, a satisfactory one. In the case of new-comers it required (1) six months' notice of intention to apply for naturalisation; (2) two years' continuous registration to qualify for naturalisation; (3) five years' continuous registration after naturalisation, in order to fulfil the time conditions for obtaining burghership. Other conditions relating to good conduct and property qualifications were also laid down.

This proposal has been ridiculed as preposterous by those unacquainted with the restrictions with which most European States hedge the franchise. Some of the particular restrictions proposed were undoubtedly vexatious, and must have been removed in order to make the measure one of practical relief. But, inadequate as it was, it marked a distinct concession, and Sir A. Milner admitted that it was "a considerable advance on the existing franchise law."

Instead, however, of treating this "considerable advance" as a first step in a diplomatic descent, Sir Alfred flaunted his whole demand, and, because it was not at once conceded, broke off the conference. " The result of your memorandum is, that you and I have failed to come to an agreement in the most important points of the subjects discussed by us, and we are at present in the same position as we were previous to the conference; therefore this conference is altogether at an end, and there is no obligation on either side as an outcome thereof."

Is it possible to conceive a ruder banging of the door of conciliation than this ?

In considering the Bloemfontein Conference two salient facts present themselves. First, that the franchise is recognised as the one and only object of diplomatic pressure. Secondly, that Great Britain definitely refuses to submit her differences to arbitration. It is true that Sir A. Milner admitted that "there is a class of questions regarding which Her Majesty's Government would be prepared to arbitrate," but he stated in the same breath "there are subjects about which Her Majesty's Government most clearly cannot arbitrate;" and when Mr. Kruger proposed arbitration "regarding disputes with reference to the manner of interpreting documents" (the proper sphere for a court of arbitration, according to the Hague Conference), he shirked the issue, saying, "I have no authority to speak on this matter."

That the British policy at this time was expressly directed and confined to the franchise is still more strikingly proved by Sir A. Milner's speech at Cape Town on June 12th, in which he said, "To have pressed for the redress of the Outlander grievances one by one, to say nothing of the other subjects of difference, would have been to engage in an irritating controversy and to spoil the chance of an amicable compromise on broad lines going to the root of the differences. . . . It seemed best to strike straight at the root of the evil by giving the people whose interests Her Majesty's Government is bound to defend such a share of political power as would enable them gradually to redress their grievances themselves, and to strengthen, not to weaken, the country of their adoption in the process."

Had the policy thus outlined, of a settlement upon a franchise basis, been adhered to, there is every reason to believe that the peace could have been kept. Had Great Britain been willing to submit all other outstanding differences to arbitration, the peace could have been kept. But the subsequent course of British diplomacy shows, first, a progressive departure from the Bloemfontein position; secondly, a stubborn refusal to submit the rest of the case to an impartial arbitration.

It is of urgent importance to understand that Great Britain steadfastly set her face against arbitration as a full mode of settlement.

In the earliest despatch to the Transvaal Government following the conference (that of August 2), it was stated that "His Excellency the High Commissioner is prepared to discuss anything which the Government of the South African Republic wishes to bring forward, including arbitration, without the interference of foreign Powers." But that Sir A. Milner was not prepared to adopt such arbitration as a means of settlement appears from the language of his despatch to our Government dated June 14th, in which he says, "I was quite prepared to advocate the settlement of differences between the two Governments —*or some of them*—by an impartial tribunal, if such could be found, involving no foreign interference whatever."

This reservation of an unknown and unstated quantity of subjects from arbitration is observable in all cases where we handled the subject, and completely destroys the *bona fides* of our proposal or acceptance of this mode of settlement.

After the Bloemfontein Conference was over a Reform Bill was submitted by Mr. Kruger to the Raad, granting the suffrage after seven years' residence upon certain conditions of registration, &c. This bill, which was passed by the Raad, marked one more distinct concession on the part of the Transvaal Government; it abated some of the time conditions of the President's proposal at Bloemfontein, and it removed certain other limitations. Though still cumbrous, and not wholly satisfactory as a working instrument, it was welcomed by the Cape Ministry as a measure of substantial justice capable of improvement in detail.

That this was at first the view adopted by the British Government is proved by the fact that their next step took the form of a proposal of a joint-commission of inquiry into the operation of the new franchise law (contained in a despatch of July 27), the substance of which was communicated to the Transvaal on August 2.[1]

[1] The British proposal was not formally communicated until August 23.

Now this proposal of a joint-inquiry the Transvaal was at first evidently reluctant to accept, having a not unreasonable fear that it would become a precedent for further infringement upon that liberty of internal government acknowledged in the Conventions.

The State Attorney first sounded the British Agent at Pretoria, to ascertain whether a simplified franchise law, with a clear seven years' franchise, and a further increase of seats in Outlander districts, would be accepted as an alternative to the proposal of the joint-inquiry. Failing to get a satisfactory answer, the State Attorney induced the Transvaal Government to make another signal step, which virtually conceded all that Sir A. Milner had asked at Bloemfontein, and more, upon certain conditions. This proposal of a five years' franchise on conditions was made under the following circumstances. In the first place, it was arranged that, in order to avoid a formal rejection, the terms should first be submitted informally to the Colonial Minister, and then, if a favourable answer was received, the formal communication should be made. In the second place, it was expressly understood that this offer, if made, should not be taken as an answer to the proposal of a joint-inquiry into the seven years' law, and should not prejudice the right of the Transvaal to adopt that proposal.

After the terms of the informal communication had been agreed upon by Mr. Smuts and Mr. Greene, the British Agent, they were cabled to Mr. Chamberlain, and the following answer was received:—" If the South African Republic should reply to the invitation to a joint-inquiry put forward by Her Majesty's Government by formally making the proposals described in your telegram, such a course would not be regarded by Her Majesty's Govern-

DIPLOMACY LEADING UP TO WAR 171

ment as a refusal of their offer, but they would be prepared to consider the reply of the South African Republic on its merits." Now Mr. Smuts felt in considerable doubt, as he well might, about the interpretation of this telegram, and asked Mr. Greene how he understood it. Mr. Greene replied, "You can see they are inviting your proposal, and they would never have done this unless they were prepared to accept it." When the proposal was, as they held, rejected, the Transvaal Government alleged that it had been "induced by suggestions given by the British Agent to the State Attorney," and charged the British Government with "breach of faith." This charge was not, as sometimes represented, made against Mr. Greene, who was always well regarded by the Transvaal Government, but against Mr. Chamberlain, who was charged with wording his telegram so as to evoke an offer of a five years' franchise, with which he intended to make play afterwards, upon conditions which he had no real intention of considering "on their merits." The only charge made against Mr. Greene was that he, quite honestly, misunderstood it. Of course, if it were a fact that the Transvaal offer was virtually accepted, as Mr. Chamberlain afterwards declared, the charge of ill-faith falls altogether to the ground.

But what was the offer, and was it accepted?

The substance of the offer (August 12) was: (1) "A five years' retrospective franchise, as proposed by his Excellency the High Commissioner on June 1, 1899." (2) Eight new seats in the First Volksraad, and, if necessary, also in the Second Volksraad, for the population of the Witwatersrand, accompanied by a guarantee that the representation of the goldfields should not in future fall below the proportion of one-fourth of the whole. (3) The new burghers were to have equal rights with the old burghers; and (4) Friendly suggestions on all details from the British Government would be considered.

The following conditions I quote verbatim.

"In putting forward the above proposals, the Government of the South African Republic assumes: (*a*) That Her Majesty's Government will agree that the present intervention shall not form a precedent for future similar action, and that in the future no interference in the internal affairs of the Republic will take place: (*b*) That Her Majesty's Government will not further insist on the assertion of the suzerainty, the controversy on the subject being allowed tacitly to drop: (*c*) That arbitration (from which foreign elements, other than the Orange Free State, is to be excluded) will be conceded as soon as the franchise scheme has become law."

This was followed by a brief telegram explaining that the words "assuming that" must be understood to mark express "conditions" of the five years' offer.

Now to this offer Mr. Chamberlain sent a reply (August 28), which he described as "a qualified acceptance." The crucial passages are these:—

"With regard to the conditions of the Government of the South African Republic—first, as regards intervention, Her Majesty's Government hope that the fulfilment of the promises made, and the just treatment of the Outlanders in future, will render unnecessary any further intervention on their behalf; but Her Majesty's Government cannot, of course, debar themselves from their rights under the Conventions, nor divest themselves of the ordinary obligations of a civilised Power to protect its subjects in a foreign country from injustice. Secondly, with regard to suzerainty, Her Majesty's Government would refer the Government of the South African Republic to the second paragraph of my despatch of July 13. Thirdly, Her Majesty's Government agree to a discussion of the form and scope of a tribunal of arbitration from which foreigners and foreign influence are excluded."

Now, is this "a qualified acceptance"—an acceptance of "nine-tenths" of the Transvaal conditions, as Mr. Chamberlain asserted in the House of Commons? In form it is, in substance it is not. Take the three conditions; first, the two which Mr. Chamberlain says he fully and at once accepted, suzerainty and arbitration. Asked "not further to insist on the assertion of the suzerainty," he refers to a statement in a former despatch, addressed not to the Transvaal but to Sir Alfred Milner, in which he stated that the British Government "have no intention of continuing to discuss this question with the Government of the Republic, whose contention that the South African Republic is a sovereign international State is not, in their opinion, warranted either by law or history, and is wholly inadmissible." That is to say, his formal acceptance of the Transvaal condition is couched in an oblique reference to a passage which reasserts in the strongest way the very doctrine whose further assertion is supposed to be renounced.

So much for suzerainty; now for arbitration. "We accepted it," said Mr. Chamberlain. But what was the proposal of arbitration that they accepted? The Transvaal had throughout consistently urged that "all other outstanding differences," and in particular the interpretation of Convention or Conventions, should be submitted to arbitration. This was the arbitration they proposed. Was this accepted? That it was not is proved by the very words of Mr. Chamberlain which follow his statement, "We accepted it;" for he continues, "We had been negotiating on that basis. We proposed it at Bloemfontein." Now the arbitration for which England negotiated, and which Sir Alfred Milner proposed at Bloemfontein, was one which expressly excluded a number of subjects, unnamed, from the sphere of arbitration. Indeed, the very telegram [1] in which Mr. Chamberlain expresses his "qualified acceptance" concludes with a paragraph which denies arbitration as a basis of negotiation. "Her Majesty's Government also desire to remind the Government of the South African Republic that there are other matters of difference between the two Governments which will not be settled by the grant of political representation to the Outlanders, and which are not proper subjects for reference to arbitration." This was in effect, not merely a refusal of the condition of arbitration, in the meaning consistently given to that term by the Transvaal, but it served to destroy all possibility of a proper settlement on the basis of the Transvaal offer, by dragging into the field new unnamed issues.

The third condition, that of non-intervention in the future in the internal affairs of the Transvaal, Mr. Chamberlain did not claim to have accepted, but only to have evaded by his answer. In form, however, his answer might be taken as a part acceptance, for the Transvaal always expressly admitted the right of Great Britain to interference under the 1884 Convention or under ordinary international usages. It is, however, in complete accordance with the provocative character of Mr. Chamberlain's diplomacy that he uses the term "Conventions" instead of Convention, thus reasserting by direct implication the doctrine of suzerainty in the very despatch in which he alleges he has dropped

[1] August 28.

DIPLOMACY LEADING UP TO WAR 175

it. Moreover, he studiously abstains from directly pledging Great Britain to abstain from interference in matters which neither fall within the Conventions nor under ordinary rights of nations. But since Mr. Chamberlain admits he would not give the pledge required by this condition of the Transvaal, his statement must rank as a refusal.

Though every acceptance was indirect, qualified, and offensively worded, while finality was directly denied and the denial deeply emphasised, it is just possible that the Transvaal Government, like a few politicians in this country, might have been led to consider the answer as a favourable one. But here enters rightly a consideration of the circumstances at Pretoria. Two days before this despatch of "qualified acceptance" reached the Transvaal, Mr. Chamberlain made his Highbury speech. I am able to bear direct testimony to the fatally injurious effect which it produced upon the Government and the burghers of the Transvaal. That speech was not cabled *in extenso;* only the denunciatory and provocative sentences, including the "squeezed' sponge" metaphor, reached Pretoria. It is not possible to exaggerate the effect it produced. Up to that time several members of the Government and many of the better informed citizens believed in the probability of some peaceful settlement, knowing that the Government, if pressed, was prepared to give a liberal and genuine franchise and representation, and to submit all other outstanding issues to conference or arbitration. The Highbury speech shattered these hopes; the men who had held them felt and said, "This means war, for it is ' a direct refusal of all finality to British demands." When Mr. Chamberlain, a couple of days later, issued that despatch which he asserts to have been a "qualified acceptance," adopting nine-tenths of the Transvaal proposals, he must have known that these carefully culled passages of his Highbury speech, interpreted in hostile fashion by the British press of South Africa, had just fallen upon the minds of the people at Pretoria. The tone and wording of that speech undoubtedly influenced, and even dominated, their interpretation of the carefully involved despatch which followed so closely on its heels. Not only the Government, but every one I met in Pretoria, and all the British newspapers I saw, regarded the despatch as a qualified refusal. This certainly was my own impression upon reading it with the words of the Highbury speech still ringing in my ears. The South African League and the Outlander Council, fearful lest a settlement upon a five-year basis should be made, had already made vigorous representations, pushing forward nearly a dozen new issues for immediate settlement. They and their organs certainly did not read Mr. Chamberlain's despatch as a qualified acceptance.

That Mr. Chamberlain did not really at the time intend his despatch to be understood as an acceptance is indicated by his subsequent telegram of September 8 (C. 9521, p. 64), in which he says: "Her Majesty's Government understand the note of the South African Republic Government of the 2nd September to mean that their proposals made in their note of the 19th August are now withdrawn, because the reply of Her Majesty's Government contained in their note of the 30th August, with regard to future intervention and suzerainty, is not acceptable." Now if, as he subsequently asserted, the pledge asked for with reference to further assertions of suzerainty was actually given in the despatch, this was evidently the time to point out that the non-acceptability was based upon a misreading of that despatch. But instead of taking this obvious and natural course, Mr. Chamberlain proceeds in the very next paragraph to give reasons for the refusal of the very proposition regarding suzerainty which in Parliament he said he had not refused. " Her Majesty's Government have absolutely repudiated the view of the political status of the South African Republic taken by the Government of the South African Republic in their note of the 16th April 1898, and also in their note of the 9th May 1899, in which they claim the status of a sovereign international State, and they are therefore unable to consider any proposal which is made conditional on the acceptance by Her Majesty's Government of these views." As a matter of fact, the Transvaal condition that the subject of suzerainty should be dropped was in no sense a reiteration of their former claims made in the notes he mentions, but Mr. Chamberlain on September 8 still evidently regards them as being such, and upon this understanding actually defends the refusal he afterwards declared he did not make.

The five years' proposal having been made by the Transvaal on the express understanding that it should not be taken as a refusal of the proposal of joint-inquiry into the seven years' franchise law, and having been according to their reading of the British despatch, refused, the Transvaal Government, without delay, reverted to the proposal of the joint-inquiry and accepted it in a despatch received September 2. This despatch is badly worded, and opens with a repetition of the objections originally made to the utility of either a bilateral or a unilateral inquiry; but it does not press these objections so far as to refuse the inquiry. On the contrary, section 10 con-

M

tains an acceptance of the joint-inquiry in the following terms :—"Assuming that it is not intended thereby to interfere in the internal affairs of this Republic, or to establish precedent, but simply to gain information and elucidation whether the measures already taken are effectual or not, and if not, to show this Government where such is the case, this Government would be glad to learn from Her Majesty's Government how they propose that the Commission should be constituted, and what place and time for meeting is suggested." Lest there should be any doubt that acceptance was here intended, the Government of Pretoria and Bloemfontein cabled to the British Government stating that the despatch was an acceptance. In spite of Mr. Chamberlain's declaration in the House and elsewhere that the Transvaal refused the joint-inquiry, his own despatch of September 8th shows that he read it as an acceptance, for it declares: "Her Majesty's Government cannot now consent to go back to the proposals for which those in the note of 19th August (*i.e.* the five years' proposals) are intended as a substitute;" words which are meaningless save on the assumption that the Transvaal's despatch was understood as an acceptance of the joint-inquiry.

This despatch of September 8, in which Mr. Chamberlain withdraws the offer of a joint-inquiry into the seven years' franchise law, which he had himself proposed, and which (allowing for the interlude of the Transvaal proposal in substitution) was accepted without delay, precipitated the crisis. It was regarded both by the Transvaal and the Free State Governments as a signal evidence of the *mala fides* of British diplomacy. Following the Highbury speech and the refusal (as they understood it) of the five years' franchise proposal, elicited by promise of "favourable consideration," this withdrawal may be considered as rendering war inevitable. If any doubt about the object of this withdrawal existed, it disappears as we read the full paragraph of the despatch announcing it: "Her Majesty's Government cannot now consent to go back to the proposals for which those in the note of 19th August are intended as a substitute, especially as *they are satisfied that the law of 1899, in which these proposals were finally embodied, is insufficient* to secure the immediate and substantial representation which Her Majesty's Government have always had in view, and which they gather from the reply of the Government of the South African Republic that the latter admit to be reasonable. Moreover, the presentation of the proposals of the note of the 19th of August indicates that the Government of the *South African Republic have themselves recognised that their previous offer might be with advantage enlarged*, and that the independence of the South African Republic would be thereby in no way impaired." The despatch proceeds to say that the British Government will accept the five years' franchise without the conditions attached thereto.

Consider how this despatch must have presented itself to the Republican Governments.

The Transvaal had objected to a joint-inquiry at the outset as an infringement on their rights of internal government. But a joint-inquiry has the form of a fair, impartial tribunal. Now, when it has been accepted, they are informed for the first time that it is withdrawn, because a one-sided *ex parte* inquiry had already been made and had reported unfavourably. They knew quite well that no proper or sufficient inquiry had or could have been held. The British Government had no facilities for holding any adequate inquiry. They knew quite well that certain representations had been made by the heads of the Outlander Council and the South African League to Sir A. Milner, and that the only evidence available to the British Government proceeded from this quarter. If Sir A. Milner is pressed to disclose the nature of the inquiry alleged to have been held, this will be manifest.

The feelings aroused by the bad faith of the withdrawal upon these flimsy grounds were further embittered by the debating point which Mr. Chamberlain made in the second of the italicised portions of this paragraph. Having elicited by misrepresentation, as has been shown above, a carefully-conditioned offer, he now affects to regard the offer as an unconditioned offer, admitted by the Transvaal to be safe and reasonable. Of course the Transvaal Government regarded the conditions as an integral part of the offer, and as necessary not only to induce the Raad to endorse the offer, but to safeguard their country against further external interference on behalf of a political party consisting of new burghers. Is it really credible that Mr. Chamberlain, after having, according to his own account, virtually accepted the five years' offer with conditions, should now seemingly propose to get this same offer, with some new further demands, unconditionally ? At the close of this despatch occur the words, "If, however, as they most anxiously hope will not be the case, the reply of the South African Republic Government is negative or inconclusive, Her Majesty's Government must reserve to themselves the right to reconsider the situation *de novo*, and to formulate their own proposals for a final settlement." These words were described both by the British and the South African press as an ultimatum. It was felt that the proposals were tendered formally, with no chance of acceptance, and simultaneously with the issue of this despatch large drafts of troops were ordered from England, in addition to those previously ordered from India.

The Transvaal despatch of September 16th, in reply to Mr. Chamberlain, renews the expression of surprise at the withdrawal of the joint-inquiry; denies that a sufficient inquiry can have been made "before the law has been tested in its operation;" "cannot understand on what ground of justice" it should be expected to grant the five years' franchise without the conditions; and finally, deprecating the idea of formulating new proposals, urges the British Government to keep its word "to abide by its own proposal of a Joint-Commission."

The British Government did not now proceed to formulate its new proposals, for it was not ready with the necessary forces to support them. Time was required. Some of this requisite was obtained by means of an interim despatch, September 22nd, which simply reiterated in other words the demands of the despatch of September 8th. On September 30th the Transvaal Government expressed a desire to know by October 2nd what decision the British Government had taken, and received a reply that the despatch would "not be ready for some days." Meanwhile Parliament had been summoned, the reserves called out, troops brought into the country and moved towards the borders. Another full week passed and no despatch from Mr. Chamberlain. On October 9th the Transvaal issued what is regarded as an ultimatum, a despatch which, after an appeal to its status under the Convention of London and a reference to the spirit of conciliation and concession which had induced it to consent to discuss matters that were clearly within the competence of its Government, concluded by a request that all points of mutual difference should be regulated by the friendly course of arbitration; and that Great Britain should withdraw her troops from the borders and cease to land and push forward other troops. The conditions of this despatch are described in the brief answer of the British Government dated October 10th as being "such as Her Majesty's Government deem it impossible to discuss."

The diplomatic intercourse between Sir A. Milner and President Steyn of the Free State, which took place on the very eve of the conflict, is not in itself of supreme importance, but two points deserve attention. The first is the strange lack of accurate intelligence respecting the feelings and intentions of the Free State Government and burghers manifested by Sir A. Milner in the despatch of September 19th, in which he "looks to the Government of the Orange Free State to preserve strict neutrality and to prevent any military intervention by any of its citizens." This is no mere diplomatic feint of ignorance: it denotes the generally prevalent belief, even in the best-informed circles of our Government, that the burghers of the Free State were divided in their sympathies, and that a powerful party, opposed to common action with the Transvaal, existed. This delusion was maintained up to the very eve of hostilities, and is one more illustration of the false information upon which our policy has relied throughout.

The other point is of even more serious import, reflecting as it does directly upon the common honesty of our diplomatic methods. During the month of September the President of the Free State, in repeated despatches, sought to intervene with a view to pacific settlement, and at the last moment addressed a long and weighty appeal to the British Government through Sir A. Milner. This critical document Sir A. Milner, alleging its "enormous length," refused to transmit in its entirety. For this course there might have been some justification, but for the deliberate mutilation of that part of the despatch which he professed to transmit there could be none. In his communication to the British Government[1] Sir Alfred thus describes the despatch from President Steyn :— "After recapitulating the history of the negotiations from their point of view, he (*i.e.* President Steyn) continues"—then follows what purports to be the *ipsissima verba* of the President. In point of fact, a number of important passages laying stress upon the feasibility of a pacific settlement, even at this critical juncture, are omitted from the despatch without the slightest indication of such omission. I print as an appendix to this chapter the portion of the despatch which the High Commissioner professed to transmit in its entirety, italicising the passages which he deliberately omitted. The despatch is, as any reader will perceive, of great importance, as indicating the strenuous efforts for peace maintained up to the last by the Government of the Free State, and the thorough conviction of that Government that the Transvaal Government was prepared to make most liberal concessions, if the British Government would once for all formulate its definite and final demands. The mutilation of President Steyn's despatch throws a most sinister light upon the pacific professions of the High Commissioner and the British Government.

[1] C. 9530, p. 36.

APPENDIX

MUTILATED DESPATCH OF PRESIDENT STEYN

(The portions printed in Italics were omitted by SIR A. MILNER.*)*

THIS Government are still prepared and tender their services to further the interests of peace, and to continue in their endeavours to procure a satisfactory solution of existing difficulties on fair and reasonable lines. They feel themselves, however, hampered now as in the past (a) by a want of knowledge as to the definite object and extent of the desires and demands of the British Government, compliance with which that Government consider themselves entitled to insist on, and as to the grounds on which such insistance is based; (b) by the fact, notwithstanding the repeated assurances of the British Government that it does not wish to interfere in the internal affairs of the government of the South African Republic nor to disturb its independence, it has pursued a policy which seems to justify a contrary conclusion. To give but one instance, *which could not be otherwise than calculated to be a most disturbing element in the conduct of negotiations,* I may mention the enormous and ever-increasing military preparations on the part of the British Government, indicating a policy of force and coercion, *during the whole course of negotiations which were stated to be of a friendly and conciliatory nature; those preparations, in the absence of any apparent cause justifying the same, being not unnaturally looked upon as a direct menace to the South African Republic, after all that has been done by the South African Republic to meet the views of Her Majesty's Government for a Joint-Commission to inquire into the scope and effect of those measures, and whether immediate and substantial representation would thereby be assured to the Outlanders willing to avail themselves of the provisions thereof.*

This Government cannot conceive it possible that the points

of difference that may exist on this subject justify those extensive and ever-increasing military preparations being carried out on this border, not only of the South African Republic, but also of the Orange Free State, and they are therefore reluctantly compelled to conclude that they must be intended to secure other objects at present unknown to the Government of this State, and the knowledge whereof, if they prove to be fair and reasonable, might induce this Government to make necessary representations to secure their attainment, and enable them to continue their efforts to secure a speedy, peaceful, and satisfactory settlement of the difficulties and differences existing between Her Majesty's Government and the Government of the South African Republic. *I beg to add that I am firmly convinced and feel sure that any reasonable assurance could be obtained.* We are firmly convinced—(the repetition is due to an alteration of Sir Alfred Milner's)—that the Government of the South African Republic has been sincerely desirous to maintain in its integrity the Convention of London 1884, both as regards its letter and its spirit, and that they do not contemplate or assert a claim to any absolute political status without the qualification arising out of Article IV. of that Convention. *And accordingly it does not appear to me that there is any misunderstanding hereon that could not promptly and without difficulty be settled.* I feel assured that there is no difference between their contention on that point and the communication made on behalf of Her Majesty's Government by Her Majesty's High Commissioner to the Governments both of the South African Republic and of this State on February 27, 1884, as to the import of that Convention; that communication was as follows: "Same complete internal independence in Transvaal as in Orange Free State; conduct and control intercourse with foreign Governments conceded; Queen's final approval treaties reserved."

In the expectation that Her Majesty's Government will share my views that no effort should be spared to effect a peaceable settlement *if possible of the points in difference between them and the South African Republic, and that consequently all causes of irritation likely to delay or prevent such settlement should be removed, or at least not be aggravated*, I trust that Her Majesty's Government may see their way clear, pending arrival of the further despatch intimated as about to be sent to the Government of the

South African Republic, and pending further negotiations, to stop any further movements or increase of troops on or near the borders of the South African Republic and of this State, and further to give an assurance to that effect to allay the great excitement and irritation naturally aroused and increased thereby; and if Her Majesty's Government should be pleased to accede to this request, this Government would be glad to be favoured with the views of Her Majesty's Government on the points raised herein, and more particularly as to the precise nature and scope of the concessions or measures the adoption whereof Her Majesty's Government consider themselves entitled to claim, or which they suggest as being necessary or sufficient to ensure a satisfactory and permanent solution of existing differences between them and the South African Republic, whilst at the same time providing a means for settlement [of] any other that may arise in the future.—M. T. STEYN, States-President.

PART II

THE POLICY OF RAND CAPITALISTS

CHAPTER I

FOR WHOM ARE WE FIGHTING?

It is difficult to state the truth about our doings in South Africa without seeming to appeal to the ignominious passion of Judenhetze. Nevertheless a plain account of the personal and economic forces operative in the Transvaal is essential to an understanding of the issue, and must not be shirked. A few of the financial pioneers in South Africa have been Englishmen, like Messrs. Rhodes and Rudd; but recent developments of Transvaal gold-mining have thrown the economic resources of the country more and more into the hands of a small group of international financiers, chiefly German in origin and Jewish in race. By superior ability, enterprise, and organisation these men, out-competing the slower-witted Briton, have attained a practical supremacy which no one who has visited Johannesburg is likely to question.

It should be distinctly understood that the stress which my analysis lays upon the Jew has reference to the class of financial capitalists of which the foreign Jew must be taken as the leading type.

Before I went there, the names of Beit, Eckstein, Barnato, &c., were of course not unknown to me; the very ship in which I crossed bore many scores of Jewish women and children. But until I came to examine closely the structure of industry and society upon the Rand I had no conception of their number or their power.

I thus discovered that not Hamburg, not Vienna, not Frankfort, but Johannesburg is the New Jerusalem.

Although their strength does not really consist in numbers, the size of this Hebrew population is very considerable. Public statistics are most deceptive in this matter; many of these persons rank as British subjects by virtue of a brief temporary sojourn in some English-speaking land, and as for names, Smith, Newman, Phillips, Gordon, Bruce are just as good as Marks or Cohen, and are often preferred. So the census of Johannesburg, taken in July 1896, only recognises 6253 Jews. But while the total population of Johannesburg has probably not increased since that date, it is generally agreed that the Jewish population is very much larger. A well-informed Jew, drawing his conclusion from synagogic and other private sources, told me there must be at least 15,000 Jews in Johannesburg and the district. The evidence of the directory, borne out by the casual testimony of the streets, would lead me to believe this an under, rather than an over, estimate. The great majority are undoubtedly Russian, Polish, and German Jews (commonly classed under the generic title of "Peruvians"), who ply the business of small shopkeepers, market salesmen, pedlars, liquor dealers, and a few rude handicrafts. These are everywhere to be seen, actively occupied in small dealings, a rude and ignorant people, mostly fled from despotic European rule, and contrasting sharply with their highly intelligent, showy, prosperous brethren, who form the upper crust of Johannesburg society. It is with the latter we are directly concerned if we would understand the economic and political import of the present movements.

It is not too much to say that this little ring of international financiers already controls the most valuable economic resources of the Transvaal.

The first and incomparably the most important industry, the gold-mines of the Rand, are almost entirely in their hands. The following brief enumeration of the leading companies, which represent the recent consolidation of many mining interests, will serve to show the extent of their power. First comes Wernher, Beit & Co., more commonly known by the name of the managing director as the "Eckstein Group." This comprises twenty-nine mines and three other financial businesses. The nominal capital is £18,384,567, but the market value at the beginning of August 1899 was over £76,000,000. This Eckstein Group is the leading member of a larger, effective combination, which includes, for most practical purposes, the Consolidated Goldfields, S. Neumann & Co., G. Farrar and A. Bailey. Of these, the largest is the Goldfields (virtually Beit, Rudd, and Rhodes), with nineteen mines, and a nominal capital of £18,120,000. Next in size comes Neumann, with a capital of £8,806,500. In more separate working, but virtually under the same ultimate control, are two other important groups of mines, largely repositories of German capital, Goetz & Co. and Albu & Co. The financial connection, according to my information, consists in the fact that Brassey, representing Rothschild, has a controlling interest in Goetz & Co., while Albu & Co. have behind them the Dresdener Bank. Now Rothschild stands for the Exploration Company, which is in effect Wernher, Beit, and Rothschild, while Wernher and Beit are believed to be large owners of the Dresdener Bank. These statements are made to me on evidence which I am naturally unable to check, but I believe them to be correct, and even if only approximately true, they indicate a close consolidation of the greater part of the Rand mining industry. Outside of them, the chief businesses are J. B. Robinson, with nineteen mines, and other estates at a nominal capital of £14,317,500, and the less important Barnato firm. It is also well to bear in mind that Wernher, Beit, Rudd, and Rhodes, Barnato, and Rothschild are associated as chief owners and life governors of De Beers.

The last few years have seen large steps towards a consolidation of the entire industry under the supremacy of Eckstein, the chief instrument of which is the Chamber of Mines. The primary object of the Chamber, started by Eckstein in 1889, was to secure returns of output, wages, &c., from the various companies, and soon most of the leading companies, with the exception of Robinson, joined it. Robinson, followed by the now rising French and German companies, formed in 1895 the Association of Mines, which was in effect a rival combination. Hostilities were maintained until 1898, when Goetz and Albu were forced back into the Chamber, which has since attained a paramountcy that extends not only to the mining industry, but widely controls the industrial and indirectly the political life of Johannesburg, forming the nucleus of a monopoly which may become to the Rand what De Beers has been for some years to Kimberley. This, however, is not the place to discuss the present and probable future of the power possessed by the Chamber, and Messrs. Eckstein, who actually wield it. This brief sketch is only designed to indicate the dominance of international finance over the vast industry whose capital had recently a normal value of some £150,000,000, and which is and will remain the great source of wealth in the Transvaal. It is, I think, correct to say that the

FOR WHOM ARE WE FIGHTING? 193

destiny of almost all these leading companies is controlled by foreign financiers. There is, moreover, no reason to believe that the capital thus wielded is chiefly owned by English shareholders. Though no means of close calculation exists, there is good reason to suppose that the French and German holdings, taken together, largely outweigh the English interest in Rand mines.

But while the power of this capitalism is based on gold, it is by no means confined to it. Whatever large or profitable interest we approach, we find the same control. The interests are often entirely severed from, and even hostile to, the mining industry, but they are in the hands of the same class. This is the case with the dynamite monopoly. Every name connected with the present and past of this scandalous economic episode is significant: Lippert, Lewis and Marks, Vorstmann, Phillip, Nobel. The rich and powerful liquor trade, licit and illicit, is entirely in the hands of Jews, from the supreme control of the liquor kings, Messrs. Lewis and Marks, down to the running of the meanest Kaffir bar. That greatest of gambling instruments, the Stock Exchange, is, needless to say, mostly Jewish. The large commercial businesses are in the same hands, in particular the important trade in horses, and other highly speculative businesses. The press of Johannesburg is chiefly their property: they control the organs of Outlander agitation on the one hand, the *Star* and the *Leader*, while the Government organ, the *Standard and Diggers' News*, is under similar control. Nor has the Jew been backward in developing those forms of loan and mortgage business which have made his fame the world over. A rich and ably organised syndicate exists which operates through branches in all the little towns, lending sums of money or furnishing credit through retail shops, which they control, to the neighbouring Boers, and thus obtaining mortgages upon their farms. I am informed that a very large proportion of the Transvaal farmers are as entirely in the hands of Jewish money-lenders as is the Russian moujik or the Austrian peasant. No one who knows the fluctuating and precarious character of Transvaal agriculture will feel surprised that the Boer should succumb to this common temptation set so carefully in his path.

It thus appears that the industrial and agricultural future of the Transvaal is already hypothecated to this small ring of financial foreigners, who not merely own or control the present values, but have, by buying up mining properties and claims of a contingent future value, secured an even more complete supremacy over the economic future.

The Transvaal is a country especially adapted to the money-lender and the stock-jobber, a land of hazards and surprises, booms and slumps, where the keen-sighted speculator and the planner of bold complex combinations has unrivalled opportunities.

Dull and depressed as was Johannesburg when I visited it, the savour of gambling was in the air. Though talk of stocks and shares was in abeyance, not so the gambling side of sport. One final testimony to the supreme genius of the European speculator stood plastered upon every wall. Sweepstakes upon races are in Johannesburg not a casual caprice of a sporting few, but an important, well-organised, and enduring trade, supported apparently by a very large proportion of the men, and even the women, of the place. A "sweep" upon a single race meeting often amounts to £120,000

FOR WHOM ARE WE FIGHTING? 195

or £150,000, a sufficient evidence of the popularity of the demand, which extends to every class of the community. This novel industry owes its local origin to a Jew known by the name of Phillips, who kept a bar in Johannesburg. Phillips runs four big " sweeps" every year and a score of little "sweeps," which are advertised on every wall and by copious handbills. The business basis of the "sweep" is that prizes shall cover 90 per cent. of the money subscribed, the other 10 per cent. going to cover expenses of management and profits. The "industry," I am told, is a most remunerative one. Phillips has now a good handful of competitors: the names of Moss, Legate, Hess, and Herff stare upon you from the back of every newspaper. It is needless to dwell on the demoralising influence of this great and growing gambling trade. Its success is alike indicative of the place and of the people that control it.

The practical paramountcy exercised by financiers, the recognised leaders of whom are foreign Jews, over the economic interests of the Transvaal, extends also to the social and the recreative side of Johannesburg life. Many of the recognised leaders of society are Jewish. The newspapers of September 13th contained the announcement: "There will be no performance at the Empire (music-hall) to-day by reason of the Jewish Day of Atonement." The Stock Exchange was also closed upon that day.

When the British arms have established firm order, this foreign host will return with enhanced numbers and increased power. During the distress of last autumn they bought up, often for a song, most of the property and businesses that were worth buying, and as soon as a settlement takes place, they will start upon a greatly strengthened basis of possession.

It may be said, granting this story of a Jewish monopoly of the economic power is true, it does not justify the suggestion that the political power will pass into their hands, and that there will be established an oligarchy of German Jews at Pretoria.

But a little reflection shows that while this class of financiers has commonly abstained in other countries from active participation in politics, they will use politics in the Transvaal. They have found the need for controlling politics and legislation by bribery and other persuasive arts hitherto: the same need and use will exist in the future. Politics to them will not merely mean free trade and good administration of just laws. Transvaal industry, particularly the mining industry, requires the constant and important aid of the State. The control of a large, cheap, regular, submissive supply of labour, the chief corner-stone of profitable business, will be a constant incentive to acquire political control: railway rates, customs' laws, and the all-important issues relating to mineral rights, will force them into politics, and they will apply to these the same qualities which have made them so successful in speculative industry. In a word, they will simply and inevitably add to their other businesses the business of politics. The particular form of government which may be adopted will not matter very much. Government from Downing Street may perhaps hamper them a little more than the forms of popular representative government; but the judicious control of the press and the assistance of financial friends in high places will enable them to establish and maintain a tolerably complete form of boss-rule in South Africa.

A consideration of these points throws a clear light

upon the nature of the conflict in South Africa. We are fighting in order to place a small international oligarchy of mine-owners and speculators in power at Pretoria. Englishmen will surely do well to recognise that the economic and political destinies of South Africa are, and seem likely to remain, in the hands of men most of whom are foreigners by origin, whose trade is finance, and whose trade interests are not chiefly British. If all I say be true, it gives no ground for any final judgment on the merits of the war. This international oligarchy may be better for the country and for the world than the present or any other rule; and England may be performing a meritorious world-service in establishing it. But it is right for us to understand quite clearly what we are doing.

CHAPTER II

THE POLITICAL METHODS OF THE OUTLANDERS

WHAT are the instruments and methods by which Great Britain has been forced into war with the Republics of South Africa? Sir Alfred Milner and Mr. Chamberlain have indignantly repudiated the suggestions of a capitalist agitation. They see a genuine and earnest movement of the intelligent middle classes of the Outlander population, the professional and commercial classes, followed in their demands by a large body of respectable mechanics and miners, filled by a natural disgust at bad government, and eagerly bent upon political reforms. It has been shown that many of "the grievances" were unsubstantial, and that some which were real directly touched only the interests of a few; but a certain residuum remained which might seem to afford a basis for a true popular agitation. What were the forces actually at work, and what their *modus operandi* ? The most visible instrument of agitation has been the South African League, to which much notoriety has been given in Bluebooks and elsewhere. It has been the chief function of this League to impose upon the public mind this notion of a spontaneous liberative movement.

The League appears to have been originally formed early in 1896 by a little group of men who distinguished themselves by an outrage committed upon a Transvaal burgher named Edwards, who had fought with the Boers against Jameson at Dornkop, and whose action was so bitterly resented by these sympathisers with the Raid that they seized him at a railway station as he was travelling to the Colony, tore him away from his children, and tarred him. This clique of men shortly afterwards started an organisation entitled the Anglo-African League, an avowed anti-Dutch society. Its name was soon afterwards changed into the South African League. The prime mover and first president was Dr. Darley Hartley, a virulent Jingo, who toured South Africa, working up the League by his inflammatory speeches. After the first congress Dr. Hartley was replaced by Captain Brabant, member of the Legislative Assembly, a gentleman whose attitude of mind may be gauged by his saying that he "wished he had two thousand men to walk over the Transvaal." Captain Brabant was succeeded at the annual congress at Kimberley last April by Mr. Rhodes.

The general principles of the League are thus stated in its constitution :—

"(a) An unalterable resolve to support the existing supremacy of Great Britain in South Africa, and a strenuous opposition to any attempts that may be made to weaken or destroy that supremacy.

"(b) The promotion of good government within and amicable relations between the various States and colonies in South Africa."

It might be argued that (a) is realised by setting up the bogey of a Dutch conspiracy in order to display valour in combating it, and that (b) is realised by becoming the chief instrument of electoral corruption in the Colony, and by fanning the flames of race hatred in South Africa.

As an influence in the Transvaal agitation, however, the League has been unduly magnified. Neither in *personnel* nor in activity does it merit the prominence attached to it. The only visible connection of the Transvaal Province of the League with mining capitalists is found in the fact that several of its leading men—Messrs. Wybergh, Webb, and Ogilvie—have been, according to my information, employed by the *Mining Journal*, an organ of Eckstein's. The officials of the League in the Transvaal state that their income and expenditure have only amounted to a few hundreds a year, and though their opponents talk much about a large secret service fund, I could find no signs of work requiring any large expenditure of money in the Transvaal, corresponding to the large outlay made by the Colonial Province of the League in procuring the election of Progressive candidates at the recent elections. Until this year the League had little influence in Johannesburg. Few men of wealth or position were among its members, and, so far as I could ascertain, it was regarded by solid business men in Johannesburg with no sympathy and with some contempt as a futile instrument of agitation. It was never in any sense representative either of the respectable middle-class or of any other class of the community, but was the name of an insignificant clique. The monster meeting which it held after the killing of Edgar first floated the League into wide notoriety, and stimulated it to redouble its efforts by means of public meetings on the Rand and the Outlanders' petition for the redress of grievances. Although I found it impossible to get any authentic documents describing the work and expenditure of the League, and the sources of their income, I am disposed to regard the Transvaal branch of it as, in the main, a genuine middle-class society, managed, and perhaps financed, by men earnestly devoted to a struggle for rights, though I cannot acquit them of gross exaggeration in the presentation of grievances and of reckless audacity in the means by which they sought to press their case on the Imperial Government. Large numbers of signatures to the petition were obtained from persons in complete ignorance of the nature of the document they signed, not a few signatures were actually forged, while many were obtained from black and coloured persons, to whom it was never proposed to grant the franchise, the demand for which stood at the head of the list of grievances.

As for the meetings held last spring in the mining centres of the Rand, by which a certain semblance of popularity was given to the Outlander political movement, Mr. Wybergh and the League leaders assert that not merely were they not instigated by the capitalists, but that they were held in the teeth of the declared hostility of the mining magnates. Their opponents utterly deny the accuracy of this statement, alleging that, if the mine managers had been really opposed, as was pretended, to political agitation, they could without the least difficulty have prohibited the men from attending the meetings, and would have done so without scruple. A point in favour of the League's contention is made out of the undoubted fact that Mr. Wybergh himself was dismissed from a lucrative post in the Consolidated Goldfields for taking part in the political movement. Though it is maintained by some that the dismissal of Mr. Wybergh was designed to throw dust in the eyes of the Government, and that his martyrdom was merely nominal, this sinister conjecture is not warranted by the necessities of the case. It seems far more reasonable to suppose that the "Goldfields," implicated more than others in the Jameson Raid and the Reform movement of Johannesburg in 1895, was genuinely averse to any prominent part being taken by its staff in another movement, which, before it was taken over by the Imperial Government, appeared doomed to futility, and that its London directors insisted upon a policy of abstinence. Mr. Wybergh informed me, and I believe his word, that when he approached Mr. Rhodes upon the subject of the League last November, the latter threw cold water upon the entire project, advising him to lie low and wait for the development of Rhodesia. This indeed may have been only a word of characteristic cunning from one who knew that he had secured a far more competent tool to work his will than the League. I see no reason to deny that the League has represented in Johannesburg a certain small quantity of genuine reform energy, and that some of its most active members have been disinterested workers for reform. But so long as the League depended on these persons its influence was nil: only when the mining capitalists took it up last spring as a convenient tool did it exert any power or claim any public consideration. What money was then required was found for it, though the limited scheme of its operations made no large demand upon the purse of the political mine-owners. The Cape Colony Province of the League, which has conducted an elaborate and expensive agitation, and which was an instrument of the wholesale corruption practised by the Progressive party at the polls last year, has doubtless been heavily financed by the political capitalists, but there is no reason to suppose that the Transvaal Province of the League received large subsidies from this quarter.

POLITICAL METHODS OF OUTLANDERS 203

The capitalist influence is, however, more obvious in the formation and direction of the Outlander Council, which came into existence last June, when the willingness of the Imperial Government to proceed to extreme measures on behalf of the Johannesburgers was clearly manifest, and when the gold magnates had made up their minds once more to enter the lists, not this time as secret conspirators, but as Imperialists. The opportunity evolved naturally enough from certain semi-official negotiations, which had been going on early in the year, between the State Secretary with two other high Transvaal officials and a half-dozen mining capitalists, through the mediation of Mr. Lippert. At their meetings a number of issues, having a direct and important bearing on the mining industry, were discussed, such as dynamite, bewaar-plaatsen, finance, and auditing. But it was natural, and indeed necessary, that certain questions of political grievances should arise, and chief among them that of franchise and representation. In dealing with these last-named matters the mining representatives consistently adopted the position that they were in no way qualified to speak for the Outlander population, which in its entirety was entitled to be consulted. This view was endorsed by the State Secretary, who even suggested that the body of the Outlanders should be invited to express their opinion. In order, as I understand, expressly to achieve this object, a committee of Outlanders was formed early in May, under the chairmanship of Mr. H. S. Caldecott, a well-known solicitor, and a public meeting was convened to test the opinion of the Outlander population. But though nominally summoned for an impartial consideration of the issue, the management of the meeting was actually in the hands of members of the South

African League, and of certain ex-Reformers who were at this juncture finally released from their obligation to take no part in politics. There was nothing strange or reprehensible in this fact. The conduct and results of a great public meeting are almost always manipulated by a few interested persons, who impose their will upon the meeting under the guise of popular votes. The large and enthusiastic gathering of June 10th, which passed resolutions to stiffen the back of Sir A. Milner, and which ended by appointing by a vote *en bloc* a number of gentlemen to form the nucleus of an Outlander Council, did its work admirably, and at its close a number of strongly committed and violent Jingoes stood as the accredited agents of the Outlanders of Johannesburg. Nearly half of those elected had taken part as members of the Reform Committee of 1895 in the conspiracy to upset the Government with the aid of Jameson. These men afterwards associated with them on the Council an equal number of so-called representative working-men, chiefly miners. A study of the composition of this Council shows that almost all the really active members are closely connected with the mining industry: mine-owners, such as Messrs. Pullinger, Evans, and Dalrymple; dealers in mining machinery, like Mr. Hosken; legal advisers of mining companies, such as Messrs. Hull, Mullins, and Solomon; or mining engineers, like Mr. Wybergh; or mining journalists, like Mr. Webb. Very few, no doubt, of these men rank as great capitalists. Most are professional men, but they are distinctly to be regarded as the mouthpieces of the great capitalist groups whose financial heads have used a handful of genuine political enthusiasts to bring about a *bouleversement* of the existing political order, which should enable them to handle,

POLITICAL METHODS OF OUTLANDERS

either in their persons or through their nominees, the reins of government. Those who predict so confidently that the strong hand of the Imperial Government will render such manipulation of politics impossible know very little of South African conditions, or of the ingenuity which the " capitalists " are there exhibiting.

I have perhaps dealt with these political organisations at greater length than they deserve. They have not exerted any great influence upon the movement in South Africa, except in so far as they have served as instruments to mould public opinion in England by representing the Outlander movement as the passionate appeal of an oppressed and outraged multitude of our fellow-subjects against the tyranny of a Boer oligarchy.

CHAPTER III

A CHARTERED PRESS

THIS war is often described as press-made, but few of those who use this expression understand the all-important part which the great factory of public opinion has been made to play. Everywhere the less reputable organs of the press are rightly regarded as disturbers of the public peace, living upon strong sensations; unwilling, and often unable, to check the accuracy of the wild rumours which they promulgate. The "Yellow Press" is a danger in every "civilised" country to-day. It is not, however, necessary to assume that this Yellow Press is engineered by outside interests making for war; its own trade interests may often suffice. South Africa presents a unique example of a large press, owned, controlled, and operated in recent times by a small body of men with the direct aim of bringing about a conflict which shall serve their business interests.

When Mr. Rhodes, failing to obtain forcible control of the Rand by the clumsiness of Dr. Jameson and the vacillation of his confederates in Johannesburg, spoke of an appeal to "constitutional means" for gaining his ends, he well knew what he meant to do. He designed to use the armed forces of the British Crown and the money of the British taxpayer to obtain for himself and his fellow-capitalists that political control of the Transvaal which was essential to his economical and political ambitions. To do this, it was above all things necessary to apply an adequate motive-power to the minds of the British Government and the British people. For this work he found the press by far the aptest instrument. Some considerable time ago he had acquired, with Messrs. Eckstein and Barnato, a leading interest in the *Cape Argus*, the evening paper at Cape Town. The Argus Company has now so far expanded its field of operations as to own also the *Johannesburg Star*, the *Bulawayo Chronicle*, the *Rhodesia Herald*, and the *African Review*. The *Cape Times*, the most influential paper in South Africa, has come under the control of the same body of capitalists, half its shares having been bought by Mr. Rutherfoord Harris, the well-known director of the Chartered Company, and the active coadjutor of Mr. Rhodes in many financial exploits. Last year the *Diamond Fields Advertiser*, of Kimberley, passed into the same control, under significant circumstances. Its owner had previously rejected two offers to surreptitiously purchase the property. The first offer, made several years ago, sought to buy a half interest for £8000, and a guaranteed salary of £2000 a year for the editor, provided he were willing to keep quiet the fact that the paper had changed owners. A couple of years later, another offer was made to the proprietor of £20,000 and £1000 compensation for the acting editor, who was to be replaced by a man with "proper" views, the condition of this sale being that the paper should still continue to bear the imprint of being owned and managed by its former proprietor. Eventually the proprietor was compelled to retire for reasons quite independent of these negotiations, and the paper was actually sold to the general manager of the *Cape Times* (a brother-in-law of Mr. Harris), who purchased it outright for £12,500, professedly upon his own account. Several other papers at Port Elizabeth, Durban, and other popular centres are credibly stated to be subject to the same control, and unsuccessful attempts have been made upon others. In particular, the *Midland News*, an able and honest journal, circulating widely among the farmers of the entire Colony, and taking a strong independent attitude upon political issues, has been several times solicited from the same capitalist quarters, but in vain. Since the Jameson Raid the entire weight of the capitalist press has been thrown into the scale of a drastic Imperialist policy, the "constitutional means" which Mr. Rhodes, with or without the express assent of Mr. Chamberlain, had devised. So far as the Colony was concerned, this engine of education was directed to sow aspersions of disloyalty against the Bond and their British supporters, and to drill into the public mind by constant droppings the notion of a Dutch conspiracy throughout South Africa. Defeated at the colonial elections, the chief part of this press energy was then directed to exasperate the British colonists of South Africa and the British nation against the Transvaal, working up every misdeed or mistake of the Government, and inventing others as they were required.

When the capitalists of the Rand had determined upon a *coup*, and possessed the full assurance that the British Government was behind them, they redoubled their efforts to precipitate a crisis. For this purpose notable changes were made in the press of Johannesburg. The directors of the *Star* imported from England a young and vigorous journalist, Mr. Monypenny, to aid in bringing matters to a crisis, the post having been offered to three well-known London journalists, one of whom, asking as a condition of acceptance that he should have a three years' engagement, received the significant answer that six months only would be given. Although several morning dailies, sprung up within the last few years, had proved notorious failures, an addition to the militant press was made in the establishment of the *Transvaal Leader*. The circumstances attending the production of the *Leader* are peculiarly instructive. The company was registered on April 18 with a capital of £15,000 in £1 shares. The first two directors were Mr. W. Hosken (chairman of the Chamber of Commerce, virtually an appanage of the Chamber of Mines) and Mr. J. J. Hoyle, a local solicitor. The great bulk of the shares, no less than 14,878, stood in the name of Mr. Pakeman, a former sub-editor of the *Star*, who had been brought at a most liberal salary to edit the new paper, and whom no one believed to be capable of venturing so large a sum of money upon so precarious an investment. The other shares, with the exception of two allotments of fifty each to the two above-named directors, were registered in the names of twenty-two persons holding one share each, the majority of whom are known to have been in the employ of a firm of solicitors who act for Messrs. Beit and Eckstein.

The immediate capital outlay considerably exceeded the total capital of the company, for £10,000 was paid at once for the plant of the defunct *Johannesburg Times*, and £7000 to Mr. J. B. Robinson for the property on which the offices stand. Moreover, the expenses of the new paper were utterly disproportionate to its nominal resources, and indicated a free supply from some large external source, generally believed to have been Eckstein's. It is, I am informed, admitted that the cable service alone cost the *Leader*, during its short tenure of life, no less than £3000 per month—a sum which considerably exceeds the ordinary expenditure of any London penny paper. The actual loss of running such a paper in Johannesburg must have been enormous, but the end doubtless justified the outlay in the eyes of those who bore it. The single aim of the *Star* and the *Leader* during the six months preceding October was to inflame the passions of the Outlander by harping upon the Cape "Boy," the Edgar, the Appelbe outrages, and to harden the hearts of the Government by a constant tirade of abuse and insult directed against them.

There is something distinctly humorous in these papers parading among the Outlander grievances the Press Law, at a time when, day after day, they were permitted to use language which, even in times of ordinary tranquillity, would have ensured the arrest and prosecution of editors and publishers in any other country of the world except England and the United States, and which in either of these last-named countries would have evoked popular reprisals at least as formidable from patriotic citizens.

The arrest of Mr. Pakeman and the attempted arrest of Mr. Monypenny of the *Star* in September last were represented in England as a terrible outrage upon liberty of publication. I do not seek to defend the policy of the Transvaal Government at this crisis, but it is right to remember that the two laws under which action took place were regular and not unreasonable statutes, and such as exist and are enforced in England as well as in Continental States. The language of the *Leader* clearly brought it under the law of High Treason of 1877, one of the last laws passed before the British Annexation, and expressly endorsed by the subsequent proclamation of the British Government. In order that no semblance of undue harshness might attach to this arrest, the Public Prosecutor did not even press the charge of high treason, but brought the matter under the Press Law of 1896, in order that Mr. Pakeman might be let out upon the bail which he presently caused to be estreated by his non-appearance to take his trial.

I will ask readers to consider a few samples of the language by which this Capitalist press was allowed to stir up rebellion in the Transvaal, and to provoke the armed intervention of an outside nation for many months, before any step was taken to stop them.

Take first the following paragraph from a leading article entitled "Justice in the Transvaal," on July 17th:—

"But nothing is easier than to rig justice in the Transvaal if only the interested parties are of the beloved Burgher flock. The wily Koetser, doubtless backed in influential quarters, appealed to that excellent institution the High Court, with a result that his term of imprisonment was reduced from six months to one. The Executive has also reduced the penalty in the case of the other offenders. It is this sort of thing that breeds contempt for the very name of justice as administered in the Transvaal. It will soon become impossible to get a Boer punished, no matter what his crime. We venture to think that there would have been precious little clemency had the offenders not been burghers of the State. It is doubtful whether in such a case the distinguished Chief Justice would have suspended the operation of the High Court. But the woman's name was O'Neill, and the offender's name was Abraham Koetser, and that makes all the difference."

Would such a flagrant contempt of court be permitted to an English newspaper? How much less reason to permit it where it is made a part of an organised attempt to overthrow, not merely the respect for justice, but the entire Government?

As weeks went on the language of the two Johannesburg papers, particularly of the *Leader*, became still more inflammatory. From a considerable number of articles advocating internal rebellion or external coercion, I select the following, which were among those read in court at the preliminary examination in the Pakeman case:—

"Even yet there is time for some strong and just man to arise and lead the burghers to Pretoria and sweep the gang from power, to annul the decree of the Raad by a *coup d'état* and eject the dynamitards from the State. We fear it will not be done, and the misled and abused burghers will be led to battle to defend a national crime. Prayers and humiliation are of no avail in such an issue as this, nor can a reverent man feel that Heaven will uphold him in the struggle. The die is cast, the siege is finished; yet those who have risked their lives and have seen their fellows die around them will remember the vanity of attempting to conceal guilt by guilt, and will visit the black crime upon those who have cheated them to their fate."

In the same issue there appears an article headed, "The End of Patience," which concludes as follows:—

"We will have no half settlements, and if we can't win a full and honourable citizen rank as British subjects, we shall win it in another way."

In an issue of the *Leader* of August 29th appeared the following:—

"The abolition of the Republic is not the end that

we anticipated and hoped for; yet we fully recognise the necessity for the step in view of the hopeless attitude of this Government. We had hoped that the burghers themselves would have found a strong leader and have put their house in order, boldly purging the country of the robbery and shame that have brought the State to such a ruinous pass. Although some have talked of the necessity for reform and many have bewailed the disgrace brought upon the country by the tactics of the junta at Pretoria, nothing effective has been done, and it remains for the Paramount Power to effect what the people have shrunk from."

I will only refer to an article entitled "Fundamental Savagery," which appeared in the *Leader* on August 10th. It is couched in the following terms:—" In this pastoral and pious community, or, if you prefer it, in this common (or garden) department of the British Empire, crime succeeds crime and outrage grows upon outrage with a fecundity that stupefies the most romantic imagination. Yet this last outrage—the climax in a series of financial jobberies, hocus conspiracies, detective corruptions, constabulary violence and national treason—cannot be allowed to pass with the usual protest of a single article, or be suffered to remain in brutal potentiality upon the Statute Book till the moment shall arrive when protest is fruitless and murder is done upon a defenceless population in the pre-sanctified name of the pious and pastoral Boer. The ratification by the Raad of Article 74 of the Concept Grondwet is in the opinion of the *Leader*, and, we believe, of every thinking man, a deliberate proclamation of a state of Constitutional Savagery in this Republic. There is not another country in the white man's world where a Minister dare propose such a measure. This article, empowering an experienced diplomatist like Mr. President Kruger, by and with the consent of another quaintly conditional person like Mr. Cronje, of a puppet like Mr. Schalk Burger, of an influence like Mr. Executive Judge-begetting Kock, of a strange-mannered nonentity like Mr. Reitz, to proclaim 'martial law,' and oblige every inhabitant to undertake military service against each and all-comers, be they his friends or his foes, is the most infernal depth that the Republic has reached in its effort to touch an independent bottom. . . ."

Consider the circumstances of the country where these passages are published. The Outlanders, dwelling undisturbed in the very heart of the country, are actually negotiating with the enemy of that country, a far more powerful State with possessions bordering on the Republic, to induce an invasion. The same Outlanders, a little more than three years before, had actually conspired and instigated a secret attack, endorsed, assisted, and condoned by important officials of the British Government. Yet in a case of such grave extremity, after they have permitted the full virulence of these dangerous attacks to flow unchecked for many months, a howl of virtuous indignation is raised because the author of this printed matter is at length laid by the heels, and his fellow-editor is driven out of the State. How long would the British Government allow such matter to be published by an influential journal in Ireland, in India, or even in London?

But so far I have only presented the first link in the chain of this press conspiracy. Those who understand the *modus operandi* of a party press will know that the combined power of these chartered libertines of print vastly exceeds the mere sum of the units. The financial relations between the newspapers which I have named found constant and vigorous expression in their columns. A common line of policy imposed upon, or sympathetically adopted by, the editors of papers at Johannesburg, Kimberley, Cape Town, and Bulawayo gave a powerful lead to the other members of the English press throughout South Africa, whose natural proclivities were Imperialist and anti-Dutch, and who were eager for a masterful policy. A new piece of tactics, or a sensational anti-Boer tale, first issuing from the *Johannesburg Star* or the *Kimberley Advertiser*, was immediately communicated to the *Cape Times* or the *Argus*, and ran the round of the Rhodes press, gathering an accumulation of authority in the process, until, by combination and reiteration, it had fastened a misjudgment, an exaggeration, or too frequently a falsehood, upon the public mind. The opinion of the British in South Africa has been the plaything of a press which, working in closest union, has practised the most unscrupulous ingenuity in driving the fooled public along the road designed for it to go.

But the inflammation of the credulous mind of South Africa was a task comparatively simple and of subsidiary importance. The chief object of this press conspiracy, to attain which every nerve was strained, was the conquest of the Government and the conscience of Great Britain. I have no hesitation in saying that a large proportion of the outrages and other sensations emanating from the press of Johannesburg and Cape Town were designed chiefly, if not exclusively, for the British market. Over and over again I have heard strong Outlander politicians of Johannesburg express their astonishment and indignation that their press, having so good a cause, should damage it by gross exaggeration and positive falsehoods. The stories of Zarp atrocities and Boer assaults upon women did not even obtain wide credence at the Cape. But faithfully reproduced, and duly endorsed by the most reputable colonial papers, they passed by wire and mail to the great newspapers of London, and were there received with an implicit confidence which must have brought a grim smile into the face of the colonial inventor.

What I am describing is nothing else than an elaborate factory of misrepresentations for the purpose of stimulating British action. To those unacquainted with the mechanism it may seem incredible that with modern means of communication it has been possible to poison the conscience and intelligence of England. But when it is understood that the great London press receives its information almost exclusively from the offices of the kept press of South Africa, the mystery is solved. Until just before the outbreak of hostilities the three most important London Unionist journals were served directly from the office of the *Star* with their cable news from the Transvaal, Mr. Monypenny himself serving the *Times*. That at so critical a juncture the *Times* should subject its policy to the inspiration and direction of a young journalist of the Rhodes press, just arrived in South Africa and completely unfamiliar with its life and politics, is matter for serious reflection.

Another London Conservative paper was instructed from the *Leader* office; one of the chief general cable services, widely used by most important English newspapers, was fed from Johannesburg by a prominent member of the Executive of the South African League. The London "Liberal" paper, whose perversion from the true path of Liberalism has inflicted the heaviest blow

A CHARTERED PRESS

upon the cause of truth and honesty in England, was fully and constantly inspired by the editor of the *Cape Times*, upon which office, I am informed, no fewer than three other important London dailies relied for their Cape Town intelligence. The *Cape Times* and the *Argus* offices also supplied two great general channels of cable information to the English press.

When it is borne in mind that this great confederation of press interests is financially cemented by the fact that Rand mining magnates are chief owners of at least two important London daily papers and of several considerable weekly papers, while the wider and ever-growing Jewish control of other organs of the press warrants a suspicion that the direct economic nexus between the English press and Rand finance is far stronger than is actually known, we shall have a clear comprehension of the press conspiracy which has successfully exploited the stupid Jingoism of the British public for its clearly conceived economic ends.

One of the humorous reliefs of the tragic movement of events has been the righteous indignation displayed by this Rhodesian Press-gang against the papers subsidised, or reported to be subsidised, by the Transvaal Government. The insolent provocation and the malignant falsehoods of certain members of the Hollander press, such as the *Rand Post* and the *Volkstemm*, and of two English papers at Pretoria and Johannesburg reported to be in Government pay, certainly played into the hands of the Imperialist war party, on the one hand, by rousing the passions and feeding the overweening confidence of the ignorant Boers, on the other hand, by furnishing printed matter which their enemies interpreted as representative of the general Boer sentiments and ambitions.

In speaking of this war as press-made, it is right to mete out a fair share of reprobation to this Krugerite press, though neither in circulation nor in real influence can it compare for one moment with the power of its antagonists.

On the whole, the press of South Africa has during the last year, for skilful and detailed misrepresentation, directed to a single end, attained a record in the annals of journalism. I cannot here fully prove or illustrate the accuracy of this judgment; to do so would require an accumulation of minute evidence, with an elaborate running commentary, such as would weary the most industrious reader. But I will indicate a few of the chief features of the campaign as I watched it during the summer and autumn months. "Filling up the cup" was the first phase which came within my view. Day after day the corruption of officials and of judges, narratives of crime winked at by the police, maladministration of the Liquor and the Press Laws, the dynamite scandal, the education grievance, were pressed home with an extravagance of unproved assertion and an absolute ignoring of all extenuating circumstances, which were clearly designed for no other purpose than to preserve an open sore between the Transvaal and the British Governments. This was the time when a Seven-Year Franchise Law was passed, and a genuine panic seized the moving spirits of the agitation lest a peaceful settlement upon a basis of fair representation should be attained. To keep all the other outstanding grievances well to the front, so as to prevent a settlement upon the basis of Sir Alfred Milner's Cape Town speech and the subsequent concessions of the Transvaal, was then the single object of this procession. It laboured to stiffen the back of the High Commissioner and the Cabinet, while feeding the slow-rising Jingoism of the English public, which in the early summer was notoriously averse from the coercive policy required of it.

As soon as diplomatic intercourse had taken on a tone of increased acerbity, the game of the Johannesburg press was to breed panic among the Outlanders, and to precipitate a business crisis which should create throughout South Africa, and by reaction in England, a forcible conviction that a conflict of armed forces was inevitable, though in truth the state of diplomatic intercourse at that time warranted no such assurance. With this object the Johannesburg press filled its columns day by day with tit-bits, carefully culled from the most rabid Dutch newspapers, and seasoned with preposterous surmises of the coming Boer atrocities, the ill-treatment of Outlanders who should be found in Johannesburg at the outbreak of hostilities; and, in particular, the danger to which miners would be subjected. If any hot-headed Boer in his cups, such as Ben Viljoen, made, or was said to make, some brutal speech about Englishmen, struck on the sounding-board of the Johannesburg press, it reverberated through South Africa; every idle word of the most insignificant official was treated as if it were the avowed policy of the Government. All this in order to create and sustain a scare which should drive the citizens of Johannesburg first to send away their families into Natal or Cape Colony, and then to follow them. One result of this policy has been that many people of moderate means and timid temperament, who "cleared" early in the summer, have almost ruined themselves already by the needless expenses of their premature flight and long protracted absence. As the strain between the Governments became more serious and war became really imminent, the rumours of coming atrocities, the "commandeering" of British subjects, the starvation and ill-treatment of those who stayed, became more startling; and long before war was actually declared the bulk of the inhabitants had taken to flight. Having got them out of Johannesburg, the press followed the refugees down the line, and the Cape press took up the running with tales of Boer insults and assaults at the stations, told with a wealth of circumstance that carried conviction to nine persons out of ten. How Boers struck English women with clubbed rifle or sjambok, spat in the faces of passengers, dragged them out of their carriages and forced them to shout for Kruger, refused them the right to purchase food, and in general behaved like savages—all this sort of thing occupied the Cape papers for some ten days. Exactly how large the grain of truth might be in this vast conglomerate of falsehood it was not possible to ascertain, because, although the tales of outrage were otherwise lavishly equipped with detailed circumstance, the names of the sufferers were for good reason almost invariably withheld. Two exposures at last killed this particular class of lies. In one instance a prominent political Outlander, whose brutal maltreatment by Boers and subsequent death in prison furnished a leading case for several days, turned up alive and free. The other case, where a number of armed Boers were stated to have flogged with sjamboks unarmed passengers who were peaceably entering a village near a station to purchase food, was still more discreditable in its recoil. It was proved, and reluctantly admitted by the press, that a number of rowdy Outlanders, coming by an earlier train that day, had outraged a girl in the very station grounds, and that, to prevent any recurrence of such conduct and to keep the public peace, police had been put at the station barriers to prevent passengers from leaving the station. Some men in a later train, disregarding these orders and forcing their way past the guards, were driven back by armed Boers in the neighbourhood.

In another case, where a free fight took place at a station, it turned out that a number of miners insisted upon standing on the platform and singing "Rule Britannia," a proceeding which was not unnaturally resented by young Boers in the station. Under the circumstances of this helter-skelter flight many hardships were inevitable, and it is likely enough that insults and threats were flung at the passengers by coarse and ignorant yokels inflamed by the war fever and hatred of Englishmen. The "commandeering" of money in excess of a certain sum practised upon passengers in some of the last trains was bitterly resented by them and their friends; but war had then been declared, and I venture to think that under similar circumstances in any European country some similar restrictions would have been placed upon the amount of property which expelled subjects of the hostile State could carry away.

So far as could be ascertained, very few cases of personal injury or insult took place, and in most of these direct provocation was given. The outrages to women and children I believe to be entire fabrications. Danger to "women and children" had figured in the historic letter which was taken to justify Jameson's raid; it was now used again with brazen-faced effrontery to fan the flames of revenge. Those who know the Boer character are aware that such outrages are not within the sphere of vice; but knowing well the methods of the Jingo press and the gullibility of the English mind, I have not the slightest doubt that these railway outrages were played for all they were worth. When cable intelligence indicated that these lies had done their work, they disappeared almost at once from the columns of the Cape press, though congested trains full of the poorest and most belated refugees continued to pass down the lines. The hose of mendacity was now switched on to a different theme; war was now beginning, and every art of false imagination was enlisted in the work of defaming the honour and courage of the enemy. A conscientious reader of the *Cape Times* and the *Argus* during the opening days of hostilities would have come to the conclusion that the Boers divided their time pretty equally between firing upon the white flag and upon the red cross. Another class of irritant is best described by an illustration from the *Cape Times* of October 18th:—

MURDER THE ENGLISH.

An Appeal in the Taal.

Natives Incited to Murder.

MARITZBURG, *October* 18.—[From our own Correspondent.]— A lady who arrived here with her family from Barberton last night gives a piteous account of things in that neighbourhood.

She says that renegade Englishmen are rampant in the outlying districts, and are threatening and bullying all whites.

A circular emanating from the office of a Dutch newspaper, printed in the Taal, calls upon all Boers, as a sacred and religious duty in the event of a reverse, to use their utmost endeavours to incite the natives to outrage and murder all English women and children.

The alarm in the isolated places is intense, and a repetition of the massacres of the Indian Mutiny is feared.

A CHARTERED PRESS

Though the *Cape Times* was appealed to for the name of the Dutch newspaper, and for a more satisfactory account of the circular, no more was heard of this incident: it had performed its part and passed away. This method was systematically applied: vague words full of sound and fury from anonymous mouths, unverified and impossible of contradiction! Another class of stories was engaged in showing that the Boers were stirring up rebellion among the Basutos, tampering with certain of their chiefs, and in dwelling upon the ill-treatment sustained by Basutos leaving the mines at the hands of the Boers. The drift and purpose of this "news" was to furnish beforehand a sort of justification for a Basuto inroad on the Free State, should such an event take place, and to stimulate such an event by suggestion. I do not deny, nor do I doubt, that there have been many cases where Boers have robbed the travelling Basutos on leaving the mines; but the incessant harping on these incidents is only to be understood as part of a general scheme for turning native feeling against the Dutch, a project the infernal malignity of which is only understood by those familiar with the great, dark shadow in the background of South African life, the fear of a native rising. A peculiarly infamous variant of this appeal to colour hatred is supplied by statements in the Cape press that black combatants were seen in the Boer commandos. It is hard to believe that the correspondent responsible for this lie was unaware of the fact that under no circumstances would Dutchmen employ armed Kaffirs, while they commonly took them in their campaigns to look after their horses.

The "outrage" manufacture of the Yellow Press was

accompanied by a never-ceasing tirade of imputations of treason against the Cape Dutch, which was calculated to expand the field of hostilities from the Republics to the whole of South Africa. It may appear reckless to impute so terrible a motive, but no one in Cape Colony could converse freely with British colonists without evoking over and over again expressions of a keen desire to open up the whole issue between Dutch and English, to force into the light of day the "hidden conspiracy" of the Bond, and once for all to establish by a signal, overwhelming blow the supremacy of the British over the whole of South Africa. A victory over the Republics, however complete, would not satisfy these people, who form, I think, a large majority of the British. They had persuaded themselves that the snake of Afrikanderism would then be only scotched and not killed, and that the larger task would remain to be done afterwards.

Numbers of men told me, when I pointed out the efforts made by the Ministry and Mr. Hofmeyr to preserve quiet in the Colony, that they regretted the success of these efforts, and that they would sooner have the matter fought out once for all.

I do not charge the more responsible organs of the Colonial press with a deliberate pursuance and a consistent advocacy of this reckless policy, but their treatment of the natural sympathy which the Colonial Dutch feel with the Republicans as evidence of treasonable conspiracy has been one of the most effective means to implicate the Colony in a race war.

After the outbreak of hostilities, a still more insidious mode of provocation was introduced by articles and letters suggesting that a satisfactory settlement required such interference with representative government in Cape Colony as would ensure the domination of the British. These open menaces of the press were so dangerous as to evoke at last from Sir A. Milner the proclamation denying that any such interference with elective institutions was designed.

No opportunity has been neglected by the Cape press of seeking, by misrepresentation of facts or perversion of language, to support the charges against the Cape Dutch. Let me quote a typical example. The *Cape Times* of October 25 contained the following paragraph:—

"Mr. M. J. du Plessis, M.L.A. for Cradock, addresses a letter to his constituents through the medium of the local Dutch paper, in which he tells them: 'The Transvaal people are our kith and kin, and it is only natural that we should sympathise with them. There is no honest man, no matter of what nationality, who will not admire us for doing that.'"

Mr. du Plessis is a prominent member of the Bond party in the Assembly, and this paragraph is calculated to fasten on him a charge of stimulating co-operation of the Republican forces. Now compare this sentence with a literal translation of the entire letter which Mr. du Plessis addressed to his constituents, and which may be taken as a fair example of the tone generally adopted by the Dutch members:—

"CRADOCK, *October* 14, 1899.

"TO MY FELLOW-CITIZENS,—

"Beloved fellow-citizens, the times in which we live are serious, and as I shall not have the opportunity of meeting you at present to address you, and to inform you of what is in my mind, I use the columns of *The Afrikander*, as the matter brooks no delay. The inhabitants of the Transvaal and the Free State are one in blood with us, and it is impossible for us not to sympathise with them. There is, moreover, no right-thinking person, of whatever nationality, who will not approve this sentiment. However, I desire to say to all my fellow-citizens, 'Men, sympathise and feel with and for our relatives and friends as much as you please, but do not forget that we are subjects of her Majesty, our revered Queen Victoria, and let us not commit any excess to mar the last years of her reign. Let us stay still and leave the issue which is so momentous for the whole of South Africa in the hands of Him who judgeth justly, and who will make all things end in the best way.—Your fellow-citizen,

"M. J. DU PLESSIS, M.L.A."

Can any language be more loyal, more dignified, more appropriate, and more remote from the meaning borne by the garbled sentence of the *Cape Times?*

Nowhere in the world at the present time has the press an unsullied reputation. But for carefully conceived and brilliantly executed mendacity, directed by widely diverse paths towards a single goal, the recent conduct of the capitalistic press of South Africa holds the record.

Unfortunately, as the copy-book instructs us, perfect success is seldom attainable. Put into more vulgar language, some one generally gives away the game. I have pointed out that it has not been necessary for Mr. Rhodes and his friends to buy and control directly the whole press of South Africa, because many organs of British African opinion were already in devoted sympathy with the Jew-Imperialist design that is in course of execution. The bulk of the Natal press is in this case. It did not need buying. But it would have been better to buy it. For if the *Times of Natal*, one of the oldest and most influential organs of South Africa, had been subject to the careful manipulation of the master hand, it would never have set forth the following interesting theory of press ethics :—

"Franchise, paramountcy, and so forth, have been all very useful in the evolutionary process of education. But before we shall have finished we have to reach that point when home opinion shall have come into line with opinion in Natal, as to the necessity for a clean sweep of the present order of things in the Transvaal and Orange Free State, and of the Bond in Cape Colony. To do this there is but little cause now to harp upon old well-worn grievances. Those have already become fairly well understood at home. The best object lessons we can now employ are those atrocities to our women and children. If we are to disarm those who are now against us at home, and who will endeavour in the day of our triumph to restore as much of the Boer power as possible, out of a misplaced sentiment for a weak foe, and who could go frantic over atrocities in Bulgaria, then, if they require atrocities to assist their comprehension of facts, and to disarm their opposition, so be it. It should not now be difficult to supply the necessary chapter of horrors to strike the imagination even of these good people."

The powerful English press of South Africa, thus owned and controlled by a handful of rich men bound together by closest financial bonds, succeeded first in inflaming the public of South Africa and afterwards in communicating the passion to the mind of the British public.

One last link in the chain deserves notice. It was necessary not only to deceive the British public as to the true position in South Africa, but also to deceive South Africa as to the state of feeling in Great Britain. I need not describe in detail how this was done; how intelligence from Europe was selected, distorted, heightened or suppressed, in order to support the agitation among the British Colonists and Outlanders, and to goad on the Governments of the Republics towards the precipice of war. The virtual unanimity of all parties in England, with the exception of a mere despicable handful of "Little Englanders," the support of the entire British press, the endorsement of a drastic policy by European Governments—these points were enforced by every art of the *suppressio veri* and the *suggestio falsi*. The chief intention and the sure result was to breed despair of any amicable settlement among the Republican politicians. The torpor of this despair I witnessed gathering in the minds of the leading men at Pretoria and Bloemfontein, and the latest intercourse between Sir A. Milner and President Steyn bears striking testimony to the diabolical success of the press policy.

That the burden of the Outlanders was so intolerable and so urgent that immediate redress was essential, that such redress could not be won by ordinary peaceful diplomacy, that the Boer Governments would yield before a sufficient display of armed force—these were the central falsehoods which the capitalist wreckers through their press drove into the British mind. That England was one-minded in her aggressive policy towards the Transvaal Government, that she had no intention to accept a fair franchise and representation as a basis of genuine and final settlement, but that she designed to enforce her suzerainty and supremacy by an interminable series of subsequent demands which implied a total loss of "independence"—these were the representations of the policy and feeling of England by which the same press goaded the Republics into defiance and despair.

CHAPTER IV

FOR WHAT ARE WE FIGHTING?

IN former chapters I have shown who the persons are that have brought about this war and the methods they have employed—a small confederacy of international financiers working through a kept press. It remains to describe the nature and the size of the gain which is their object.

There is no secret about the matter. This war is a terrible disaster for every one else in England and South Africa, but for the mine owners it means a large increase of profits from a more economical working of the mines, and from speculative operations. Mr. Fitzpatrick puts into the mouth of "leading men of the Rand" the following statement of grievances in 1896. "If you want the chief economic grievances they are. The Netherlands Railway Concession, the dynamite monopoly, the liquor traffic and native labour, which together constitute an unwarrantable burden of indirect taxation on the industry of over two and a half millions sterling annually." In other words, the mining capitalists stood to gain an income of two millions and a half by a successful political or military coup. Mr. Hays Hammond, of the Consolidated Goldfields, "would regard the sum of 6s. per ton as a conservative estimate of the direct and indirect benefits of good government," while Mr. J. B. Robinson takes 6s. as a minimum statement of the gain. Now, Mr. Hammond shows that a saving of 6s. per ton works out at "an increase of annual dividends by £2,413,268, based on last year's tonnage of ore crushed "—an independent corroboration of Mr. Fitzpatrick's former estimate.

Here is something worth spilling the blood of other people for. How is this prize to be won? Mr. Hammond's report contains an ingenuous admission that "in the Transvaal economics and politics are so closely connected," which throws light upon the ways and means of mining economy. Each one of the "savings" he specifies depends upon politics being managed in the interest of the mines. Into the details of these politics I cannot enter. It must suffice to say that dynamite, railway rates, gold thefts, and other matters which figure prominently here and elsewhere are of quite subordinate importance.

The abolition of the dynamite monopoly, for instance, cannot possibly account for more than a quarter of a million increased profits, while a most generous reduction of railway rates, and the best possible administration of the gold theft law would not furnish another tithe of the anticipated gain.

The one all-important object is to secure a full, cheap, regular, submissive supply of Kaffir and white labour. Wages form about 55 per cent. of the working expenses of the mines, and of the 6s. per ton in which Mr. Hammond expresses the advantages of "good government," another expert, Mr. Curle, estimates that 5s. would accrue from a full supply of labour, with proper administration of the Pass and Liquor Laws, which keep the Kaffirs from deserting their employment, and prevent them from obtaining drink.

The attitude of the mining industry towards the Transvaal Government in respect of the labour question is instructive. Witnesses before the Industrial Commission at Johannesburg were unanimous in maintaining that it was the duty of the Government to procure a steady and sufficient supply of Kaffirs for the mines. The Government was called upon to accredit and assist agents of the mining industry to obtain native labour, to "pay premiums to Kaffir chiefs," to furnish extra pay to native Commissioners for the same object, to convey this labour "under supervision" to the mines, erecting "compounds" along the road, reducing railway fares to one-third of the existing rate, and in a dozen other ways spending public money to serve the private interests of the mines. Why "politics and economics are so closely connected" that the public purse should be used to keep down the wages-bill of the mines is not intelligible to English people. But it is perfectly clear that under a "reformed" Government the mine owners will take every care to press these claims.

Put in a concise form, it may be said that this war is being waged in order to secure for the mines a cheap adequate supply of labour. This need has been a pressing and a growing one. The last report of the Chamber of Mines puts the matter thus: "Under the permanent condition of shortage of supply which has prevailed, it is clear that under stress of competition the tendency would have been to gradually increase wages." Last June this "shortage" was estimated at 12,000, in spite of every effort of the Native Labour Association, which scoured Africa to procure Kaffir workers. Sierra Leone, the Gold Coast, and Liberia have been approached by the mine owners, and serious proposals have been entertained to import Hindoo or even Italian labour.

If the output of gold is to be enlarged, on terms which will yield a maximum of profits, a large expansion of the labour-market is essential. It is this issue which beyond all others has driven the capitalists into politics, marking out for them, on the one hand, an imperialist, on the other, a domestic policy. The sources of native labour in the Republics and the Colonies are quite inadequate. The natives of Zululand, Basutoland, Swaziland, and Natal are fine workers, but can seldom be persuaded to go underground, while the Bechuanas and Cape Kaffirs are capricious, and form a very small proportion of the supply. A larger but very unreliable supply comes from the extreme north of the Transvaal: it is significant that no natives from the neighbourhood can be induced to enter the mines. By far the most important supply comes from the Portuguese territories on the east coast, and it is to this quarter and to the lands north of the Zambezi that the mine owners are looking for this increased supply.[1]

It is thus manifest that the pressure of the powerful mining interests will continually be used to drive us into political interference with countries which lie outside our present possession and control. By persuasion or coercion, labour must be got from Mozambique and from the north.

[1] The following schedule of the Native Labour Association gives the numbers obtained from these several sources during the period November 1896 to December 1898:—

Mozambique	32,271
North Transvaal	12,535
Zulu and Swaziland	511
Basutoland and Cape Colony	5,963
Bechuanaland and Marico	2,068
Rhodesia	263
	53,611

A careful investigation conducted along the entire main reef by the Rev. C. Baumgarten in June 1899 gives the following results:—

		Percentages.
Zulus	8,402	9
Up country, N. Transvaal, and Bechuanas, &c.	18,196	18
Colonial and Basuto	8,740	9
East Coast	56,830	64
Total	92,168	100

For this reason our international capitalists are expanders of the British Empire.

The difficulty of raising, at a sufficient pace, the required supply from these distant regions will, however, prove very great, and these sources must be supplemented by bringing more pressure to bear upon the reluctant natives of South Africa, among whom underground work is unpopular.

"They should," as Mr. Rudd recently urged, "try some cogent form of inducement or practically compel the native, through taxation or in some other way, to contribute his quota to the good of the community, and to a certain extent he would then have to work." Not only would he have to work, but he would have to work cheap, for, as Mr. Hays Hammond said, "With good government there will be an abundance of labour, and with an abundance of labour there will be no difficulty in cutting down wages."

The thin edge of the wedge of "forced labour" has been introduced in several directions outside of Rhodesia, where, under a thin disguise, it is still in practice; even in Cape Colony Mr. Rhodes, by his Glen Grey Act, has essayed to teach "the dignity of labour" to reluctant natives who prefer to work or idle for themselves, while the forced indenturing of captive Bechuanas charged with, but not convicted of, rebellion, is a line which may be profitably followed in the future, when the present conflict of white races has borne its certain fruit of native disturbances. The Boer treatment of natives in the Transvaal has never been enlightened or humane, and a form of indenture not widely differing from slavery has always prevailed. The fact that some philanthropic persons believe the present war justified by the need of redressing native grievances will not deter our economic lords from adapting the temper and the forms of Boer institutions to their profitable use.

An interesting passage in a recent speech of Earl Grey, referring primarily to Rhodesia, has a likely bearing on the Transvaal mines:—

"They must dismiss from their minds the idea of developing their mines with white labour. Means had to be sought to induce the natives to seek, spontaneously, employment at the mines, and to work willingly for long terms of more or less continuous service. In time, he believed, the education of the natives would cause them to seek work to gratify those growing wants which were the certain result of increasing contact with civilisation. Meanwhile, an incentive to labour must be provided by the imposition of a hut-tax of at least £1, in conformity to the practice of Basutoland, and also by the establishment of a small labour-tax, which those able-bodied natives should be required to pay who are unable to show a certificate for four months' work."

There is a humorous impudence in the suggestion that "spontaneous" and "willing" work is to be induced by hut and labour taxes. This is the spirit of South African capitalism all over: the Rand differs from Rhodesia only in being a little less free-spoken—the men are the same, the motives and the economic needs are the same, the conduct will be the same.

There is in reality but one idea of handling the labour problem throughout South Africa, that of "forced labour," thinly disguised under the cloak of taxation, voluntary contract, indenture, or imprisonment. Mr. Rhodes has frequently and openly avowed the economic principle, and has practised it unblushingly in Rhodesia, as the official report of Sir R. Martin testifies.

Mr. Rudd recently maintained with some real show of *à fortiori* reasoning the following interesting thesis:—

"If under the cry of civilisation we in Egypt lately mowed down 10,000 or 20,000 Dervishes with Maxims, surely it cannot be considered a hardship to compel the natives in South Africa to give three months in the year to do a little honest work."

The only obstacle Mr. Rudd sees is the fact that "there is a morbid sentimentality among a large section of the community on the question of the natives"; in other words, the moral feelings which according to Mr. Hugh Price Hughes and his friends are the chief justification of this war. In his examination before the Industrial Commission Mr. Albu gave the following interesting evidence upon the wage question:—

"The native at the present time receives a wage which is far in excess of the exigencies of his existence. The native earns between 50s. and 60s. per month, and then he pays nothing for food or lodging, in fact he can save almost the whole amount he receives. . . . If the native can save £20 a year, it is almost sufficient for him to go home and live on the fat of his land. In five or six years' time the native population will have saved enough money to make it unnecessary for them to work any more. The consequences of this will be most disastrous for the industry and the State. This question applies to any class of labour, and in any country, whether it be in Africa, Europe, or America. I think if the native gets enough pay to save £5 a year, that sum is quite enough for his requirements, and will prevent natives from becoming rich in a short space of time."

"You say the native does not require luxuries, and if he has worked for a year he has saved enough to go back to his kraal and remain idle?"

"Yes."

"Can you suggest any remedy for this?"

"The only remedy I can suggest is that we pay the native a wage which, whilst enabling him to save money, will hinder him from becoming exceptionally rich. . . ."

"Is it in the control of the mining industry to regulate the wages of Kaffirs?"

"To a great extent it is, provided that the Government assists us in bringing labour to this market."

So much of Kaffir wages, now of white:—

"Are you of opinion that the wages paid to (white) miners at the present moment are abnormal?"

"In some instances they are abnormal."

"Is there any chance of getting these abnormal wages reduced now that there are so many out of work?"

"Certainly there is: I think the white labourers are prepared to accept the lesser of two evils. If we close down the mines a lot of white labourers will be thrown out of employment."

This is a perfectly straightforward policy and would be endorsed by almost all South African capitalists, excepting that most of them would be sufficiently discreet to keep silence about their intention of reducing white wages, content to carry out the plan when they have got the power into their hands.

The instrument for complete control of the native and white labour market will be the Chamber of Mines. That body, which represents the gradual concentration of the entire industry for fighting purposes in politics and economics, has long concerned itself with this question; forcing a common rate of wages on the trade and inspecting the books of the companies to see they keep the rule, it has already once effected a reduction of wages, and has only been prevented from further action by the disorganised state of the country. Through its annex, the Native Labour Association, it has already gone far to crush the private enterprise of unauthorised labour touts and to get into its own hand the available supply of labour. With the political machinery of the Transvaal in its hands or under its control, it will be greatly strengthened in its efforts to compel " voluntary " labour and to bring it safely and cheaply to the mines at the expense of Government.

This drawing of labour from a distance, assisted by hut and labour taxes, will be reinforced by a policy of maintaining close at hand a large, safe, well-regulated supply. The Chamber of Mines indignantly repudiates the intention of establishing the Kimberley " compound " system which converts a labour contract into a period of imprisonment with hard labour and a truck system of wages; mine owners and managers examined by the Industrial Commission explained that the " compound " system was inexpedient, because it would " injure the industrial community." But none the less a widely prevalent belief has existed in Johannesburg that the " compound " would be adopted when the time was ripe. " Why," it is asked, " should the mine owners be deterred from an obvious economy by consideration of the commercial classes in Johannesburg? When the system was adopted at Kimberley there was no consideration of the ruined shopkeepers there; the interests of the Rand capitalists in the town values of Johannesburg are insignificant when compared with their interests in the mines, and will not stand in the way of any really profitable reform." On the whole, however, it seems more likely that another solution of the native labour question will be found, and that, instead of the Kimberley "compound," a system of native locations along the Rand will be adopted. While the "compound" system gives the companies a full control of the labour during the period contracted for, it does not secure a permanent supply upon the spot, which is the thing most desired. If, on the other hand, a large number of able-bodied natives can be induced to break up their tribal agricultural life in distant parts and plant themselves with their families in a dense population upon lands belonging to the companies and adjoining the mines, a really more effective control will be obtained. Once there, their old tribal life abandoned, prevented from wandering by the rigorous administration of the Pass Law, deprived of the opportunity of getting land enough to earn a living, they can only keep themselves and their families by regular employment on the mines for a wage determined by the Chamber. Such a system of native locations, assisted by Pass and Liquor Laws, a Hut and Labour Tax, will furnish a serf population, *ascripti glebae*, who, nominally free, will be virtually compelled to devote themselves and their families to the service of the mines. This course will have many advantages; it will save the cost of bringing labour from longer and ever longer distances, it will keep the labour when it has been got, and furnish a regular, reliable, cheap and experienced body of workers, some of whom may be taught to do skilled work which will displace white labour: their presence will raise the value of surrounding lands and will, by forcing the wages to be spent upon the spot, enable the mining capitalists to take another profit out of shops owned by the companies or built upon their land.

Another advantage of this method of "locations" is

that it is adaptable, without the name, to the case of white labour. The white miners at Kenilworth, the suburb of Kimberley, are absolutely under the control of De Beers Company: drawing their wages from De Beers, living in houses owned by De Beers, trading with shops controlled by De Beers, they are the political and social serfs of the company; if they object to any terms imposed upon them by the company, they must quit not only their employment but their homes, and must leave Kimberley to find a means of living outside the clutches of the diamond monopoly. The same will be the position of the white miners who may be induced to bring their families and settle down upon the Rand. The mining companies do not even now genuinely compete for labour; white wages as well as black are fixed by central authority, and workers dismissed from one mine cannot easily get employment in another. The rapid consolidation of mining interests, and the virtual supremacy of Eckstein's in the Chamber of Mines, will speedily perfect the control over white labour. The "independence" of the Cornish miner has hitherto consisted in the fact that, being single, he could save a large proportion of his wage, and could leave for home if he were ill-used or dissatisfied. If he can be placed, with a family to keep, in a house belonging to the mines, with no option of any other work, and with no power of saving enough to break up his home, and remove his family, his "independence" will be gone, and his wages can and will be reduced as often and as far as the convenience of the companies requires.

Though less has been said, for obvious reasons, about reducing white wages, miners are well aware of the intention of the managers, and Mr. Albu's sentiments are known to be widely entertained. The matter is well put in a recent article by "An Outlander" published in the *Mining World* :[1]—

"White wages have not been reduced in the past, because the Outlanders desired to work together for political salvation, and any attack upon the white labourers' pay would have caused a split in the ranks. However, when new conditions prevail, white wages must come down."

Indeed, the saving to be effected out of white wages is greater than out of black, for the aggregate of the wages paid to white miners has hitherto been larger than that paid to black, though the numbers of the latter are eight times as large.

If this war can be successfully accomplished, and a "settlement" satisfactory to the mine owners can be reached, the first fruits of victory will be represented in a large, cheap, submissive supply of black and white labour, attended by such other economies of "costs" as will add millions per annum to the profits of the mines. It is no extravagance to argue that the blood and the money of the people of Great Britain are being spent for this purpose; that at present no other definite tangible result of the conflict can be shown. The men who, owning the South African press and political organisations, engineered the agitation which has issued in this war, are the same men whose pockets will swell with this increase; open-eyed and persistent they have pursued their course, plunging South Africa into a temporary ruin in order that they may emerge victorious, a small confederacy of international mine-owners and speculators holding the treasures of South Africa in the hollow of their hands.

[1] December 16, 1899.

PART III

TOWARDS A SETTLEMENT

CHAPTER I

DUTCH AND BRITISH IN SOUTH AFRICA

BEFORE any proposals of settlement can be usefully considered certain important issues, relating to the economic and political present and probable future of South Africa, require discussion. What are the present number and distribution of Dutch and British colonists in South Africa, and how far is it likely that the near future will change these factors of race supremacy? What is the mining future of South Africa, in particular of the Transvaal, and how long will it last? Is a great agricultural development possible, and, if so, what part will British colonists play in it? Are large manufacturing industries likely to rise in the Transvaal? How will the "native question" open out (a) as regards the labour market, (b) as regards education and the franchise, (c) as a possible military danger? How can the disturbing factors of the Cape "boys," the Indians, and the "mean whites" be dealt with? Some of these really fundamental questions lie beyond the scope of this volume, to others at least a tentative answer can be given by consideration of certain large unassailable facts.

As is usual, the first difficulty is to get certain common necessary measures. In seeking to discover the respective numerical strength of British and Dutch colonists and dwellers in the two Republics we are met by serious obstacles. No racial record is attempted in either colonies or Republics, and in default of this we are obliged to rely upon imperfect records either of church membership or of burghership. Turning first to Cape Colony, the religious record in 1891 classed the whites as follows:—

Protestants	356,960
Catholics	14,853
Jews	3,007
Mahometans	31
	374,851

Of the Protestants 228,627, or 60.65 per cent., belonged to the Dutch churches. If we suppose all the other Protestants to be of British descent, and even include as British the entire body of the Jews and Roman Catholics, though many Germans and other foreigners are present amongst them, the result will be 228,627 Dutch against 146,224 British. In Natal we are destitute even of this religious census, and no reliable statistics from other sources take its place enabling us to distinguish British and Dutch. It is, however, admitted that of the 61,000 whites estimated to be living in Natal in 1898 the vast majority were British. A rough estimate assigning 10,000 as the number of the Dutch would probably be near the mark. In the Transvaal the best available basis of computation is the latest estimate of the Staats Almanak, which gives the white population as 288,750, together with the burgher list, comprising males over the age of sixteen, which contains 29,279 names. A more recent burgher census, taken last summer, is said to contain about 35,000 names, but, since there is no means of comparing this with a census of the whole white population, it is safer to take the earlier list in

DUTCH AND BRITISH IN SOUTH AFRICA

comparing Dutch with British. These figures by no means bear out the popular notion that the Outlanders are three-quarters of the population. If we suppose the proportion of ages and sexes to be the same in the Transvaal as in this country, 29,279 as the male population over sixteen will represent a total Boer population of about 125,000, leaving an Outlander population of 163,750. Recent events certainly indicate that the Boer population is at least as large as the figure above named—125,000. What proportion of the computed Outlander population, 163,750, is to be called British in race, in language, or in sympathy, once more we have no means of calculation, but it certainly includes very many thousands of Hollanders, Continental Jews, Germans, and Americans. Personally I do not believe it is likely that as many as 100,000 of these Outlanders are of British descent, but the general opinion would probably assign a larger number, say 120,000, and this may be provisionally accepted. When we come to the Free State, with its population of 77,716 in 1891, we are again thrown upon church membership for our estimate of Dutch and British. Of this number 68,940 belonged to the Dutch Reformed Church, and if we add half of those, 3970, who gave no statement of church membership, and class the rest, including even a few Lutherans and Jews, as British, we reach the following result: Dutch, 70,925; British, 6791. It is highly probable that the number of British colonists in the Free State has since 1891 increased somewhat faster than the growth of the Dutch colonists, but how large this increase may be we have no means of knowing, and in any case the numbers are too small materially to affect the total balance either for the Republics or for South Africa.

Now, assuming these figures to be approximately accurate, we reach the following distribution of British and Dutch colonists over South Africa, omitting Bechuanaland, Basutoland, and Rhodesia:—

	British.	Dutch.
Cape Colony	146,224	228,627
Natal	51,000	10,000
Transvaal	120,000	125,000
Free State	6,791	70,925
	324,015	434,552

If Bechuanaland and Rhodesia were thrown in there would be a gain of a few thousands to the British as compared with the Dutch total, but from our existing means of information it is evident that the Dutch Afrikanders are numerically far stronger than the British over South Africa, and it is highly probable that there is a considerable Dutch majority over the genuinely British population in the two Republics taken together.

Supposing this calculation to be approximately true, it has important political implications. One inevitable effect of the present war will be to accentuate the race cleavage as a political division throughout South Africa. In so far, therefore, as representative government prevails in any federation of these States, the Dutch will exercise in virtue of their numbers a practical dominance. In Cape Colony, even under a reformed distribution giving increased representation to the towns, the solidarity of race which the present trouble has established will give the Dutch an easy superiority. In the Free State, and even in the Transvaal, if any reasonable time qualification for the franchise is retained, they will at present retain the supremacy at the polls. In Natal alone is the British power really dominant. If any system of federal government in South Africa is established upon the basis of a popular franchise, it is pretty evident that the Dutch Afrikanders will control that government.

But, it is maintained, the firm establishment of British paramountcy throughout South Africa, and in particular a state of good settled government in the Transvaal, will induce so large and rapid an immigration of British settlers as to turn the scale of racial superiority in a few years. Setting aside for the present the highly hazardous speculations as to the future of Rhodesia, it is upon the growth of a distinctly British population in the Transvaal that everything depends. It is popularly believed that this growth will be so great as soon to give the British colonists an absolute superiority of numbers not merely in the Transvaal but in South Africa as a whole. In considering this assumption it must not be forgotten that the tendency, apart from immigration, has been for the Dutch settlers to increase at a considerably faster pace than the British. No exact measurement of the relative rate of growth is obtainable, but common knowledge attests the statement that almost all the Dutch farmers throughout South Africa marry young, have large families, and, though infant mortality is considerable, rear successfully a large number of children. In most countries the birth-rate and the growth of population is larger in the country than in the towns, when the natural rate of growth alone is taken into consideration. And this brings up a most important factor in the situation—the coincidence of an economic with a racial cleavage throughout South Africa. The British are townsmen, the Dutch are countrymen. This local and industrial division is of prime importance in any calculation as to the future. So far the division of occupations has gone very closely upon racial lines, a fact fraught with most important economic consequences. The modes of rural industry chiefly in vogue, cattle and ostrich farming, have had little attraction for British settlers, and although certain considerable districts of the Eastern Province, where soil and conditions favour arable farms, are largely peopled by men of British descent, while even in the most distinctively Dutch regions a sprinkling of English blood is found, no general tendency is seen for Englishmen to take to country life and work in Cape Colony or the Republics. Hitherto the real "settlement" of South Africa has been Dutch; the British comers have not for the most part been "settlers," but rovers, not even attaching themselves very strongly to any single town or any single industry, but moving to and fro, with the economic and political changes of this most eventful country, from Cape Town to Kimberley, and thence to Johannesburg or to Bulawayo, as the spirit of speculative industry might lead them. Not merely in the Transvaal, but all over South Africa, there is this radical difference between Dutch and British Afrikanders, that the former have definitely severed themselves in fact and feeling from Europe, and regard South Africa as their country and their only home, while the British Afrikander, though his family may have been for three generations living in South Africa, not only continues to speak of England as "home," but continually contemplates a return to it. This is a fact of prime political significance; those who really regard South Africa as home, and are in thought and in interests firmly rooted there, both must and ought to have a greater influence in determining its destinies than those

DUTCH AND BRITISH IN SOUTH AFRICA

who are mere sojourners or hold their occupation of the land more lightly. It is not right or good for any country that birds of passage, mere temporary gain-seekers, should by force of numbers dominate the policy of that country, nor will it, in fact, be easy for them to do so. The superior political strength of the Dutch Afrikander is derived not merely from his numbers but from that greater solidarity of interests associated with the more fixed settlement he has effected. If the British are to be really paramount as a race in South Africa by other means than Imperial tyranny from Downing Street, it can only be by a substantial immigration into South Africa of British people who will settle down to the permanent agricultural and industrial development of the country, with the fixed intentions of making their homes in the country and of building up a distinctively British Afrikander society. Whether this is desirable, and how far it is possible and likely to occur, are speculative questions which should find some sort of answer before terms of settlement can be discussed.

CHAPTER II

THE AGRICULTURAL OUTLOOK

WE have seen that, however great may be the formal paramountcy of Great Britain in South Africa, the reality of her ascendency, her power to mould the future policy either of a federation or of separate states, must depend upon the increase of the proportion of British Afrikanders, as compared with Dutch, more than upon any other condition. Hitherto there is reason to believe that the Dutch stock has been more prolific than the British, and that the latter has not made good its deficit by immigration. If a secure and efficient government, upon the basis of equal rights for civilised races, is established after the conclusion of the war, will a stream of immigration be maintained into South Africa from Great Britain?

This is a crucial question. For some time the issue may be shirked by keeping military or other coercive control over parts of South Africa where "disloyalty" is suspected. But ultimately, and not remotely, the self-government of the white races must be frankly and fully conceded under such nominal control as we exercise over Canada and Australia. Will free representative institutions give the upper hand to Dutch or British stock? But for recent events, the fusion of blood, and of economic and social interests, which had long been taking place, might have gained such acceleration as to have made this question of little import. It may, however, be taken for granted that for many years to come this wholesome fusion is entirely stopped, and that politics will run upon strictly racial lines. Therefore, unless there is so large and rapid an influx of new British population as to out-number and out-vote the Dutch Afrikanders, the essential object of British policy, viz., to secure a practical British ascendency, will be frustrated.

Primarily, our question is an economic one, and depends for its answer upon the probable industrial development of South Africa. In treating this matter we may discard the remote future, nowhere more incalculable than in Africa, and restrict ourselves to more immediate probabilities. How far are agriculture, mining and manufacturing industries likely to develop fast enough to find profitable employment for large numbers of British immigrants within the next few decades? Those who see immense areas of land marked on a map, and are informed that the population for the Colonies and Republics is less than one and a half persons per square mile, and that the climate and soil are favourable to white colonists, may entertain the notion of some great scheme of settling British agricultural labourers or small farmers in South Africa. But the least reflection and investigation of the country will serve to check such wild optimism. In the first place, no really substantial migration of agricultural population from this country is taking place, or is likely to take place, even to the United States. A small number of men with the requisite skill and capital take to colonial farming upon a large scale. The Eastern Province of Cape Colony has drawn some of these who have done fairly well, a sprinkling is to be found in Natal, in the Free State, Bechuanaland, and Rhodesia. But this migration all told is insignificant, nor is there any reason to believe that a "settlement," which shall fasten the formal ascendency of Great Britain upon all South Africa, will furnish the requisite conditions to tempt any large migration from the dwindling agricultural population of these isles. Even if there were the men to go, why should they choose South Africa? The most valuable lands in the Colonies and the Free State are already occupied, those in Rhodesia are owned by syndicates with whom hard bargains must be driven.

Moreover, the proportion of really serviceable land, even for grazing, is extremely small, while arable farming and other kinds of cultivation are attended by dangers and difficulties which probably exceed those experienced in any other country. Rinderpest, the tsetse-fly, and horse fever have periodically swept off the live stock; droughts, hail-storms, locusts destroy the crops of whole districts. Preventive and curative measures for dealing with some of these afflictions are doubtless available; rinderpest has been successfully repressed over large areas, and a gallant attempt to combat the plague of locusts by fungus poison is being made. But Africa is a land of surprises, and its agriculture is painfully prolific in new dangers which take the heart out of progressive agriculture. To the low fertility of most of the soil, and the constant recurrence of these destructive pests, must be attributed the poor and conservative farming of the Boers. Land where a sheep requires six acres to furnish it a bare subsistence, as is the case on the Karoo, or where a farm of 5000 morgen (10,000 acres) often proves inadequate to support a family, as is the case over large parts of the Free State, will scarcely tempt the enterprising British yeoman. He would have to adapt himself

THE AGRICULTURAL OUTLOOK 253

to a life and a mode of agriculture entirely foreign to his habits and his inclinations, and would, at the best, earn the scant and precarious livelihood which seems to satisfy the rude Boer frontiersman. No doubt there are vast areas available for ranching, provided the pressure of agricultural population in Great Britain made large migration essential, and governmental or other grants of land and capital were available so as to plant them securely on South African soil. But does any one seriously suppose that this will be done? The overwhelming majority of British who go to South Africa have settled down to mining or town life and will continue to do so. The character of the country, and the kind of life imposed, do not suit the British agriculturist. It is a country of vast grazing farms, where the farmer leads a dull, solitary, monotonous life, and hires or coerces Kaffir labour to do the hard manual work for him. Each farmer is, to all intents and purposes, a little serf-holder, and generally suffers, as is natural in these circumstances, a descent into a torpid unprogressive life. Such ranching spread over large tracts of country can never absorb any large quantity of British labour. Mr. Bryce has excellent grounds for his statement: "On a large grazing farm the proportion of white men to black servants is usually about three to twenty-five; and though the proportion of whites is of course much larger in the small towns which supply the wants of the surrounding country, still any one can see with how few whites a ranching country may get along."[1]

Even when there is a great show of fertility, as is evinced by the astonishingly rapid growth of trees, the soil is not rich to any depth and has very little staying

[1] "Impressions of South Africa," p. 437.

power. The Free State is the only South African State which really keeps itself in food and has to spare, exporting to the market of the sister Republic food stuffs for man and beast amounting to a value of nearly £1,000,000 per annum in recent years. But even there the wheat-growing area is comparatively small, and consists almost entirely of the rich lands bordering on the west frontier of Basutoland. As for the prospect of the Transvaal "finding itself" in bread, Captain Younghusband presents the serious climatic obstacle: "It is said that wheat cannot be grown in summer because the rain falls in that season and causes rust, and in winter there is all sun and no rain, so that to grow wheat irrigation must be resorted to."[1]

The enormous size of these farms renders impossible any true social life; the family sometimes keeps together until it forms a little clan, but for the most part economic necessity scatters families at such wide intervals, that anything in the way of regular society, even of a few neighbours, becomes impossible. To Englishmen such a life is intolerable: even if the men could bear it, it is not endurable for women and children to be cut off from all society and means of education. It may be said that the conditions here described are not eternal. New crops may be introduced and developed. Creditable qualities of tea and sugar are already produced in Natal. Transvaal tobacco has peculiar merits which are recognised throughout South Africa. Cotton, coffee, and rice have a possible future. But there is no evidence to show that South Africa presents any peculiar advantages for these and any other agricultural products which will induce a large application of capital and labour.

[1] "South Africa of To-day," p. 17.

It is often said that the low fertility of the soil may be overcome by irrigation and by other arts of scientific agriculture. No doubt this may be possible, though the low rainfall of many otherwise desirable districts, the absence of rivers, and the hazard attending the sinking of wells, are serious obstacles; but the expense of any effective considerable system of irrigation would be so great that we may place it out of serious consideration in dealing with the near future. Unless a very large, near, regular, and high-priced market for agricultural produce existed in South Africa, it would be quite impossible to induce any considerable number of British agriculturists to settle on the soil. Even where the land is British territory, as in Bechuanaland and Rhodesia, it is pretty evident that in a few years Dutch trekkers from the Republics and colonies will largely outnumber colonists of British descent.

There can be no spontaneous independent British agriculture in South Africa which shall produce a new class of British yeomen comparable in numbers or character to the Boer, who, by the process of several centuries' use and selection, has become assimilated to his hard and changeful environment, chiefly by accustoming himself to bear the hardships, and by adopting so simple and conservative a mode of farming that the changes and caprices though they cripple enterprise do not destroy him.

Any large development of progressive profitable farming which shall tempt British agricultural settlers can only follow in the wake of a great industrial and mining development. The notion of an agricultural community of British settlers living a substantially self-sufficing life, and taking their manufactured goods as imports from England, while giving in exchange the fruits of the soil raised under the pressure of ordinary motives, is entirely chimerical. If there is to be any considerable and rapid increase of agricultural population in South Africa, it must presuppose a large increase of mining and town population, and even then the increased farming would almost certainly be done by Dutch rather than by British Afrikanders. These conclusions relating to the early future will, I think, be pretty generally admitted by those who have considered the conditions.

CHAPTER III

THE PROBABLE INDUSTRIAL FUTURE OF SOUTH AFRICA

WHEN confident predictions are made of a large and rapid growth of British population in South Africa, they are based upon the belief that the country possesses a great mining and manufacturing future. There are many who look forward to the swift development of the rich and varied mineral resources, which the country is known or believed to possess, as the sure guarantee of British supremacy, maintained by the numerical superiority of members of the British race.

In order to test the value of such predictions, it is best to start from known facts. Gold and diamonds are the two solid assets of this order in South Africa. Diamonds, first discovered in quantity in 1869-70, brought a considerable growth of population into the neighbourhood of Kimberley during the next fifteen years, while the mining claims remained in many hands, and competition ruled the output and the price. The growth of this mining population was attended by a corresponding growth of traders and of general town population in Kimberley. This tendency, however, received a signal, sudden, and final check by the amalgamation of mining interests in one great company, De Beers, achieved by Mr. Rhodes in 1885. Since that time the quantity of the output has been virtually stationary, though a slow rise in the value per carat, under the stress of an almost complete monopoly, gave a certain inconsiderable rise in the aggregate annual value prior to 1890. Since 1890, after De Beers had secured almost perfect control of other small mining properties, output, value, and, what is more important for our present consideration, number of white employees remained stationary. The following short table will serve to make this clear. The weight and value given refer to diamonds exported from and imported into the district of the Kimberley mines, the imports representing diamonds taken in the River Diggings :—

Year.	Carats.	Value.	Labour.
1891	3,255,545	£4,174,208	1592
1892	3,039,062	3,906,992	1709
1893	2,758,827	3,821,443	1793
1894	2,507,409	3,013,578	1553
1895	3,355,863	4,323,308	1593
1896	3,283,439	4,195,651	1740
1897	3,220,367	4,024,040	1696
1898	3,232,057	4,124,170	1653

These figures will suffice to make it evident that the economic conditions of the great De Beers monopoly are such as to render it impossible to anticipate any increase of employment for British labour in this important industry, the importance of which may be measured by the fact that it provides about one quarter of the total export trade from Cape Colony.

It is evidently upon gold, not upon diamonds, that we must rely if we anticipate a large and rapid demand for British labour. Now gold is known to exist and has been worked in various places in Africa south of the Zambesi. In Natal, Zululand, Swaziland, in Northern

Bechuanaland, and in Cape Colony quartz reefs containing gold have been found and worked to some slight extent. But the fairly unanimous judgment of experts indicates that none of these known reefs is likely to contribute anything considerable to the gold output. Although great hopes have been entertained of the secondary goldfields of the Transvaal, and one or two of them are sedulously boomed for speculative purposes, they do not make any large or increasing contribution to the aggregate output, nor is there any reason to expect any considerable development in the future. Twelve years ago the Potchefstroom district was believed to have a profitable future, but only one or two mines of any importance remained open in 1899. The reputation of the Heidelberg district during the last ten years has lived upon the success of a single mine, the Nigel, upon the strength of which some dozens of worthless mines have been floated.

Barberton, the first of the goldfields to be discovered, is now ranked as "a failure" by Mr. Curle, the author of "Goldfields of the World," who thus summarises the condition of the De Kaap district: "Of about forty mines in existence, or recently in existence, at De Kaap, there is only one, the Sheba, which has ever attained the position of a permanent mining enterprise."

Of Lydenburg, which has generally been considered the most promising district next to the Witwatersrand, the same authority says: "The reefs are usually narrow, and frequently irregular in value; they are difficult to mine, and, on the whole, have proved disappointing."

The following table of the quantity and value of the gold output for 1896 and 1897 will serve to indicate the comparative insignificance of the subsidiary goldfields of South Africa:—

	1896.		1897.	
	Quantity.	Value.	Quantity.	Value.
	Oz.	£	Oz.	£
Witwatersrand .	2,280,892	7,864,341	3,034,678	10,583,616
De Kaap . . .	121,390	439,685	113,972	398,902
Lydenburg . .	50,387	148,778	50,942	178,296
Klerksdorp . .	38,818	125,109	84,781	296,733
Zoutspansberg .	5,602	15,807	225	791
Swaziland . .	...	...	4,979	17,427
Other districts .	857	3,293	141	...
	2,497,946	8,597,013	3,289,718	11,475,765

Of the future of Rhodesia it is of course unsafe to speculate. The same expert who condemns the future of the secondary Transvaal goldfields believes that Rhodesia "is about to become a prominent and permanent gold-producer," and that within the next few years some thirty payable mines will be either at work or in process of development. No one, however, believes that any goldfield comparable, either in richness or in reliableness, to the Rand is likely to be established in Rhodesia or elsewhere. I believe that a general consensus of opinion among men who are not definitely interested in optimistic judgments endorses the conclusion thus stated by Mr. Bryce:—

"It seems probable, though not certain, that in many districts a mining industry will be developed which will give employment to thousands, perhaps many thousands, of natives, and to hundreds, perhaps many hundreds, of white engineers and foremen. Should this happen, markets will be created in these districts, land will be cultivated, railways will be made, and the local trades which a thriving population requires will spring up. But the life of these gold reefs will not be a long one. As the gold is found in quartz rock, and only to a small extent in gravel or other alluvial deposits, the mining requires capital, and will be carried on by companies. It will be carried on quickly, and so quickly, with the aid of the enormously improved scientific appliances we now possess, as to exhaust at no distant period the minerals which the rocks contain."[1]

Present probabilities thus do not indicate that any great development of gold-mining outside the Rand is likely to afford employment for such a large amount of British labour as will materially strengthen the proportion of British colonists to Dutch. If we turn from vague speculations of interested "boomers" to the evidence of sober facts, the Witwatersrand remains the one large solid *fait accompli*, and it is to the further development and life of this goldfield that we must look for the required stimulus to British immigration.

The political future of the Transvaal and of South Africa evidently depends, more than upon any other economic factor, upon the growth of the gold output of the Rand, the demand for white labour attendant on this growth, and the duration of the large profitable working of these mines. It must be remembered that the gold of the Rand is now believed to have been thoroughly explored, and although there is no precise agreement as to the depth at which gold can be profitably worked, the aggregate value of the gold which it was estimated in round numbers, some three years ago, could be taken from these mines was put down at £700,000,000. The evidence of several American experts, apparently accepted by the Chamber of Mines, and placed in evidence before the

[1] Page 439.

Industrial Commission in 1897, supports this computation, though Mr. Hays Hammond and some other engineers, having regard to the development of more favourable conditions enabling lower-grade ores to be profitably worked, consider this figure too low. But let us take as the basis of our calculation a higher estimate of the wealth of the Rand, and placing it at £800,000,000 instead of £700,000,000, deduct from that total £50,000,000, as approximately representing the actual output of the last few years since these estimates were formed. On this computation there will remain £750,000,000 of future output. Now, in considering the political and social influence of this industrial asset, it is convenient to begin by considering the probable duration of this industry. How long will the Rand last? Fifty or sixty years, with a probable extension, is the general answer that is given. Captain Younghusband, who went pretty thoroughly into the matter, thinks "it is a safe forecast to say that fifty years hence the gold resources of the Transvaal will not have been exhausted," and evidently looks forward to a considerably longer life than this; while Mr. Bryce holds that "it is practically certain that this production and population will go on increasing during the next few years, and that the mines will not be worked out before the middle of next century at earliest." But this opinion of Mr. Bryce, and the general opinion with which it coincides, is evidently based upon the supposition that the output of 1898, amounting to some £15,000,000, was a sort of maximum. Now can we accept such a limit? It is to the economic interest of the mining financiers to suggest a long life to the mines, but it is to their interest as mine owners to get out of the mines in any given time the maximum output which can be profitably got. The

INDUSTRIAL FUTURE OF SOUTH AFRICA

actual figures, indicative of the growth of the Rand output since its discovery, do not justify the belief that £15,000,000, or any such limit, can be set upon the annual output; indeed, they make it tolerably certain that under a more secure Government, favourable to the mining industry, the next few years will see a very large increase of output. The following table of the yield since 1887 makes this quite evident:—

Year.	Value.	Output.
		Oz.
1887	£81,022	23,125
1888	726,821	208,121
1889	1,300,509	369,557
1890	1,735,491	494,817
1891	2,556,328	729,268
1892	4,297,610	1,210,868
1893	5,187,206	1,478,477
1894	6,963,100	2,024,163
1895	7,840,779	2,277,640
1896	7,864,341	2,280,892
1897	10,583,616	3,034,678
1898	15,141,376	4,295,608

Seeing that the gold production of the first eight months of 1899, in spite of the disturbed political and economic state of the country, exceeded that of the corresponding eight months of 1898 by nearly 30 per cent., it is pretty certain that the value of this year's output would have reached nearly £20,000,000.

Following these figures, we see a continuous rapid growth, checked only by the effects of the Raid, and even then but for a single year. There is no reason whatever to suppose that £20,000,000 or any other limit can be set upon the annual output. Indeed, it is made manifest by recent speeches of mining magnates that a large increase, not only of proportion of profits to expenses, but of output is expected to follow a settlement of the Transvaal under British supremacy. It is precisely upon this expectation that the prospect of a large British immigration, which shall give British settlers an unquestioned predominance of power, depends. There will, it is maintained, be a large demand for British labour in the mines and for the subsidiary industries upon the Rand, while Johannesburg will exhibit a great and rapid increase of British population.

Now, if we base our expectations of a large British population in South Africa upon the gold industry of the Rand, we seem to be confronted by the following dilemma. The belief in any considerable increase of the mining and subsidiary population rests upon the assumption that the output will proceed by leaps and bounds, as has been the case since 1886. But if this occurs, it results that the prospective treasure will be exhausted in far less than half a century. Our provisional estimate of £750,000,000 would last only twenty-five years if we suppose the average output to be £30,000,000 per annum, which output would be attained in about two years' time at the rate of growth manifested during recent years. Indeed, it is evident that those who talk confidently of the need of at least 150,000 Kaffirs for the mines contemplate at least so large an increase of output, for the maximum number of Kaffirs employed in 1899 in mining processes was less than 100,000 all told.

If a settlement, bringing improved railway communication with the north, better relations with the Portuguese, and safer transit to and from the mines, provide an indefinitely expanding supply of native labour at a price as cheap as or cheaper than the present, there is every probability that the growth of output may be far larger than that which I have named. As the richer mines are rapidly worked out, the output would of course decline, and some amount of gold-mining might linger for a considerable time. But the probabilities seem all against the maintenance of a large, tolerably regular industry, giving employment to great quantities of British labour. The remarkable regularity of the gold deposits, which distinguishes this from all other goldfields of the world, is no guarantee of a corresponding regularity of output or of employment. The tendency will not be that which we found in the diamond mines, to maintain a steady output. Even if the economic structure of the Rand should lend itself to an amalgamation as complete as that of Kimberley, no corresponding regularity of output would ensue. In the case of diamonds, restriction of output is due to the fact that any increase beyond the calculated limit would, by its effect on market prices, reduce the aggregate profit; no such results would follow in the case of gold. The tendency of the Rand mine-owners, whether they form a working combination or compete, will be to increase the present output to the utmost, restrained only by the difficulty of obtaining a sufficiently large, cheap, and efficient supply of labour. The only direct economic check upon such increase of output would be the fall in the general purchasing power of gold (*i.e.* a general rise of prices), and a fall in the rate of interest for money loans, which would ensue were vast quantities of gold forced on to the mints of the world. But the diminishing part which the gold supply plays in determining prices, and the increased demand for gold currency which is taking place in modern times, would so far mitigate such tendency as to make it an inconsiderable check upon the general tendency to get the gold out of the ground as fast as possible.

From the evidence tendered to the Industrial Commission it is clear that business men with a wide outlook contemplate a very rapid expansion of the mining industry beyond the present limits. One of the ablest of the American engineers upon the Rand, Mr. W. Hall, expressed the following opinion:—

"Aside from the city of Johannesburg, under the most favourable conditions, there is a possibility for employing, say, 30,000 whites and 250,000 blacks on the Rand. It is not, for purposes of my point, necessary to assume the full figures. We might accept 25,000 whites and 200,000 blacks outside of the city population as a not unreasonable probability, if very substantial reliefs are granted, and this within ten years; always provided that the black population can be made to come, stay, and work faithfully at the lower wage necessary for the development of this state of things."[1]

Mr. J. G. Hamilton, another well-known mining capitalist, recently calculated that in eight years' time the number of stamps used in the mines would be trebled.[2]

Now it is obvious that if such a forecast is even approximately true, it contemplates an output per annum nearly three times as large as that of last year, and the gold of the Rand, got out at such a pace, would not, according to the most liberal estimates, last twenty years. It is doubtless true that, if any such expansion of the mining industry took place, it would furnish employment for a considerably larger number of white miners than are at present there, and that a corresponding expansion

---

[1] Industrial Commission Report, p. 428.
[2] Report, Chamber of Mines, p. 463.

of the white trading population of the Rand might be anticipated. So far as this accession to the mining population was concerned, it would be predominantly British. Not so, however, the trading classes: foreigners, in particular German and Polish Jews, have for the last few years been taking an ever-increasing portion of the trade, and the trading future of the Rand belongs to them. A temporary boom in the building and related industries may draw into the country some British artisans, but most of the manual labour which lies beyond the present skill of Kaffirs is already in the hands of foreigners, and Johannesburg cannot be expected to furnish steady employment to any large number of British working-men.

It is distinctively to the growth of the white mining population that we must look for the numerical increase of British influence. If our power stands ultimately upon voting strength, it must reside in the persons of British miners who have settled down and made their home in the Transvaal. Now does present evidence indicate that any such large permanent settlement is probable? The dilemma which confronts us may be briefly stated thus. If so big and rapid an expansion of the Rand mining takes place as will double or treble the employment of white miners, the mines cannot last out a single generation, and no reasonable motive is furnished for Englishmen to make a settled home and to identify themselves with a country which can provide no permanent economic basis for their maintenance. If, on the other hand, an output is maintained which enables the mines to hold out for fifty years or more, no considerable increased demand for white labour is provided. So far as the past affords any clue to the future in South Africa, one would be driven to deny that any regularity of output and employment was probable. Taking into consideration the certainty of political disorders and financial fluctuations, it is unreasonable to believe that any considerable number of British miners will be provided with a steady permanent livelihood in the Transvaal. That a great burst of mining activity will follow any specious "settlement," I make no doubt. Probably within the next few years great quantities of gold will be got out; but that a few years of such prosperity will be followed by a signal collapse is quite as certain. The likelihood is that neither an enormous output over a small number of years, nor a smaller output over a large number of years will be maintained, but an irregular, incalculable blending of the two tendencies,—a condition of affairs peculiarly adverse to a safe permanent settlement of British citizens in the Transvaal.

Even if regularity and duration could be safely predicted of the Rand mining, it would not afford the required basis of British population in the Transvaal, for mining is not distinctively a white man's industry. Apart from certain skilled work in construction, the white man's part is chiefly that of overseer, and one of the chief "economies" of a progressive industry is the reduction of this class of labour. White labourers have hitherto been reckoned as about one to eight or ten of Kaffir labourers. There is, however, reason to believe that the proportion of white labour has been considerably reduced of late years, and that in the future the reduction will be far greater. Whereas the number of native labourers in regular employment on the Rand grew from 47,000 in 1896 to 67,000 in 1899, the number of white labourers during the same time increased from 7430 to 9476, a distinctly lower rate of increase. These numbers are considerably lower than the maximum employed at the close of 1898, when, according to the Chamber of Mines, there were upwards of 88,000 Kaffirs in employment. About the middle of last year the figures of black and white labour were approximately 95,000 and 11,000 respectively. Now the extremely high wages paid to white labour, an average of some £28 per month, furnish a more than usually powerful incentive to reduce the proportion of white workers. Though nine times as many blacks as whites were employed in 1895, a most careful analysis of expenses proves that white wages absorbed 34.3 per cent. of the working expenses of the mines, as compared with 28.6 per cent. wages of Kaffir labour. To reduce the wages of both white and black miners is, we observe, a fixed policy of the mining companies, but almost equally important is it for them to reduce to a minimum the employment of expensive British miners. How far it may be possible to displace white miners' labour, for skilled mechanical work and for superintendence, is doubtful; but if Zulus and Basutos can be got upon terms which oblige them to stay and undergo the necessary training, it is believed that some economy of this sort can be effected. But, quite apart from this, the progress of the mining industry on the Rand favours a reduction of white labour. Hitherto an enormous proportion of the labour has been in the work of construction and development, especially since the discovery of the deep levels. Now the statistics indicate that it is precisely for this work of construction and development that the largest proportion of white labour is required.[1] Though much work of this order must remain to be done, it will bear an ever diminishing importance as compared with the actual processes of getting gold. Thus the natural order of events favours an economy of British labour in the mines.

[1] *Cf.* Mr. Seymour's tables, Report, Indust. Com., p. 171.

If, therefore, we suppose the annual output raised for a certain number of years from £20,000,000 to £30,000,000, we cannot anticipate an increased population of more than 5000 British and other white miners, together with a much less than proportionate addition to the British portion of the trading and artisan classes of Johannesburg and other mining centres.

But, it may be said, what about the other great mineral resources, the coal and iron, the silver, copper, tin, and other undeveloped treasures? Have we not here the guarantees of a great industrial future, with large manufacturing towns furnishing a market for agricultural produce, which will likewise yield employment for a great farming population? The answer to these questions is that most of these treasures are at present mere paper assets, whose existence depends upon the assertions of interested "boomers"; they may or may not have a substantial basis, but at present they must be regarded as merely hypothetical resources. Of the reality of coal we do indeed possess assurance; it exists in large quantities, and is worked in the proximity of the Witwatersrand mines, in the Boksburg and Heidelberg districts, and also in the Middelburg, Lydenburg, and Pretoria neighbourhoods. But though a certain market for such coal is furnished by the mining industry, we have yet no assurance that its quality will make it pay either for steamship coaling or for ordinary manufacturing purposes. According to a recent official report, "the testimony of a prominent South African steamship owner is to the effect that Transvaal coal is not suitable for marine purposes;"[1] though it is only fair to add that the mining companies claim that their best coal, some of which is "little inferior to Cardiff

[1] C. 9073, p. 17.

INDUSTRIAL FUTURE OF SOUTH AFRICA

coal," cannot be put upon the market until railway communications are extended. There is no doubt that plenty of coal of low and medium qualities has been found, and that, if there were already in the country a dense, accessible industrial population, a big coal-mining industry could be established; but whether the existence of this coal can call into existence the requisite economic conditions for its working is quite another question. Those who talk of a speedy growth of manufactures and manufacturing towns add to the speculative optimism regarding coal a still more speculative optimism regarding iron. Captain Younghusband has some highly interesting suggestions about a great iron industry which he thinks possible. Since one of the most obvious external features in South Africa is the vast consumption of iron, it is only natural that the possibility of manufacturing it upon the spot should occur to the speculative economist. "Johannesburg is, one might almost say, built of corrugated iron, and among all the thousands of houses there I have seen only one which had not a corrugated iron roof. Even the houses of the Boers are now being roofed with this material instead of thatch. Might not all the corrugated iron required in the little townships, now everywhere springing up in the vicinity of the coal and gold mines, be manufactured here? Might not iron sleepers, rails, iron telegraph posts, lamp-posts, and many other things of simple manufacture, and requiring little more than casting or rolling, be turned out in this country?"[1] Possibly they may. It may even be that the day will come when steam-engines and complex mining machinery are produced along the Rand. But all this is purely hypothetical. There is nothing in the shape of solid achievements upon which we can rely for these

[1] "South Africa of To-day," p. 15.

sanguine hopes. Iron has been tested in various places; we hear of "a reef of magnetite, from 20 to 40 feet wide, extending for several miles alongside the coal, and of such quality as to yield 70 per cent. of metallic iron." We have little doubt that, within the next few years, the European investor will be invited to put his money into iron-mining companies in the Transvaal; but as yet the hard fact remains—iron has not been worked. Several things are needed to establish an iron industry which shall even furnish the simpler forms of manufactured goods. The first of these is the existence of abundance of good iron ore near to good and abundant coking coal; the second is a sufficient, a reliable, and a cheap supply of skilled white, and unskilled but trained, native labour. Even if the first requisite exists, which is, *pace* Captain Younghusband, still very doubtful, the second is conspicuously lacking, and must continue to be lacking for a long time to come, if for no other reason, for this, that the demand of the gold-mines, and their superior ability of enforcing their demands, will enable them to have the first pull upon every new labour market which may be opened in the north and along the east coast.

Although the existence of iron ore has been known for some years, no serious attempt has been made to utilise it; nor will the magical words "British supremacy" wield any spell to draw pig iron from the soil and put it into steel rails or corrugated sheets. The essential natural conditions for a successful iron industry are not yet shown to exist, and the economic conditions for working it are known to be wanting.

At present there is no solid basis of a manufacturing development in the near future: iron and coal are not worked or workable in any quantity. Indeed, the safest

INDUSTRIAL FUTURE OF SOUTH AFRICA

criticism upon the reckless language which interested *entrepreneurs* and their journalistic victims employ in painting the swift industrial emergence of the Transvaal is furnished by the sober figures indicating the small dimensions and slow growth of coal-mining [1]:—

Year.	Tonnage.	Value.
1893	548,534	£257,454
1894	791,358	359,694
1895	1,133,466	516,215
1896	1,437,297	612,561
1897	1,600,212	612,668
1898	1,683,004	...

A study of known facts and probabilities does not warrant any belief that South Africa has before it a bright immediate future, which, by the simultaneous development of mineral, manufacturing, and agricultural resources, shall implant a large British population with a practical political control of the country. An agricultural development presupposes a large industrial population; industrial development presupposes large mining and agricultural classes, whose needs it will supply by home manufactures; the profitable working of minerals implies the existence of large industrial centres. Each resource requires the prior development of the others for an effective stimulus. There does not exist such legitimate confidence as will evoke the simultaneous development of the related and dependent factors. The entire structure is aerial and unsubstantial. It is indeed possible, perhaps reasonable, to expect that, besides an addition to the unstable British population of the Rand, there will be some immigration into other industries in South Africa. Such an accession

[1] From C. 7093, and Report, Chamber of Mines, p. 401.

to the British Afrikander population might be a valuable political and social factor, if these new comers settled down, married, made homes, and reared families in South Africa. An examination of mining statistics shows how small a percentage of them have hitherto done this.

There are, however, those who confidently predict that a settled government under the British flag, with proper control of import duties and railway rates, will fix large numbers of these men as permanent colonists. They are probably mistaken. In the first place, as has already been indicated, the new Government is hardly likely to become cheaper than the old, even if it be somewhat more efficient. The taxation of the Transvaal, though accused of being excessive, has not been so much per head of the white population as the taxation of either of the British colonies. It is indeed complained that an undue proportion of this burden has fallen upon the Outlander population, but it is admitted that this same population owns the vast majority of the valuable property, both real and personal, in the country, and no system of taxation can be devised which can shift the incidence of taxes from the shoulders of the "haves" on to those of the "have-nots." It is quite likely that the proportion of the war expenses which the Transvaal will be called upon to pay, together with the expense of maintaining a large military force in the country, will more than balance any economy arising from more capable and less corrupt finance. Bearing in mind the low financial morality of the economic masters of the State, in whose hands the chief political power will actually be placed (attested by a long admitted practice of corruption), we cannot expect the future of the Transvaal to be distinguished by pure and disinterested administration and finance. Again, does any one acquainted with South African affairs believe that the disestablishment of the dynamite, the Netherland Railway, and other public concessions or monopolies will not be accompanied by a growth and extension of all sorts of private economic monopolies organised by Jewish rings?

Nor is there reason to expect any considerable reduction of import duties. The reckless charges made against the Transvaal Government of extortionate duties upon necessaries of life are groundless since the change of tariff in 1897, which shifted the chief strain of taxation from necessaries on to luxuries. A comparison of the duties on prime food-stuffs in the Transvaal and Cape Colony shows that the colonial taxation is considerably higher. I am assured by careful housekeepers who have lived in Johannesburg and Cape Town, that for articles of ordinary consumption the prices in the former are not appreciably higher. Many luxuries are somewhat more expensive; house rents in Johannesburg are considerably higher than in Cape Town, though not much, if any higher, than in Kimberley. Some fall in expenses of living may perhaps be likely to occur within the next few years, but there is no reason to anticipate any great reduction in the cost of maintaining family life along the Rand. When we bear in mind that the mining companies are counting on any reduction in expense of living, which may be effected, to enable them to make corresponding reductions of money wages, we perceive that no motive is provided which will induce white miners or other workers on the Rand to make a permanent settlement with their families. It will still continue to be cheaper and more desirable for them to live as single men, sojourners in a foreign land, saving money, sending it home and returning home themselves when they have made enough, or are tired of the arid life in a new and essentially uninteresting country.

It is impossible to converse freely with all sorts and conditions of men upon the Rand without being struck by the fact that very few regard it as containing the possibility of a satisfactory home. Underneath a certain superficial effervescent enthusiasm, partly the glamour of gold and speculation, partly the riotous zest of a free licentious life in a stimulating atmosphere, a profound dissatisfaction lurks. No number of Britons will cast their lot permanently in this bare land and build homes for posterity; they will go there and live in luxury (though not in comfort) for a term of years, if they are paid to do so, but they will not stay. What is particularly true of the Transvaal applies with considerable force to South Africa in general. People go to South Africa to make money, whether as capitalists or as workmen, when they have made it they intend to come away and generally do so. It is a common grievance, seriously impairing the economic prospects of the country, that almost every African millionaire deserts the land where he has made his wealth, settles in Europe, and drains Africa from a distance. The same is true of a large proportion of the professional men and traders in Cape Town, Port Elizabeth, East London, Durban. The men who have succeeded in making money in these places generally return to England with their families. The exceptions largely consist of men who have taken longer than they thought to make their pile, or have failed to make it; some of these, marrying out in the Colony, are tied by the needs and expenses of a family, who can be better launched in life out there than in the old country, which all British South Africans speak of and regard as "home." There are, of course, a certain number of well-established British colonial families, but there is no tendency for the number greatly to increase: the peculiar enthusiasm for South Africa which is the staple factor in Afrikander nationalism belongs chiefly to the Dutch country folk and seldom to the English townsman, nor is it likely that any new political condition or speedy economic change will graft it upon any number of newcomers. Least of all is the British working-man who migrates under the temptation of high wages likely to make his abiding-place in a country where the economic conditions are such as to give the virtual control of his life and work into the hands of a small number of international capitalists, in whose grip he will be helpless.

Even if there should be an industrial boom in South Africa which will draw a large number of British workers, they will not play the part required of them as a political factor: they will be a fluctuating population, following the changes of this most incalculable country, not fitting themselves by residence or other fixed status for the duties and privileges of sound citizenship, and possessing neither the political capacity nor the moral right to rule the destinies of a country which is not in any true sense "their own."

If we are guided in our judgment of the probable economic development of South Africa by the known and measurable facts of the past and present, instead of lending an ear to the unfounded generalities and the enticing speculations of financial or political promoters, we shall find no ground to suppose that a great British immigration, either into the Transvaal or into other regions of South Africa, is about to set in, which will enable "British supremacy" to be achieved and maintained by the process of giving equal rights and privileges to all civilised men south of the Zambezi. On the contrary, there is every reason to believe that the Dutch Afrikanders will continue to outnumber the British in any confederation of South African States, and in the several States, with the exception of Natal and the Transvaal, while in this last State the small British majority which, though not hitherto existing, may come into existence, will by its fluctuating character and conflicting interests be unable to muster a steady elective power which will meet the dogged and closely-welded political organisation of the Boers.

APPENDIX

TAXATION ON NECESSARIES OF LIFE

THE following table shows the comparative taxation of chief necessaries of life in the South African Republic and Cape Colony. The otherwise free list of the former is qualified by an *ad valorem* duty of 7½ per cent., while a similar duty of 3 per cent. must be added to the Cape Colony import duties. The result of this comparison is to show a far more liberal tariff in the South African Republic than in Cape Colony.

	Cape Colony.			S. A. R.		
	£	s.	d.	£	s.	d.
Tea, 100 lbs.	2	10	0	0	5	0
Chicory, 100 lbs.	0	16	8	0	7	6
Butter, per lb.	0	0	3	0	0	¾
Cattle for slaughter (each)	1	10	0	Free.		
Sheep and goats, ditto	0	5	0	Free.		
Meats (preserved in any form, including ham, bacon, beef, and mutton), per lb.	0	0	2	Free.		
Meats (tinned and potted), per lb.	0	0	2	Free.		
Meat (frozen), per lb.	0	0	2	Free.		
Vegetables (preserved), per lb.	0	0	2	Free.		
Lard, per lb.	0	0	2	Free.		
Coffee beans, raw, 100 lbs.	0	6	3	Free.		
Coffee beans, roasted, 100 lbs.	0	16	8	Free.		
Cheese, per lb.	0	0	3	Free.		
Kaffir corn, 100 lbs.	0	2	0	Free.		
Wheat, 100 lbs.	0	2	0	Free.		
Mealies, 100 lbs.	0	2	0	Free.		
Mealie meal, 100 lbs.	0	4	6	Free.		
Meal, wheaten, 100 lbs.	0	4	6	Free.		
Flour, 100 lbs.	0	4	6	Free.		

CHAPTER IV

THE NATIVES IN SOUTH AFRICA

IN all parts of South Africa the native races, roughly grouped under the generic title Kaffir, comprise the overwhelming majority of the population, and if the principle of the greatest good of the greatest number is to prevail in South Africa, their claims should be paramount. Though no exact figures are available, except in the Colonies, the natives seem to be about three times as numerous as the whites in Cape Colony and the Transvaal, twice as numerous in the Free State, ten times as numerous in Natal, while in Rhodesia, Portuguese territory, and other British and German protectorates, the proportion is much larger. While the total white population south of the Zambezi cannot much exceed 800,000, the blacks probably muster nearly 8,000,000. Probably three-quarters of these live in tribes under the direct rule of chiefs, many of them untouched by European influence, though others, like the Zulus, Basutos, and Bechuanas, are subjected to some slight control through white magistrates and native commissioners. Even in the Colonies hundreds of thousands live the old tribal life in locations especially assigned to them.

Not only is this Bantu population very large, it is growing more rapidly than the white population, owing to the restraints put upon tribal wars, execution for witchcraft, and the decimating influence of famines. Dr. Theal gives a large amount of evidence to show that the birth-rate is far higher among the natives than among the whites, and that in health and duration of life the superiority also lies with the native, and his general judgment is thus summarised: "A comparison between the number of people of that (the Bantu) race south of the Limpopo half-a-century ago and to-day is somewhat startling, for it reveals the fact that the increase by natural means is without parallel elsewhere."[1]

Some of these races are redoubtable warriors, armed like the Basuto, and to some extent the Zulu, with "civilised" weapons; others, like the Matabili and the Tongas, are still in a condition of crudest savagery. All of them are ignorant of the real power of their white neighbours, and few, if any, are reconciled to the restraints placed upon them and the invasions their territories have undergone. The native mind is dimly explored even by Europeans brought into the closest contact with it; the fiercer tribes are notoriously capricious, and subject to incalculable suspicions and gusts of passion. The dread of some large instinctively-concerted native rising, which should even comprise many of the tame industrial Kaffirs, is no idle fear, but one which every thoughtful statesman or soldier in South Africa has always had to keep before him. Whatever other issue of the present war there be, it is certain to leave behind it a highly dangerous disturbance of the native mind. Those best acquainted with peoples like the Zulus, Basutos, or Matabili, are aware that fear, not love or reverence, has been the chief factor in their submission, and the sight of their white masters fallen out and massacring one another is a most serious strain upon their nature. If the present conflict is con-

---

[1] Theal, "History of South Africa," vol. iv. p. 403.

THE NATIVES IN SOUTH AFRICA 281

cluded without a native rising the danger will still continue, for no one save an ignoramus believes that any other than a surface settlement is possible between Dutch and British for at least a generation. The prospect is indeed a dark one. Hitherto the two white races, however they might bicker among themselves, readily united to present a single front against the Kaffirs, and the moral influence of this race-harmony was even more potent in repressing native agitation than actual co-operation. The sudden, complete break-up of this harmony into a fierce, palpable, and lasting discord is nothing less than an upheaval of the very foundations of white civilisation in South Africa. If all the grievances of Transvaal misgovernment had been what they were described as being, nay, had the great pan-Dutch conspiracy itself been a reality, a policy entailing such grave consequences upon the fortunes of South Africa as this present war would have been too expensive and too hazardous.

But, it may be said, the establishment once for all of the British supremacy throughout South Africa will place the native question on a new and a safer footing. "The unrest, suspicions, and hostility of the natives have arisen chiefly from the oppressive and cruel treatment by the Boers, who have continually harried them by invasions, stolen their land, maltreated them as slaves or servants, denied them religious education and the rights of citizens. British rule will alter all this, and will secure them justice and protection for their lives and property, together with educational and other means of attaining civilisation."

This is the theory widely accepted in England just now, and there are many who are genuinely persuaded that one motive which justifies and purifies this war is that it will afford protection and benefit to the native races. Bold comparisons have been set forth by missionaries and politicians of the different treatment accorded respectively by English and Dutch colonists, and of the feelings entertained in return by the natives.

Now in the first place the truth has always been obscured by a long-standing feud between English missionaries and Dutch farmers. From the early decades of this century the missionaries, who were the only Englishmen closely concerning themselves with the affairs of natives, set themselves to denounce to the British Government and the British public the treatment accorded the natives by the Dutch. Many of the tales they told were true and merited the reprobation they received; the back-country farmer, usually a Dutchman, has sometimes displayed gross injustice and brutality towards the Kaffirs on his farm, groups of frontier farmers not infrequently planned raids upon desirable Kaffir lands, and both collectively and individually manifested a total disregard for black men's rights. But, as more discreet historians admit, the sympathy and the credulity of missionaries often outran their judgment, and many of the charges which they brought were unfounded or grossly exaggerated.[1] What chiefly fanned the feud, however, was the political uses made of this humanitarian crusade to prevent the Dutch farmers from defending themselves against Kaffir incursions, and to restrain them from the encroachments which they wished to make upon the lands of savages. The emancipation of slaves, which was one of the immediate causes of the Great Trek, helped to fasten this policy upon the Imperial Government, and in all treaties with the Republics and enactments for government of

[1] Upon this point compare the eminently impartial work of Mr. Cloete, "The Great Boer Trek."

Protectorates the provision of protection for natives has figured conspicuously.

All this, it may be said, surely proves that we are animated by praiseworthy sentiments of freedom and justice, and that the Imperial paramountcy in South Africa will win the gratitude and affection of the native races. And it may fairly be admitted that so far as governmental power in the administration of native affairs actually emanates from Downing Street, and from the representatives of the Imperial power in South Africa, consideration and humanity characterise the policy.

But what is not sufficiently understood in England is the fact that this humane policy, commonly styled "Exeter Hall," is denounced and repudiated quite as vehemently by the great majority of British colonists as by the Dutch. The "missionary," I might add the essentially Christian, view of the native, as a man and a brother with a soul and body of his own and a right to determine his own destiny, is no more popular among the British than among the Dutch of South Africa. I do not say there is no difference between the Dutch and British view. The former for the most part frankly regard the natives as animals which they have a right to use for their benefit as they use a horse or cow: if they are kindly persons they treat them well, if brutal they treat them ill. It hardly occurs to them that they are concerned with persons who have a right of freedom or of property: the traditions of slavery drawn from their ancestors still survive in various ways, and the notion that a Kaffir has a right to demand wages finds reluctant harbourage in many of their breasts. The British, for the most part new-comers, accustomed to social grades but not to slavery, simply look upon the Kaffir as a low type of humanity: they have no more reluctance than the Dutch in setting him to labour for their benefit, but they distinguish him a little from the rest of the animal kingdom. So far as actual treatment is concerned, there can be little doubt that the average Briton is less given to cheating and physically maltreating Kaffirs whom he employs than the average Dutchman. But that cannot altogether be accounted unto him for righteousness. Britons are chiefly dwellers in towns, where public opinion has some restraining influence and where the practical liberty of blacks is necessarily greater; the life of the Boer farmer from its isolation makes for brutality, and his power over his black servants is well nigh absolute. If we are to make a fair comparison, it must take British and Dutch in the same environment, and such comparison is very difficult. I have been often told that Kaffirs would sooner work for English than for Dutch farmers, because the former treated them more kindly and they were surer of their wages; but my informants were always British, and Dutchmen told me quite another story, insisting that the Dutchman got on better with the Kaffir because he understood more of his ways from long experience, and could handle him more intelligently.

Again, a comparison is often made between the position of Kaffirs in Cape Colony, where they can own land, move about freely, enjoy some opportunities of education, and hold a franchise on equal terms with whites, and the Transvaal, where they may not own land, cannot move without a permit, cannot buy liquor, and are destitute of political rights. But nothing can be more fallacious than such comparison as a test of race feeling. No one acquainted with the views of the Outlanders will suggest that, if the political power in the Transvaal passes into their hands, they will use it to liberate the Kaffirs from the restrictions imposed upon them now. On the contrary, we have heard from the mouths of representative men their real intentions, viz., to tighten the lax administration of those very laws which discriminate blacks from whites, and to introduce a new system of taxation which shall have the effect of "forcing labour."

I have tried to compare the Dutch and the British treatment in general terms. But if we are to assess the claims of our present crusade for the liberation and elevation of the Kaffirs, we must rather compare with the old tyranny of the Boer farmer the new tyranny of the mining capitalist. I will not call him British, for he is generally not. What this new tyranny is like to be has been sufficiently expounded on its economic side in a recent chapter: the Kaffir with his family is to be placed in a position in which he cannot refuse his labour, and that of his family, for whatever wages the mines choose to offer.

This is the very core of the native question from the standpoint of the South African capitalist. Mr. Fitzpatrick's position on the matter is thoroughly representative. "It is one upon which there is a great divergence of views between the people of Europe and the people of South Africa. South Africans believe that they view it from the rational standpoint, they believe also that Europeans, as a rule, view it more from the sentimental. The people who form their opinions from the writings and reports of missionaries only, or who have in their mind's eye the picturesque savage in his war apparel as seen at Earl's Court, or the idealised savage of the novelist, cannot possibly understand the real native. The writer holds South African views upon the native question, that is to say, that the natives are, to all intents and purposes, a race of children, and should be treated as such, with strict justice and absolute fidelity to promises, whether it be of punishment or reward; a simple consistent policy which the native mind can grasp and will consequently respect."[1]

We know what this talk about "children" means. One of our own minor poets, writing of the Boers, says they are "little children," and amiably suggests that "Some little children must be whipped with fire." The South African notion is that a race of children should be set to toil for the profit of their parents, instead of being educated for an independent manhood. This notion is to be found sometimes in England too. It is the view of some Lancashire parents, who are satisfied to send their offspring to the mills, instead of keeping them at school, that they may live in idleness on the wages of the young half-timers.

Let the friends of humanity who approve this war take due note of this "rational standpoint" and this "simple consistent policy."

"Dreams of empire," the whole mission of civilisation, when submitted to the practical test, shrivel up into this very meagre sordid reality. "We have all got to think over the proposition why the English labourer works at the rate of twelve shillings a week, why the Indian works at twopence a day, and why we pay, including food, £4 a month.... And if you ask me for a big foreign policy, it is the question whether we can bring these natives to understand the dignity of labour, and whether we can make arrangements with neighbouring States to co-operate in bringing that about."[2]

[1] "The Transvaal from Within," p. 328.
[2] Mr. Rhodes at Cape Town, as reported by the *Cape Times*, 29th October 1894.

Friends of humanity who favour this war because it will release the native from the tyranny of the Dutch farmer and make him a cheap miner, may be invited to reflect upon the working life of these black miners, huddled together in compounds, without their womenkind, and either subjected to despotic and degrading restrictions on their liberty, or else exposed to the full temptations of all the vices of European civilisation. Apart from the floggings and other brutal ill-treatment in the mines, of which we have official evidence,[1] I have found a virtual unanimity among missionaries and native commissioners as to the demoralising influence which life at the mines, particularly in the Transvaal, is exercising upon native life. The habit of strong drink, which few, if any, Kaffirs can resist, is first contracted at the mines, and is then introduced into the tribal and domestic life. It is true that the mines are generally in favour of a prohibition policy, and are strong opponents of the demoralising liquor traffic which robs them of twenty per cent. of the working time of the "boys." But it is practically impossible to keep down a trade so profitable as the liquor trade, over an area so large as that of the Rand. In spite of well-attested endeavours to enforce the law prohibiting the sale of liquor to Kaffirs, drunkenness has been widely prevalent, and will continue. There is something almost humorous in the anxiety betrayed by mine owners for the "morals" of the boys. Listening to their language one might sometimes imagine that philanthropy was a branch of the mining industry, until one is rudely recalled to sober fact by some such remark as that made by Mr. Way, a mine manager, at a recent meeting

[1] See Annual Report, Chamber of Mines, 1899, pp. 92, 94; also Bluebook of Native Affairs (Cape Colony), 1899, p. 34.

of the Chamber, who "mentioned as a striking instance" (of the evil of the liquor traffic) "that last Sunday, out of 950 boys, he had only 250 at work." Even worse are the effects of sexual vice. In the Cape Blue-books we find sandwiched in pages of dry statistics such statements as this: "Many cases of syphilis are introduced from Johannesburg and Kimberley."[1]

The following testimony to our attempts to civilise the native and teach him the dignity of labour deserves attention, coming, as it does, from a resident magistrate who has devoted many years to a sympathetic study of native questions. In reporting the condition of the natives in the district of Nqamakwe, Mr. Scully writes: "On the one hand, we are able to record a satisfactory advance in the direction of education and church building; on the other, a deplorable demoralisation on the part of the young men, who go out to work in large numbers, and return from the mines 'brutish in their knowledge.'" "The state of health of the natives cannot be looked on as satisfactory. Phthisis is steadily increasing among them. There can be no doubt whatever that this is largely due to the adoption of European clothing, which is eminently unsuited to people living in structures such as the native hut; brandy-drinking; the contrast between life as lived by the men at home and at the mines when they go to work—all these are having their inevitable effect upon the native physique. Rheumatism is becoming more and more prevalent. Among children pulmonary diseases carry off a large number, and leave many permanently weakened. I regret having to report, having reason to believe that syphilis has taken hold of the people, and that it is gradually

---

[1] Blue-book, G. 31, 1899, p. 76.

increasing. It is estimated that probably three per cent. of the local natives are syphilitic in some form."[1]

Those who are persuaded that in breaking up the natural Kaffir life, in teaching them regular habits of labour, and in instilling into them new wants and habits which British trade can profitably satisfy, we are carrying on a crusade of humanity and civilisation, may be invited to ponder this evidence.

But it may be said, "All this is no doubt deplorable, but the evils you describe are chiefly due to abuses of capitalist power, which the Imperial control will set itself to check. Neither the mine owner nor the ordinary coarse-minded colonist is going to have his way with the native. England is going to be the protector and the elevator of these lower races; she is going to secure for them the benefits of religion and education, and to give them in good time that full measure of civil and political rights which is essential to the civilisation of every people."

This is a sound and generous theory; but, unfortunately, it cannot be embodied in practice. No amiable regulation from Downing Street can secure the practice of a policy opposed to the inclinations and convictions of the overwhelming majority of the British and Dutch Afrikander populations.

Both white races are strongly opposed to the liberation and elevation of the native, and the British are no more likely to lend their aid to carry out an Exeter Hall policy than the Dutch. It is true that a vigorous educational movement has been permitted among the Cape Kaffirs, that Christian missions have been encouraged, and that an increasing number of Kaffirs have been

[1] Blue-book, G. 42, 1848, p. 82.

allowed to acquire and exercise the franchise. Here and there I have found a man who believed in the intelligence and educability of the Kaffir races, and who believed that they ought to have free scope in the future of South Africa. Among this small minority are some men of high distinction in the Colony, such as Mr. Rose Innes and Mr. Solomon. But the vast majority set aside as utterly abnormal the instance of the Fingo statesman Jabavo and the handful of other natives educated at Loveday College, and deny alike the right and the capacity of Kaffirs to place themselves on a footing of equality with whites.

There is a virtual unanimity among white South Africans that the natives must be kept down; nine-tenths of the British colonists with whom I conversed regarded the Kaffir franchise as an anomaly which would have to be removed if it became a really potent factor at elections and Kaffirs showed any capacity for political organisation on a race basis.

Even the bestowal of elementary education is considered dangerous by most, and Christianisation is only favoured or condoned so long as the management of native churches is entirely in European hands. The growing determination of the natives to manage their own congregation, and the establishment of a vigorous Ethiopian Church, is regarded by most colonists as a dangerous symptom of rebellion. Let me quote upon this point the testimony of Mr. Rhodes, given so long as five years ago: "When he was travelling in the Transkei he found some excellent schools, but they were teaching the people Latin and Greek, and turning out a peculiar class of human being, the Kaffir parson—(laughter). Now the Kaffir parson was a most excellent type of individual, but he belonged to a class that was overdone. They were being turned out by the dozen, were wearing the black coat and white tie, and the consequence was that, in the absence of suitable openings for them, they were becoming agitators, beginning to say the Government was wrong and that the people were oppressed, and, in a word, bade fair to become a dangerous class."[1]

Educated niggers are no more popular with the British in South Africa than they are with the British in India; there is not, either among the British or the Dutch, any real growth of liberal feeling upon native questions. The existence of a Kaffir vote in Cape Colony is likely to prove a serious obstacle in any scheme of federal government based on elective institutions. The British majority in Natal will no more dream of allowing political power to niggers than the Dutch majority in the Transvaal or the Free State.

Let no one deceive himself. This strong deep-rooted general sentiment of inequality cannot be over-ridden by Imperial edict. Any attempt to secure real substantial equality of rights for the natives of South Africa will involve us in hostility with British and Dutch alike, and indeed furnishes the not improbable bond of future union of the now disrupted races which will eventually sever South Africa from the control of Great Britain.

This opposition to the education and elevation of the natives is based only in part upon fears lest a power, either constitutional or political, should be formed, which would threaten the political supremacy and endanger the persons of the whites. It stands chiefly upon a solid economic sentiment which, though seldom expressed,

[1] *Cape Times*, July 27, 1894.

is everywhere operative. The white races form a permanent economic aristocracy; no hard manual work is done by whites. Not that the climate disables white men from manual work: excepting in parts of Natal, white men can stand field work even in the summer and can labour at other manual employment without injuring themselves, though there is reason to believe they cannot work so hard or so long as in Europe. The presence of large supplies of available Kaffirs has simply converted the entire white population into a parasitic class living upon black labour by methods which resolve themselves, when properly considered, into "force." This statement will only appear exaggerated to those unversed in the interplay between the political and economic arts whereby the operation of rudimentary physical compulsion is concealed. Some of the crude forms of this interplay have occasionally emerged in the shape of labour taxes, indenture, Glen Grey Acts. But the entire system of South African society stands upon various modes of coercing Kaffirs into working for the benefit of whites, by invading their territories, goading them to reprisals, depriving them of their land and cattle, breaking down their tribal system, tempting them by strong drink and guns, and in one way or another placing them in such a position of political and economic weakness that they are unable to refuse wage work upon terms offered by white masters.

Hardly any white South African seriously believes that any essential change in these economic relations between white and black races is possible or desirable. Virtually all, British and Dutch alike, acquiesce in what is to all intents and purposes a serf-civilisation. The aspirations of justice and liberty for lower races which genuinely inspire many Englishmen, have no echo among white South Africans. The genuine believers in the progressive future of the Kaffir races in South Africa are a mere handful of men looked upon as "faddists," not dangerous because they are so few and so impotent for serious action. Do not mistake me. Large numbers of South Africans believe in what they call a just and humane treatment of the natives, but what they mean is the kindly treatment of permanent inferiors, children who can never grow up, and with whom a firm considerate coercion takes the place of genuine education.

We must look forward to a continuance of the present absolute social cleavage between blacks and whites, and to the maintenance of existing divisions of economic functions. Manual work has become a badge of shame for white men, because it puts them on a level with the Kaffir: wherever working conditions are such that white must co-operate with black, the former is soon seen to have shifted what is arduous, monotonous, or disagreeable on to the back of the latter, and to have made a "servant" of him. Some skilled manual labour in mining, building, or manufacturing trades is done by whites, but all told it amounts to very little, and most of it which lies outside the range of Zulus, Fingoes, and other more educable Kaffirs, is shifted on to Cape boys and other "coloured" or half-breed men. Mr. Bryce well summarises what he found: "The artisans who to-day come from Europe adopt the habits of the country in a few weeks or months. The English carpenter hires a native 'boy' to carry his bag of tools for him; the English bricklayer has a native hodman to hand the bricks to him which he proceeds to set; the Cornish or Australian miner directs the excavation of the seam and fixes the fuse which explodes the dynamite, but the work with the pick-axe is done by the Kaffir. The herdsmen who drive the cattle or tend the sheep are Kaffirs, acting under the orders of a white."[1]

The fact is, that South Africa is not in any true sense a white man's country, for though white men live they do not work there save in the capacity of overseers of serf-labour. No satisfactory civilisation can possibly arise where two races live together without blending, one superior in cerebral development and using this superiority to impose all the burden of directly productive labour upon the other, while it despises this inferiority. This essentially parasitic life visibly impairs the moral fibre of the white peoples, and inevitably tends to the mental and even physical degeneracy which develops in all slave-owning communities.

Neither in mental attitude nor in practice does much real difference exist between British and Dutch in the treatment of the native: if the vicious habits I have described seem more crudely prominent among the Dutch, it is because they are from longer residence more firmly rooted in these oppressive habits, and by incessant and more dangerous collision with native tribes have taken on more of their savagery. The recent history of Rhodesia is enough to show, if such new testimony be wanted, that Englishmen are only too liable to the same temptations. Let those who think this war will issue in benefit to African natives remember that its first and most tangible result will be to place large new tracts of Africa north of the Zambezi and along the East Coast under the exploitation for purposes of "cheap labour" of the very

[1] "Impressions of South Africa," chap. xxi.

THE NATIVES IN SOUTH AFRICA

men who have so plainly violated the sacred trust of civilisation in Rhodesia.

Let us get rid at all hazards of the cant about a righteous war for redress of native grievances. This war may procure for us more gold and more cheap labour, but there is not much likelihood that it will issue even incidentally in any gain to natives. No betterment of native treatment can in the nature of the case be imposed upon South Africa from Downing Street: a matter of such intimate detailed internal policy must always remain in the hands of South Africans. Dutch and British South Africans do not widely differ in the view of native questions, and if they did the British could not practically control the Dutch, whose social and economic relations with the natives over most parts of the country are far closer. In so far as the future of the British in South Africa is linked with the exploitation of mines, there is, unfortunately, at present little reason to believe that the kind of man who will control this industry, and the profitable ends he has in view, will in any way contribute to that elevation of the native races which we profess to have at heart.

CHAPTER V

FEDERATION OF STATES

IF Great Britain succeeds in breaking the military power of the Boer Republics, two related questions will arise, one having reference to the treatment of the conquered territories, the other to the federation of States in South Africa. Upon the latter and larger matter history has something to say, for "federation" is no new term in South African affairs.

In 1859 the greatest of our proconsuls in South Africa, Sir George Grey, proposed to the Home Government a scheme whereby the legislatures of Cape Colony, Natal, and the Orange Free State should be empowered to form "a federal union embracing Kaffraria within their limits, and with authority to adopt into the Union, then or thereafter, all States which might wish to join them, including Native States, with large powers of self-government."[1] In a series of despatches he opened up the subject fully, and suggested the inclusion in such a Union not only of the Free State but of the Transvaal. So far as the Free State was concerned there was no slight reason to believe that she might acquiesce in such a scheme. The burghers were divided at this time, some in favour of federation with the Colony, others in favour of federation with the South African Republic. If a scheme could have been devised acceptable to the latter State, no difficulty with the

---

[1] "Life and Times of Sir George Grey," p. 281.

FEDERATION OF STATES

Free State was to be anticipated. Even apart from any general scheme of union, President Bishof and a powerful section of the Free Staters openly advocated a federation with the Colony.

The broad statesmanlike principles which animated Sir George Grey's proposals are thus stated in the address made by him at the meeting of the Colonial Parliament in 1859: "You would, in my belief, confer a lasting benefit upon Great Britain, and upon the inhabitants of this country, if you could succeed in devising a form of federal union under which the several provinces composing it should have full and free scope of action left to them, through their own local governments and legislatures, upon all subjects relating to their individual prosperity or happiness; whilst they should act under a general federal government in relation to all points which concern the general safety or weal."

Although Sir George believed that he was acting in accordance with the wishes of the Imperial Government, he was rebuked for bringing the matter before the Cape Parliament, and was recalled from his post. Sir George Grey was the first great federationist in the British Empire, and it is desirable to mark clearly the two great principles upon which he proceeded.

The first may be thus stated in the language of his biographer: "His ideas concerning federation were not exactly similar to those expressed by many of the leading statesmen of Australasia. He did not believe in a hard and fast union, regulated by law, between States dissimilar in character, separated by great distances, and existing under different climates and conditions. He rather favoured a loose federation, which should leave each portion of the federated States free to work out its own destiny, and should yet enable all to join together for any great purpose; and so, in any crisis or sudden exigence, give to the whole that strength and solidity which springs from union."[1] In other words, it was a scheme of federal home rule which Sir George Grey proposed, that would easily admit widest diversity of forms of government in the several federated States. The other vital principle is illustrated by the language of his address to the Cape Parliament. Federation must come on the initiative, or, at all events, with the free consent and goodwill of the federating units. He does not ask the Imperial Government to devise a scheme, and then attempt to impose it on the Parliaments and Raads of South Africa, but he takes the favourable resolutions of the Free State Raad, and bringing them before the notice of the Colonial Parliament, invites the latter to "devise a scheme of federal union." Sir George Grey, though both an imperialist and a federationist, was far too wise to attempt to bring about federation by imperial pressure. Home Rule, not Imperialism, was to be the directing force in the affairs of South Africa. This was likewise the view of Lord Rosmead, so vigorously expressed in the speech in which he took leave of South Africa in 1889: "There are three competing influences at work in South Africa. They are Colonialism, Republicanism, and Imperialism. As to the last, it is a diminishing quantity, there being now no longer any permanent place in the future of South Africa for direct imperial rule on any large scale. With responsible government in the Cape, with Natal soon likely to attain that status, with the independent Republics of the Orange Free State and the Transvaal, and with Germany on the west coast and

---

[1] "Life and Times of Sir George Grey," p. 327.

Portugal on the east, the idea of the permanent presence of the imperial factor in the interior—of a South African India in the Kalahari—is simply an absurdity."

It is in complete accordance with the unfortunate history of the relations between Downing Street and South Africa that, some years after, having refused federation when it was proposed by the right man, with the right method, and at a specially favourable conjuncture of circumstances, the Imperial Government should have attempted to enforce it in South Africa by the wrong men, the wrong methods, in the teeth of circumstances. Yet such was the case. When Lord Carnarvon, in 1875, devised a new scheme of confederation on his own account, and sent Mr. J. A. Froude to urge it on the Governments and people of South Africa, he had little reason to anticipate a favourable reception.

Not merely the chief sufferer, the Orange Free State, but the entire Boer population had been recently exasperated by the injustice of the annexation of the Diamond Fields of Griqualand West: the Transvaal, though severely pressed by native hostility and financial straits, was in no mood to seek a British alliance, and the Cape Colonists were affronted at the suggestion of foisting upon them a cut-and-dried scheme of federation. Resolutions were carried in the Cape Parliament condemning the Colonial Secretary and his despatch, and the presence of Mr. Froude with his personal explanations entirely failed to win over the recalcitrant people. The opposition was not a distinctively Dutch one, for large numbers of British Afrikanders were quite as outspoken in their opposition to the scheme.

Mr. Froude, learning from experience the folly of endeavouring to force on such a measure, reported to the Home Government in favour of patience and conciliation, and advised the calling of a conference, which was held in London in August 1876, attended by representatives from the South African States, under the presidency of Sir Garnet Wolseley. Two courses were open to Lord Carnarvon: one was to adopt the conciliatory course urged by Mr. Froude, and to use the unrivalled gifts and experience of Sir George Grey to get it carried out; the other, to take personal charge, to appoint a governor and other officers imbued with a strong coercive spirit, and to force confederation at all hazards upon the States of South Africa. Unfortunately native perversity and ill advice impelled him to choose the latter course. Sir Bartle Frere was sent out in 1877 to school the Cape Colonists into submission, while Mr. Shepstone had been despatched in the previous year with a Special Commission, giving him power and authority to annex any territories adjoining the British Colonies, provided he were "satisfied that a sufficient number of the inhabitants desired to become our subjects." The extraordinary character of this Commission has never been fully realised. It meant simply this, that not only the Transvaal, but the Free State, the Portuguese territory, and any neighbouring native territories might be annexed at the absolute discretion of Mr. Shepstone. Add to this that the Commission was a secret one, and the climax of impolicy is reached.

The entire career of Sir Bartle Frere is a lesson in the folly of attempting to force an Imperial policy upon South Africa. Sent out as an avowed Imperialist to drive the Colony along a course it did not choose to take, Sir Bartle Frere soon found himself in open hostility to his Cape Ministry. The Ministry, strongly opposed to federation, naturally resented all attempts to assert the Imperial authority, and were dismissed by the Governor in consequence of their objection to assign the supreme control of the troops engaged in border warfare to the Imperial military authorities. One member of the Molteno Ministry thus dismissed, Mr. J. X. Merriman, is a member of the present Cape Ministry. The immediate appeal of Sir Bartle Frere to the voice of the colonists was successful upon the point in issue, and a substantial majority of the new House approved the action of the Governor. But this triumph was short-lived and entirely fruitless. The discreditable and disastrous Zulu War, culminating in the catastrophe of Isandhlwana, and involving the early supersession of Sir Bartle Frere, was one source of failure, not merely by discrediting in England the whole policy of Lord Carnarvon and his nominee, but by impressing upon British colonists, as well as Dutch, the grave dangers of the pushful Imperialism. But the collapse of the federation design was chiefly and directly due to the treacherous annexation of the Transvaal, which was intended as a signal step in the consummation of the policy. The visible injustice and oppression of this act destroyed altogether the amicable basis upon which Sir George Grey relied, and substituted one of naked force. The appeal made by the Transvaal burghers to their kinsmen of the Colony soon broke the popularity of Sir Gordon Sprigg's Ministry, and in the Parliamentary Session of 1880 the proposal of confederation was definitely rejected by the House, and thus disappeared from the stage of practical politics in South Africa. As a plank in the platform of the new Imperialism of Lord Beaconsfield's Government, it was swept away in the flood of unpopularity which overwhelmed the Conservative party in the elections of 1880.

Although no formal step towards political federation of the States of South Africa has taken place since 1880, there have been definite advances towards a business co-operation for certain specific purposes. The most important of these is the Customs Union. The Union Tariff was brought into force in Cape Colony by Act of Parliament in 1889, and was adopted later in the same year by the Free State. Any civilised State of South Africa may be admitted to the Union at six months' notice after a formal request made to the Governor of the Colony. British Bechuanaland thus became a member in January 1891, Basutoland in July of the same year, and the Bechuanaland Protectorate in July 1893. In 1898 Natal, hitherto recalcitrant and preferring to run a lower tariff of her own, entered the Union, which now only required the adhesion of the Transvaal to give it completeness.

Co-operation in the establishment and working of railway communication, though far less advanced and attended by much friction and dissension, must nevertheless be looked upon as a practical piece of federation. Though there is no common ownership of lines and rolling stock and no common management, since the Free State withdrew the control of its railways from the Colony after the Raid, there is such amicable co-operation between the different systems as is represented by the use of one another's rolling stock and arrangements for booking through. That we can buy a ticket for Johannesburg at Cape Town, or at Pretoria for Durban or Delagoa Bay, and can travel without changing carriages, is a very real and serviceable piece of federation.

It is along these lines of practical economic and social convenience, based upon felt union of interests, that sound spontaneous federation naturally moves. The folly of endeavouring to cast the forms of political federation before these natural bonds of common interest have become sufficiently numerous and closely set, ought to be one of the most obvious lessons of history.

Outside the community of interests represented by a Customs Union, a federal system of railways, and a common postal and telegraphic system, there are doubtless many other forces making for federation of States in South Africa. Too much, perhaps, is made of the uniformity of physical conditions and the absence of strongly marked natural boundaries of States. So also the present identity of economic interests, as indicated by the common dependency of all the States upon the resources and the requirements of the Rand, cannot be regarded as a factor of such permanent importance as to control an Imperial policy of federation. But the community of race and language, the fluidity not merely of the industrial but of the agricultural population in South Africa, their wide severance from other civilised white communities and their common liability to certain contingencies of internal disturbances or external attacks, certainly supply a basis of effective political co-operation.

It seems an idle platitude to point out that federal constitutions cannot be manufactured, but must grow by voluntary action based upon a recognition of common interests. That the community of real interests will in the long run prove adequate to furnish a federal constitution in South Africa seems certain: that the time is yet ripe is far from certain. What has hitherto impeded this natural growth? Chiefly political jealousies.

and suspicions between States and races. Has the current of recent events served to increase or to abate these jealousies and suspicions? There can unfortunately be no hesitation in answering this question. The tenor of events from 1895 to the present moment has been a constant stream of separatist influence among States and races.

The formal antagonism between the Republics and the British territories in South Africa has been visibly growing during the last four years; the Free State in particular has been alienated from her close Colonial relations and has been driven into a hostile camp. The Governments and the peoples of Cape Colony and Natal are further out of sympathy than they have ever been. Underneath these divisions, and worse than them, is the fatal growth of a race antagonism exasperated by the present bloody conflict which, under the most favourable conditions of "settlement," will render any sincere co-operation impossible for generations between those parts of South Africa which are dominated by a Dutch Afrikander population and those which are of British race and sympathy. As a sequel of successful war a scheme of formal federation may be forced upon South Africa, but the forcing process in itself must nullify all possibility of successful operation. I do not merely allude to the feelings of the population of the conquered provinces. But I would put to those who look to federation of South Africa as a worthy and profitable result of our present enterprise these questions: "Does the past history of Cape Colony justify us in believing that her population, the majority of whom resent bitterly the policy of the present war, will consent at the present juncture to abrogate their rights as a self-governing colony and to receive from the hands of

Mr. Chamberlain at Downing Street a scheme of federation which is avowedly designed to establish a British Imperial control over South Africa by diminishing the independent action of the majority of the electors of Cape Colony? Will the Cape Colonists, with the last twenty years' experience in mind, and goaded almost to frenzy by the injury and insults of this strife, consent in 1900 to adopt a scheme of federation which they refused in 1880?" Such a scheme can only be forced upon South Africa by some signal abrogation of the rights of free self-government in Cape Colony, an abrogation which would be received with present applause by the party defeated at the polls last year, but which would, by loosening the very foundation of confidence in British rule, introduce as a permanent factor in colonial politics that racial disloyalty which, in spite of false accusations, has never existed in the past, and which would by its disintegrating influence destroy the reality of any federation.

Federation of States in South Africa, as elsewhere, must be of spontaneous internal origin, and must be based upon the clear recognition of a community of interests and feelings, what is called a "union of hearts." Where and when this condition is lacking, no real federation is possible. A scheme of federation imposed as a result of military conquest cannot endure; coming into being by the sword, it will either perish by the sword or collapse from internal impotence.

CHAPTER VI

THE TRUE LINE OF BRITISH POLICY

THE large space given in this volume to the causes and antecedent circumstances of the war is due to the necessity of breaking down a most dangerous fallacy which has obsessed the public mind, that once embarked upon the struggle it is idle to consider causes, and that even when the time comes for settlement, justice and expediency can be projected upon a future policy which need not closely scrutinise the past. The intellectual anarchy implied in this catastrophic view is one of the most signally injurious results of popular passion blinding a nation.

Hardly less instructive, however, are the crude notions about the future of South Africa expressed by not a few of our responsible political leaders. I may for convenience paraphrase their view as follows: "After the war has been brought to a successful close by the capture of Pretoria and Bloemfontein, British supremacy will be firmly established in the Transvaal and the Free State; the Boers, recognising they are fairly beaten, will respect the power of Great Britain, and, after the first soreness has passed away, will settle down in amicable relations with the Outlanders and the British officials, acknowledging the superior justice, purity, and efficiency of British rule; after a brief interregnum of military control, equal rights will be accorded to all whites, the proportion of the British population enabling them to exercise effective control over the internal policy of the States; while a federation of South African States will establish once for all the absolute supremacy of Great Britain south of the Zambezi, impose a uniform and superior government over the whole country, and secure humane treatment for the native races, educating them to take a proper place in the future civilisation of South Africa."

Now, if the facts recorded in the chapters of this volume are substantially correct, this view of a coming settlement is dangerously and manifoldly false.

I will not dwell upon the military aspects of the case except to remind readers that Pretoria, Bloemfontein, and the other towns of the Republics are not great centres of wealth and population, like the capitals and chief cities of European States, but little places with small populations almost entirely of Outlanders who own most of the property.

Although to take and hold the centre of government is doubtless an important step towards obtaining the practical control of a country, it is far less important in the Republics of South Africa than elsewhere, because it gives little direct hold upon the persons or the property of the burgher population.

The easy, amiable talk about the Boers taking their beating gracefully, and settling down quietly under an Outlanders' rule supported by British force, or even under a directly British rule, is contradicted by the entire tenor of the history of the Republics, as well as by the common knowledge of human nature. The crude psychology of the pugnacious schoolboys, who hammer respect and affection into one another by a bout of fisticuffs, is void of truth; it is, in fact, nothing but a paradoxical extension of the mischievous maxim, *Si pacem velis para bellum*. Boys who have fought generally hate one another, nations always do. As for respect, it is possible that individual Boers may have some increased respect for the courage of individual Britons, but that will not mitigate their hatred and abhorrence of the British power, which has used its superior weight and numbers to crush a smaller people. Why should it? What basis for legitimate respect are we offering, by bearing down through sheer numerical superiority a people who will rightly boast that we tried to meet them man for man and ignominiously failed? Should we, their not remote blood kinsmen, settle down meekly under a beating from an immensely bigger nation than ourselves?

Those who utter this preposterous surmise are possibly misled by their conviction that our just interference implies a sort of feeling among the Boers that they are in the wrong, and that a fuller conviction of this truth, following punishment, will help to teach them resignation. Whereas the exact contrary is the case. The Boers to a man believe, with a long-settled passionate conviction, that theirs is a holy war, fought to preserve the independence of their country from the assaults of greedy foreigners in their midst who have cajoled the British Government to take part in a conspiracy for territorial plunder.

No one who has witnessed the uprising of this national spirit in the Republics on the eve of war is likely to entertain for a single moment this notion of a speedy acquiescence of beaten Boer nations; no one who has read their history, and knows the root-factors of their race character, will endorse such a notion.

Will all the disillusionments we have sustained serve to teach us nothing? Shall we still fondly cling to the belief that the Boers will recognise themselves beaten, and lie down beneath the heel of a conqueror?

They will do no such thing. They will fight to the end; beaten in set battles, their chief towns taken, they may disperse to their farms, and defend them with the help of their women, or many of them may take to the open hilly country of the North, and carry on a troublesome guerilla warfare for an indefinite number of years. The Johannesburger or the town British colonist, who before the war declared the Transvaal Boer would not fight, and that in no case would the Free State enter the conflict, now declares that the beaten Boers will settle down on amicable terms with the men who got in foreign troops to crush them and to hold them down. False in their former judgment, are these people to be trusted now? These British townsmen do not know the country Dutch; those who have lived among the latter upon terms of sympathetic intimacy ridicule the notion. The selective process of several treks has made the Boers of the Republics a race in whom detestation of British rule is the most distinctive trait; is the present tribulation of their country likely to eradicate this trait?

The attempt to enforce British rule upon the Republics is likely to turn out a longer and a costlier process than we reck—costlier in blood and money, and futile in the end. It is doubtful if we can spare the strength which will be needed for keeping the Boers of the Republics as a subject race.

It may be said that this is not our policy or our intention; when a firm settlement is once effected, we shall give equal rights to all under the British flag. But will this prove a satisfactory settlement? It will evidently work out in one of two ways. Either the Outlanders will be dominant as a political party, in which case the mining magnates, who have organised this attack, will rule the Transvaal as De Beers rules Kimberley, controlling the Outlander vote by economic force; or, if the old burgher party should remain more numerous, or should detach enough of the non-British Outlanders, then the British, whose flag floats at Pretoria, will find themselves outvoted at the polls, and subjected to the practical control of their enemies, embittered by the memories of the war, and bent on every sort of constitutional reprisal. Such is one of the dilemmas which will be the legacy of this disastrous war: the choice between an oligarchy of financial Jews, and a restoration of Boer domination.

A similar dilemma besets our government of South Africa as a whole. A long protracted period of coercion, during which the self-government of the colonies is overridden or superseded by military despotism and Downing Street, while some mechanical scheme of federation is similarly administered or controlled, would not only fatally retard the natural political development of South Africa, but would, if historic precedents have any weight, sap the loyalty even of the most loyal British colonists, and at no distant date sever South Africa from the British Empire. On the other hand, if we early and honestly fulfil our loudly expressed purpose of securing a real equality of political rights for the white races south of the Zambezi, we shall be handing over, not only in the Republics but in Cape Colony, the real legislative and administrative power to the Dutch, closely constituted as a party, and bitterly antagonistic to the British townsmen; while a federation, which shall keep the power in British hands, can only be achieved by a new partition of African territory, directed by the crudest art of jerrymandering.

If my estimate of the relative numerical strength of Dutch and British races, and of their probable increase, is approximately true, it will be impossible to make a federation of existing States upon a representative basis which will not hand the federal government to the Dutch. The specious method of punishing "disloyal" subjects or "disloyal" districts by disenfranchisement might provide a temporary and a purely formal solution of the difficulty, but it would entail the heavy price of a further education in disloyalty, and an exasperation of race feeling. Not merely would it afford no settlement; it would make settlement more difficult. The same result would ensue from the jerrymandering policy already plainly advocated in the press of the two colonies. To break up South Africa into six or seven States, so arranged as to give to the British colonists a permanent majority of federal representatives, would involve not merely an arbitrary and injurious redistribution of territory, but a visible and flagrant violation of that very principle of "equal rights for all white men" which we are affecting to establish. The proposal to give Mashonaland or even Natal an equal voice with Cape Colony and the Transvaal in guiding the destinies of federated South Africa would be patently unjust, and would soon be resented bitterly by the British as well as by the Dutch settlers. That the exorbitant claims now preferred by Natal, on grounds of her conspicuous loyalty, will receive the welcome assent or even the acquiescence of Cape Colony, no one who has followed the past relations of the two colonies will be inclined to believe. A policy plainly and avowedly adopted in order to secure the immediate political supremacy for the British by contorting the forms of election so as to achieve this end, far from aiding a settlement, would lay a permanent legitimate basis of discontent, and effectually retard the processes of *rapprochement* and fusion, without which peace and security of government are impossible.

Those who seek to consummate their recent impolicy of accentuating the separation of the Dutch and British races, by securing the permanent and visible supremacy of the latter, are engaged on a futile task. The true merit of the so-called British race has ever consisted in its power to assimilate the elements of alien white races with which by emigration or by immigration it has been brought into contact. It dominates and holds down by force many coloured races; it has never succeeded in practising such rule over white races. A South Africa in which the British, as a race or as a party, shall assert supremacy over the Dutch is a practical impossibility.

Even were it possible it would be plainly detrimental to all known processes of civilisation and good government.

Equally crude and fallacious is the notion of those who defend the present conflict by the application of a "scientific" law, according to whose operation the higher civilisation, represented by the British race, must replace the lower civilisation of the Dutch. This process of competition and of conquest by the higher race they assert to be a natural law of progress, which enables them to set aside all special moral considerations or particular expediencies, and to regard the present conflict as inevitable, a painful duty undertaken in the sacred cause of the civilising mission of Great Britain.

Full discussion of this farrago of false assumptions masquerading under scientific terminology is here impossible. It must suffice to say that it has never been proved that only one type of civilisation exists, or that the type represented by the life of modern industrial peoples is higher than, as well as different from, the type of the agricultural races in such countries as Burmah, China, or the Transvaal. To say that there exists one goal of civilisation for all the races of the world, one road along which progress lies equally for all, and that the Anglo-Saxon peoples are the possessors of this goal, and therefore the sole judges of the progress of other peoples, is at least a gratuitous assumption.

Turning from the region of nebulous theory to the concrete facts of life, and to the case most in evidence, it is at any rate open to serious question whether the civilisation of Johannesburg, the typical British product in South Africa, is higher, better, or more desirable than the simpler, ruder civilisation of the burgher population of the land. An impartial student of human societies, making a thorough investigation of social life in South Africa, would surely hesitate to pronounce the life of the towns—Johannesburg, Kimberley, Cape Town, Durban— and the characters and ideals of their inhabitants, to be intrinsically finer and worthier than the life, character, and ideals of the Dutch farming population.

One last and largest assumption in our opening hypothesis requires a word. Even if the firm abiding dominion of the British race could be established throughout South Africa, it would not secure the liberties and the progressive civilisation of our "black brothers." With a very few individual exceptions, the British Afrikanders have no more belief in the education and equal political rights of the Kaffirs than have the Dutch. Loyal Natal is quite as unlikely as the Transvaal to defer to the influence of the Imperial Government, should it ever be exerted in order to procure for black or coloured folk equal political and civil power with that conferred on whites.

Both races are agreed in accepting a serf-civilisation concealed under different thin disguises; both races regard the inferiority of the Kaffirs as permanent, and living on the manual labour of these inferiors, they develop of necessity the vices of a parasitic caste. These vices take different forms in town and country life, in agricultural and industrial societies, but their essential character remains one and the same. Whenever we speak of settlement, this abiding factor of racial cleavage and oppression must be kept in mind. It presents a permanent barrier to the attainment even of that distinctively British civilisation which some contend that we are justified in fighting for. This dark background of the South African problem can never be ignored.

If, however, we confine our attention to the white races and ask what is the best basis of settlement, the immediate answer is scarcely more satisfactory. There is no settlement, only different kinds and degrees of unsettlement. The really practical question, which I will ask but will not attempt to answer, is, "What issue of the war will least disturb the moral and social elements in South African life which were making towards amicable co-operation and fusion in the past?" The *status quo ante*, we are told, is impossible. That may be so, but a calm view of the situation, with a true understanding of the origin and nature of this war, suggests that the best "settlement" will be that which approaches nearest to this *status quo ante*.

In following the lines of such a settlement it is essential to renounce one conspicuous error of our recent policy, which more than any other has contributed to this catastrophe.

The Dutch Afrikander population and their leaders

must be heard with respect and sympathy, not as a concession but as a right. The fatuous folly which has, by charges of disloyalty, sought to evoke the very spirit which it exorcises must be abandoned. The Cape Ministry, chosen by the majority of the people, and the experienced leaders of that part of the population which recognises South Africa as "home" and has lived in it for generations, must no longer be set aside, ignored, and openly flouted in favour of a clique of councillors, mostly new-comers, and all with interests opposed to the interests of the people at large.

A policy of least disturbance of anterior conditions, involving the adherence to our earlier pledges to respect the "independence" of the Republics, I would urge not so much as a counsel of obvious expediency, though it is that, but as conformable to the commonly accepted standard of morality. Whether this war be accounted a crime or a blunder matters not: it is a sound and certain rule that any apparent gain which comes to the criminal or the blunderer out of his crime or blunder is no true gain but an injury. The nation has been told that it is seeking neither gold nor territory by this war: let it be clearly seen that she gets neither, and let us equally make sure, if we can, that those who are responsible as direct causes of this evil business, make no personal gain. The wages of sin is death, and, hard as it may seem, it is in the long run best this should be so. To seek to dodge the Nemesis of misconduct is as idle for a nation as for an individual. If the facts recorded here are substantially true, and the judgments substantially sound, the British people has been led into a crime, and no juggling with territorial boundaries or political institutions will enable her wholly to escape the penalty. Pay in the present she must in reputation, blood, and material resources: her best lovers, the truest patriots, will desire that, as she comes to a gradual recognition of her error, she may have the courage to proclaim her fault, and if, as is unhappily the case, full reparation is impossible, she may at least renounce the ill-gotten fruits of such a victory as she may win.

INDEX

African Review, the capitalist ownership of, 207
Afrikander Bond, The, formation, policy, and scope, 106, 108; charges against, refutation of, 100, 101-102, 113-114; account of meeting at Burghersdorp, 110-111
Agricultural outlook of South Africa, 251-256
Albu & Co., 191, 192
Albu, Mr., statement on native and white wage question, 235, 236
Appelbe case, The, 56
Arbitration question, 146-149, 167-169, 172-174
"Association of Mines," formation and object of, 192

BARNATO interest in Rand mines, 192
Basutoland, annexation of, by England, 141
Beck, Dr., speech on Imperialism, 107
Beit (*see* Wernher, Beit & Co.)
Blackmail (*see* Bribery)
Bloemfontein Conference, 6-8, 98, 164-169
British and Dutch population in South Africa, proportion, 244, 246; Dutch increase far greater, 247; racial and economic cleavage coincide, 247, 249; future proportion of, 278
British policy after the war, difficulties to be encountered, 306-314; errors to be avoided, 314-316
Boers, The (*see* under Transvaal)
Brabant, Capt., and South African League, 199

Bribery and corruption of Transvaal officials, 73-83
Bryce, Mr., farming in South Africa, 253; gold-mining in South Africa, 260, 261, 262; on native and white labour, 293
Bulawayo Chronicle, ownership of, 207
Burghership (*see* Franchise grievance)
Butler, Sir William, comparison of Johannesburg and Australian goldfields by, 56; on British policy in South Africa, 5

CACHET, Prof. J. C., speech against Rand agitators, 111
Cape Argus, the ownership of, 207
Cape "Boys" (*see* Native labour)
Cape Colony—
 Afrikander Bond (*see* that title);
 Afrikander press in, 110
 Afrikanders, attitude of, on eve of war, 99-105
 British and Dutch population, proportion, 244, 246
 British press, attitude of, 99, 100, 157; capitalist owners of, 206-228
 Disaffected districts, The, 103-105
 Dutch attitude towards English, 124, 125; dangers of a rising, 50; Dutch conspiracy (*see* that title)
 Expenditure compared with that of Transvaal, 86
 Jameson Raid, effect upon trade, 8, 9
 Money voted for Imperial Navy by Afrikander Bond, 114
 Mauser rifles distribution, refutation of the story, 115

INDEX

Cape Colony (*continued*)
  Newlands, suburb, 119
  Parliament, attitude towards Transvaal situation, 3–9; Downing Street government dreaded by, 8
  Progressive party, action of the, 105–118
  Religious census for 1891, 244
  South African League (*see* that title)
  Taxation and import duties compared with those of Transvaal, 86, 274, 275
Cape Times, ownership of, 207; extracts from, 222, 225
"Chamber of Mines," the formation and object of, 192, 236
Capitalists. *See* Press, Gold-mines, Jewish factor
Chamberlain, Rt. Hon. J.—
  Animosity of Boers to, 43, 44
  Bloemfontein Conference, despatch concerning, 164
  Diplomatic negotiations with Transvaal immediately preceding the war, 164, 170–183
  Edgar case, speech on, 57
  Famous Highbury speech, effect in Pretoria, 175, 176
  Suzerainty, despatches concerning, 146–154, 172–173
Coal-mining in South Africa, slow growth of the industry, 270, 271, 273
Colonial Dutch Reformed Church, strong protest against war by, 117
Consolidated Goldfield Co., The, 191
Conventions of 1881 and 1884 (*see* Suzerainty)
Customs Union, The, 302

DE BEERS CO.—
  Absolute control over white employées, 239
  Check to industrial growth at Kimberley by, 257
  Plans for dynamite monopoly, 93
De Kaap gold-mines a failure, 259
Derby, Lord, intention regarding suzerainty question in Convention of 1884, 152–153
Diamond Field Advertiser, ownership of, 207
Diamond fields, discreditable method of acquisition by England, 140

Diamond mines (Kimberley)—
  Exports one-quarter of total exports of Cape Colony, 258
  History of, and exports table (1891–1898), 257–258
  Diplomatic negotiations concerning franchise reform and suzerainty preceding the war, 146–154, 161–183
Du Plessis, M. J., letter to *The Afrikander*, wilful misrepresentation of, 225
Du Toit, Mr., 106
Dutch and British population in South Africa, proportions, 245, 246; increase of Dutch the greater, 247; racial and economic cleavage coincide, 247–249; future proportions, 278
Dutch conspiracy, the alleged, 105–118, 224–225
Dynamite, half the world's supply absorbed by Transvaal, 92
Dynamite Concession, The—
  Grievance not a real one, 92–94
  History of, 26, 27, 88–95
  Jewish control of, 193
  Reduction of cost in dynamite in 1897, 18
  Result in mining profits which would follow abolition of monopoly, 230
  Total profits for 1897–1898, 90

ECKSTEIN group of financiers, widespread influence of, 191, 192
Edgar murder, The, 56, 57, 161
Education grievance, The, 33, 34, 37, 38
Educational Council, bad tactics of the, 37, 38
Edwards outrage, 198
Eloff, Mr. Frickie, 35
Emigration in the future, obstacles to, agricultural, 250–256; mining, 266–278
Esselen, Mr., progressive policy of, 16

FARMING (*see* Agricultural outlook)
Federation question, The, Sir G. Grey's scheme, 296–299; Lord Carnarvon's scheme a failure, 299; Sir Bartle Frere and Mr. Shepstone sent out, 300–301; natural bond of common interest necessary to, 302–304

INDEX

effect of the war upon, 304-305
Fischer, Mr.—
  On progressive influences and action in the Transvaal, 17
  On curse of gold-mines, 139
Fitzpatrick, Mr.—
  On native labour, 285
  On Selati Railway scandal, 77, 78
  Pretoria forts in 1887 described by, 133
Franchise grievance—
  Bloemfontein Conference (see that title)
  Malaboch campaign, franchise conferred by edict of Raad after, 24
  Outlanders wish for privileges without the duties, 24
  Reform law of 1899 and diplomatic negotiations preceding war, 169-183
  Sir A. Milner's despatches on, 162-164
  Various attitudes towards, 63-72
Frere, Sir Bartle, career in South Africa, 300-301
Froude, Mr. J. A., mission to South Africa, 299

GAMBLING trade in hands of Jews, 194, 195
Glen Grey Act, The, 233
Goetz & Co., 191, 192
Gold law of Transvaal and Rhodesia compared, 87
Gold-mines—
  Association of Mines (see that title)
  Chamber of Mines (see that title)
  English holdings in the minority, 193
  German and French holdings largely outweigh English, 193
  Heavy taxation reasonable, 86
  Jewish owners predominate, 191-193
  Native labour (see that title)
  Survey of gold districts, 259; table of outputs (1896-97), 260, 263; future of mining, 260-269; reasons for increasing output, 265; economics of black v. white labour, 268-269
Gold Thefts law enforced, 19
Greene, Mr. Conynghame, statements concerning Transvaal expenditure, 85, 86
Greene, Mr., and franchise reform law of 1899 170-171
Grey, Earl, speech on native labour in the mines, 234
Grey, Sir George, federation scheme drawn up by, 296-298
Grobler, Piet, 34

HAGUE Peace Conference, British representative works to exclude Transvaal from area of arbitration, 157
Hall, Mr. W., on future of gold-mining, 266
Hamilton, Mr. W. G., on future of gold-mining, 266
Hartley, Dr. Darley, 199
Hofmeyr, Mr., loyalty and influence of, 104, 105, 112
Hollander factor, the evil effect and diminishing influence of, 74, 75
Hollander press, The, 217, 218
Horse trade in Jewish hands, 193

ILLICIT Liquor Syndicate, The, bribery by, 82
Imperialism, quotation from Dr. Beck, 107
"Imperialism, The New," effect of in South Africa, 8
Industrial Commission, The, 90
Industrial future, 257-278 (for details, see various titles)
Iron-mining in South Africa hypothetical only, 271, 272

JAMESON Raid—
  Deterring effect on franchise reform of the, 17, 18, 20, 71
  Effect upon trade of the, 8, 9
  Engenders disbelief in British sense of justice, 155
  Expenditure on Transvaal armaments increased after, 129, 130, 132, 134
Jewish factor, The—
  Advantage of obtaining political power in Transvaal to, 196
  Financial, industrial, and economic predominance in Transvaal, 189-197
  Johannesburg, predominant in, 11, 190-195

INDEX

Johannesburg—
  Administration of justice in, 81
  Bribery and corruption in, 80, 81
  Demand for full self-government, real reasons of, 19
  Description of the city, 10; lust of gold, 12; industrial and commercial energy, 13; absence of Boer element, 13, 14
  Gambling, trade in, 194, 195
  Jewish element enormously predominant in, 11, 190–195
  Luxury, liberty, and license in, 61
  Outlanders in position of, 55, 56
  Press in Jewish hands, 193
  Reform agitation by foreigners, 17, 18
Johannesburg Star, the ownership and aggressive policy of, 207, 208, 219
Joubert, General—
  Character of, 33
  Election campaign, 1893, Liberal views and sympathies of, 16
  Wealth of, 28

KAFFIRS (*see* native labour)
Karoo, the unproductiveness of, 252
Kimberley, Lord, despatch concerning suzerainty (1881), 149
Kock, Mr., 76
Krause, Dr., 73
Kruger, Piet, 35
Kruger, President—
  Bloemfontein Conference (*see* that title)
  Character and personality of, 7, 15, 22–31
  Charges of corruption against, 26, 28
  Dynamite monopoly scandal, 89, 92
  Conception of politics, 24
  Opening of a Jewish synagogue by, 28
  Position as President, 15, 17
  Public appointments filled by members of the family, 34, 35
  Religious views of the war, 158

LABOUR question (*see* Native labour question, and White labour)
Language grievance, 33, 34, 37; speech by Rev. J. T. Lloyd, 38

Leyds, Dr., racial antagonism fostered by, 33, 74
Lippert dynamite monopoly, 88, 89
Liquor law, The, 19, 81 230, 287; bribery used to resist changes in, 82, 83
Liquor trade, Jewish control of, 193
Lloyd, Rev. J. T., statements concerning the language grievance, 38
Locust plague, efforts to combat, 252
London Convention (*see* Suzerainty issue)
Loveday, Mr., statement concerning finance of Transvaal, 85
Lydenburg gold-mines disappointing, 259

MANSVELT, Dr., educational policy of, 34, 37
Merriman, Mr., 4, 116
Midland News, The, attitude of, 208
Milner, Sir A.—
  Bloemfontein Conference, 6–8, 98, 164–169
  Boer view of, 156
  Diplomacy and despatches before the war, 161–183
  Distrust of Boer Government by 6, 7
  Ignorance concerning intentions of Orange Free State, 182
  Mutilation of President Steyn's despatch, 183–186
Mines—
  Coal-mines (*see* that title)
  Gold-mines (*see* that title)
  Iron-mining (*see* that title)
  Labour question (*see* Native labour question, and White labour)
  "Pass Inspectors," bribery of, 80
  Profits after the war, immense increase of, 229
Miners—
  Attitude towards franchise question, 66
  Native labour question (*see* that title)
  Transitory character of population, statistics proving, 68, 69
Mining World, The, extract on white miners' wages, 240
Missionaries, feud with Dutch over treatment of natives, 282

INDEX

Money-lending business in the hands of Jews, 193-194
Monypenny, Mr., 209, 210, 216
Mortgage business in hands of Jews, 193, 194

NATAL—
  British and Dutch population, 244, 246
  Expenditure compared with that of Transvaal, 86, 274, 275
  Native Element, The—
    Condition and rights of natives in Cape Colony and Transvaal compared, 284, 285
    Difficulties following upon conclusion of war, 313, 314
    Proportion of natives to whites in South Africa, 279; increase of natives the greater, 279, 280; disturbing effect of the white war upon, 280, 281; British and Dutch treatment of natives, 281-295; future outlook, 295; vice among, 287-288
  Native Labour question, 230-240; "compound" and "location" systems, 237, 238; number employed in mining, 264
  "Native Labour Association," The, 237, 268-270, 279-295
Neumann & Co., 191
Newspapers (*see* Press)
Nobel Trust (*see* Dynamite monopoly grievance)

Ons Land, loyal policy of, 105, 110
Oppenheim, Baron (*see* Selati Railway scandal)
Orange Free State, The—
  British and Dutch population in, proportions, 245, 246; Dutch increase the greater, 247; racial and economic cleavage coincide, 247-249
  British civil and political status in, 144
  Conventions violated by England, 141
  Dependent on Transvaal for markets, 143, 254
  Diamond fields (*see* that title)
  Ignorance of Sir A. Milner concerning intentions of, 182
  Model government of, 136, 143, 144

Orange Free State, The (*continued*)—
  Reasons for joining the Transvaal in the war, 17, 136-145
  Steyn, President (*see* that title)
  Telegram from Downing Street on signing of 1884 Convention, 142
Outlanders, The—
  Bribery of Transvaal officers by, 78-80
  Grievances—
    Attitude of Cape Parliament towards, 5
    Commonly received and erroneous views of, 52, 53
    Dynamite monopoly (*see* that title)
    Educational grievance (*see* that title)
    Franchise grievances (*see* that title)
    Summary of, 96, 97
  Proportions to total population of South Africa, 244-246
  Transitory character of population, 69, 70
Outlander Council, the formation of, and manipulation by capitalists, 66, 203-205
Outlander press, attitude of, 156

PAKENHAM, Mr., 209, 210
Pass Law, the, 19, 58, 230, 238
Peace Conference (*see* Hague Conference)
"Peruvians"—
  Definition of term, 190
  Large amount of trade in hands of, 267
Phillip, Mr., and South African Explosives Co., 90
Phillips, runner of sweepstakes in Johannesburg, 195
Press, The—
  Capitalist ownership of South African press, inflammatory policy of, 206-228
  London press inspired by capitalist press in South Africa, 215, 216, 217
Press Law grievances, 58-61
Pretoria Convention (*see* Suzerainty issue)
Policeman (*see* "Zarp")
Population (White), race proportions, 244-246; Dutch increase the greater, 247; racial and economic cleavage coincide, 247-

X

249 (*see* also Native element and Native labour)
Potchefstroom, 46
Public meeting, the law of, 59, 60

QUEEN Victoria, Boer veneration for, 44, 122, 123

RACE question, The—
British and Dutch, proportions, 244-246; Dutch increase the greater, 247; racial and economic cleavage coincide, 247-249; effect of the war upon, 145.
Native element (*see* that title)
Raid, The (*see* Jameson Raid)
Railways—
Co-operation of South African States, 302
Netherland South Africa Co., reduction of rates, 18
Selati Railway scandal, 26
Transvaal endeavours to divert traffic from Cape lines, 9
Rand, The (*see* Gold-mining and Johannesburg)
Refugees, stories of insults, &c., to, grossly exaggerated, 220-222
Reitz, Mr.—
Personality of, 34
Statement concerning position of Transvaal as a sovereign State, 151-152
Story of Kruger told by, 23
Rhodes, Cecil—
Boer hatred of, 123
"Constitutional means," term used by, 156, 206
"Kaffir Parson," extract from speech, 290
Knowledge of Boer character, 7
Mining interests on the Rand, 191, 192
Native labour, extract from speech, 286
Press, ownership of and influence over, 206-207
Rhodesia—
Gold laws compared with those of Transvaal, 87
Gold-mining prospects in, 260
Rhodesia Herald, ownership of, 207
Rhodesia press, aggressive attitude of, 157
Robinson, T. B., Rand mining interests of, 192

Rosmead, Lord, on Home Rule in South Africa, 298
Rothschild interest in the Rand, 191
Rudd, Mr.—
On labour question, 233-235
Rand mining interests, 191-192

SAUER, Mr., 4
Schreiner, Mr., loyal attitude of, 4, 104, 116
Schreiner, Olive—
Interview concerning Dutch feeling in the Colony, 119-125
Story of Kruger by, 23
Secret service money in Transvaal, 85
Selati Railway scandal, 77
Selous, Mr., on Transvaal armaments in 1895, 133
Settlement of South Africa after the war (*see* under War)
Smuts, Mr., 75
Soil (*see* Agriculture)
Solomon, Mr., 4, 116
South African Explosives Co., allotment of shares, 89
South African League, The—
Aggressive policy of, 64, 100, 103, 161, 176
Formation, policy, and methods of, 198-202
Steyn, President—
Pacific despatch mutilated by Sir A. Milner, 182-186
Reasons for aiding Transvaal in the war, 137, 138
Stock Exchange in South Africa, Jewish element predominant, 193
Sundry Services Account of Transvaal, 85
Suzerainty, the question of—
Cape Colony Parliament, attitude towards, 3-4
Despatches and negotiations concerning, 146-160, 172-173
Interpretation of term, 149
Revival of the claim, 146, 148

THERON, Mr., on "civil" nature of the war, 102
Times, The (London), selection of South African correspondent unwise, 216
Times, The (Natal), striking extract from, 226, 227

INDEX

Transvaal, The—
  Arbitration question, 146-149, 167-169, 172-174
  Armaments, expenditure statistics, 85, 128; inefficiency previous to Raid, and increased expenditure following upon, 132-135
  Bloemfontein Conference (see that title)
  Boers, The—
    Chamberlain, Rt. Hon. J., disliked by, 43, 44
    Character, 14, 20, 21, 44
    Commonly accepted and mistaken view of, 15
    Detachment from foreign population, 14, 62
    Distrust of British diplomacy, 6, 43, 44, 155
    Educational and progressive campaign among, 16, 17
    Enormous proportion in Government employ, 73, 74
    Family influence in politics, 34, 35
    Farms, large proportion mortgaged to Jews, 194
    Hatred of British rule fundamental and abiding, 307-309
    Intermarriage with British, 48, 49, 100-102, 121
    Life and outlook of, interview with Olive Schreiner, 120-125
    Natives, treatment of, by, 233
    Patriotism of, 48, 49
    Political education, want of, 32, 35, 95
    Rhodes, Cecil, hated by, 123
    Self-restraint of, 40, 41, 48
  Bribery and corruption of officials, 73-83
  British and Dutch population, 244-246
  Diplomatic negotiations (see that title)
  Economic grievances, abatement of, in 1897, 18
  Financial reform, direction in which it is needed, 84-87
  Franchise policy since 1890
  Gold Law the most liberal in the world, 87
  Gold-mines (see that title)
  Hague Peace Conference, Transvaal excluded from area of arbitration, 157

Transvaal, The (continued)
  Industrial Commission of 1897, 18
  Intrigue with Germany, want of evidence, 126
  Jameson Raid (see that title)
  Johannesburg (see that title)
  Joint-inquiry, the proposal of a, 6
  Justice, education, hospitals, police, expenditure statistics, 131
  Outlanders (see that title); grievances (see the various titles)
  Official incompetence and corruption, 73-83
  Political parties, violent cleavage of, 16
  Pretoria, city, 40; forts useless in 1889, 133
  Progressive movement and forces in, 20, 71
  Raad, corruption of, 82, 83; "the third Raad," 83; the present Raad, 21
  Revenue and expenditure tables (1889-97), 84
  Secret service expenditure, 85
  South African League in, 199-202
  Taxation and import duties compared with those of Cape Colony and Natal, 86, 274, 275
  Ultimatum, reason for sending the, 155-160
  War expenditure (see Armaments above)
  Working-classes, attitude towards franchise question, 66
Transvaal Leader, the capitalist organ, production and objects of, 209; extracts from, 211-214

VILLIERS, Chief-Justice De, charges England with violating Conventions, 141
Vorstman, 89

WAR, The—
  Boer attitude towards, 44, 45, 307-309
  "Civil" nature, owing to intermarriage, 48, 49, 100-102, 121
  Gains following the war, mining interests, cheap labour, 229-240
  Guerilla warfare of long duration probable, 309
  Justification by war party of, 96, 127

www.ingramcontent.com/pod-product-compliance
Lightning Source LLC
Chambersburg PA
CBHW030521230426
43665CB00010B/714